Penguin Twe

PERIOD O

SUMMER

SMALL CR.

Tennessee Williams was born in 1911 in Columbus, Mississippi, where his grandfather was the episcopal clergyman. When his father, a travelling salesman, moved with his family to St Louis some years later, both he and his sister found it impossible to settle down to city life. He entered college during the Depression and left after a couple of years to take a clerical job in a shoe company. He stayed there for two years, spending the evenings writing. He entered the University of Iowa in 1938 and completed his course, at the same time holding a large number of part-time jobs of great diversity. He received a Rockefeller Fellowship in 1940 for his play *Battle of Angels*, and he won the Pulitzer Prize in 1948 and 1955. Among his many other plays are *The Glass Menagerie* (1944), *The Rose Tatto* (1951), *Camino Real* (1953), *Cat on a Hot Tin Roof* (1955), *Baby Doll* (1957), *Orpheus Descending* (1957), *Something Unspoken* (1958), *Suddenly Last Summer* (1958), *The Night of the Iguana* (1961) and *The Milk Train Doesn't Stop Here Anymore* (1963).

Tennessee Williams died in 1983.

TENNESSEE WILLIAMS

PERIOD OF ADJUSTMENT

SUMMER AND SMOKE

SMALL CRAFT WARNINGS

PENGUIN BOOKS
in association with Martin Secker & Warburg

PENGUIN BOOKS

Published by the Penguin Group
27 Wrights Lane, London W8 5TZ, England
Viking Penguin Inc., 40 West 23rd Street, New York, New York 10010, USA
Penguin Books Australia Ltd, Ringwood, Victoria, Australia
Penguin Books Canada Ltd, 2801 John Street, Markham, Ontario, Canada L3R 1B4
Penguin Books (NZ) Ltd, 182–190 Wairau Road, Auckland 10, New Zealand

Penguin Books Ltd, Registered Offices: Harmondsworth, Middlesex, England

Period of Adjustment first published in Great Britain by Martin Secker & Warburg Ltd 1961

Summer and Smoke first published in Great Britain in *Tennessee Williams: Four Plays* by Martin Secker & Warburg Ltd 1956

Small Craft Warnings first published in Great Britain by Martin Secker & Warburg Ltd 1973

Published in Penguin Books 1982
3 5 7 9 10 8 6 4 2

Made and printed in Great Britain by
Antony Rowe Ltd, Chippenham, Wiltshire

CONTENTS

PERIOD OF ADJUSTMENT

To the director and the cast

THE CAST

The first English production of this play was at the Theatre Royal, Bristol, on Monday, 4 September 1961, with the following cast:

RALPH BATES	*Harry H. Corbett*
ISABEL HAVERSTICK	*Elizabeth Shepherd*
GEORGE HAVERSTICK	*John Franklyn Robbins*
SUSIE	*Hazel Prance*
MRS MCGILLICUDDY	*Elizabeth Spriggs*
MR MCGILLICUDDY	*Derek Smith*
POLICE OFFICER	*Pierre Aumonier*
DOROTHEA BATES	*Rhoda Lewis*

Directed by VAL MAY

Designed by GRAHAM BARLOW

The Scene

The action of the play takes place in Ralph Bates's home, Memphis, Tennessee. The time is Christmas Eve.

ACT ONE

The set is the interior and entrance of a 'cute' little Spanish-type suburban bungalow. Two rooms are visible onstage, the living-room with its small dining alcove and the bedroom. There are doors to the kitchen and bath. A bit of the stucco exterior surrounds the entrance, downstage right or left. A Christmas wreath is on the door, while above the door is an ornamental porch light, or coach lantern, with amber glass or possibly glass in several colours. The fireplace in the fourth wall of the set is represented by a flickering red light. Of course, the living-room contains a TV set with its back to the audience, its face to a big sofa that opens into a bed. The dog is a cocker spaniel. There's a rather large Christmas tree, decorated, with a child's toys under it and a woman's fur coat in an open box, but no child and no woman. RALPH BATES, *a boyish-looking man in his middle thirties, is approaching the TV set, facing upstage, with a can of beer and opener.*

TV COMMERCIAL: Millions of Americans each day are discovering the difference between this new miracle product and the old horse-and-buggy type of cleanser which made wash-day a torture to Mom and left her too tired at sundown to light up the house with the sunshine of her smile.

RALPH: *No snow!*

[*He hoists himself on to a very high bar stool facing the TV.*]

TV COMMERCIAL: So don't let unnecessary fatigue cast a shadow over your household, especially not at this –

[*He leaps off the stool and crouches to change the channel. He gets snatches of several dramatic and musical offerings, settles for a chorus of 'White Christmas', sighs, picks up a poker and stabs at the flickering *ruddy light in the fourth wall. It comes up brighter. He crouches to fan the fire with an antique bellows: the fire brightens. He sighs again, hoists himself back on to the brass-studded red-leather-topped stool, which has evidently been removed from the 'cute' little bar, which is upstage. For theatrical purpose, this stool is about half a foot higher than any other sitting-surface on the stage. Whenever* RALPH *assumes a seat on this stool he is like a judge mounting his judicial bench, except he's not pompous or bewigged about it. He is detached, considering, thinking, and over his face comes that characteristic look of a gentle gravity which is the heart of* RALPH. *Perhaps his pose should suggest Rodin's 'Thinker'.* RALPH *is one of those rare people that have the capacity of heart to truly care, and care deeply, about other people.*

A car horn, urgent, is heard out front, offstage. RALPH *slides off the stool and rushes out of the front door; he stands under the amber coach lantern. It's snowing, the snowflakes are projected on his figure, tiny, obliquely falling particles of shadow. There's a muffled shout from the car that's stopped below the terrace of the bungalow.*]

RALPH [*shouting back*]: *Hey, there, drive her up under th' carport!*

GEORGE [*Texas voice*]: Whacha say, boy?

RALPH: PUT 'ER UNDER THE CARPORT!

GEORGE: Wheels won't catch, too steep!

RALPH: Back her all the way out and then shoot 'er up in first!

ISABEL'S VOICE [*high-pitched with strain*]: Will you please let me out first, George!

[*There is the sound of a car door.* RALPH *ducks in, grinning, and seizes a carton of rice.*]

RALPH: Yeah, come on in, little lady.

[ISABEL *appears before the house, small and white-faced with fatigue, eyes dark-circled, manner dazed and uncertain. She wears a cheap navy-blue cloth coat, carries a shiny new patent-leather purse, has on red wool mittens.* RALPH *pelts her with rice. She ducks the bombardment with a laugh that's more like a sob.*]

ISABEL: Oh, no, please! I never want to see rice again in my life, not uncooked anyhow ... That fire looks wonderful to me. I'm Isabel Crane, Mr Bates.

[*She removes a red mitten and extends her hand.*]

RALPH: I thought you'd married that boy.

[Both speak in deep Southern voices; hers is distinctly Texan.]

ISABEL: I mean Mrs George Haverstick.

[She says her new name with a hint of grimness.]

RALPH [*still in the door*]: Wait'll I put m'shoes on, I'll come out!

[This shout is unheard.]

ISABEL: You have a sweet little house.

RALPH [*with a touch of amiable grimness*]: Yeah, we sure do! Wheels cain't git any traction, 'stoo damn steep.

[He shouts down.]

LOCK IT UP, LEAVE IT OUT FRONT! – I guess he's gonna do that, yep, that's what he's doin', uh-huh, that's what he's doin' ...

ISABEL: Does it snow often in Memphis?

RALPH: No, no, rarely, rarely.

[He gives her a glance. RALPH *has a sometimes disconcerting way of seeming either oblivious to a person he's with or regarding the person with a sudden intense concentration, as if he'd just noticed something startling or puzzling about them. But this is a mannerism that the actor should use with restraint.]*

ISABEL: It was snowing all the way down here; it's my first acquaintance with snow except for one little flurry of snow in Saint Louis the day befo' Thanksgivin' day, this is my first real acquaintance with, with – with a real *snow* ... What *is* he doing down there?

RALPH: He's unloadin' th' car.

ISABEL: I just want my small zipper bag. Will you please call down to him that's all I want of my things?

RALPH [*shouting*]: Leave all that stuff till later. Ha ha! I didn't know you could get all that in a car.

ISABEL: Surely he isn't removing our wedding presents! Is he *insane*, Mr Bates?

[She goes to the door.]

George! Just my small zipper bag, not everything in the car! Oh, Lord!

[She retreats into the room.]

He must think we're going to *live* here for the rest of our *lives!* He didn' even warn you all we were coming.

RALPH: He called me up from West Memphis.

ISABEL: Yes, just across the river.

RALPH: What is that car, a Caddy?

ISABEL: It's a fifty-two Cadillac with a mileage close to a hundred and twenty thousand. It ought to be retired with an old-age pension, Mr Bates.

RALPH [*at the door*]: It looks like one of them funeral limousines.

ISABEL [*wryly*]: Mr Bates, you have hit the nail on the head with the head of the hammer. That is just what it was. It's piled up a hundred and twenty thousand miles between Burkemeyer's Mortuary and various graveyards serving Greater Saint Louis. JAWGE, CAN YOU HEAR ME, JAWGE? Excuse me, Mr Bates.

[*She slips past him on to the terrace again.*]

JAWGE, JUST MY SMALL ZIPPER BAG.

[*Indistinct shout from below. She turns back in.*]

I give up, Mr Bates.

[*She ducks under his arm to enter the house again and stands behind Ralph in the doorway.*]

RALPH [*still chuckling at the door*]: What's he want with a funeral limousine? On a honeymoon trip?

ISABEL: I asked him that same question and got a very odd answer. He said there's no better credit card in the world than driving up at a bank door in a Cadillac limousine.

[*She tries to laugh.*]

Oh, I don't know, I – love Spanish-type architecture, Spanish mission-type houses, I – don't think you ought to stand in that door with just that light shirt on you, this is a – such a – *sweet* house . . .

[*She seems close to tears. Something in her tone catches his attention and he comes in, closing the door.*]

RALPH: Ha, ha, well, how's it going? Is the marriage in orbit?

ISABEL [*tries to laugh at this, too*]: Oh! Will you please do me a favour? Don't encourage him, please don't invite him to spend the night here, Mr Bates! I'm thinking of your wife, because last night – in Cape Girardeau, Missouri? – he thought it would be very nice to look up an old war buddy he had there, too. He sincerely thought so, and possibly the war buddy thought so, too, but NOT the wife!

Oh, no, not *that* lady, no! They'd hardly got through their first beer cans with – remembrances of Korea, when that bright little woman began to direct us to a highway motel which she said was only a hop, skip and jump from their house but turned out to be almost across the state line into – Arkansas? Yaias, Arkansas. I think I can take this off, now!

[*She removes a red woollen muffler. He takes it from her and she murmurs* '*Thanks.*']

What is holding him up? Why is he – ? Mr Bates, I did tell him that this is one night of the year when you just don't intrude on another young married couple.

RALPH: Aw, come off that, little lady! Why, I been beggin' that boy ever since we got out of the service to come to Memphis. He had to git married to make it. Why, every time I'd git drunk, I'd call that boy on the phone to say 'Git to hell down here, you old Texas jack rabbit!' And I'd just about given up hope he'd ever show!

ISABEL: Is he still fooling with luggage?

[*There is a noise outside.* RALPH *goes to the open door.*]

RALPH: *Hey!*

ISABEL: *What?*

RALPH: Ha ha ha! He put these bags at the door and run back down to the car.

ISABEL: *What* did he – ?

RALPH: Gone back down for more luggage. I'll take these in.

ISABEL [*as the bags are brought in*]: Those are *my* pieces of luggage! All but the small zipper which is all that I wanted!

RALPH [*calling out the open door*]: *Hey!*

ISABEL: *What?*

RALPH: *Hey, boy!* He's gotten back in the car an' driven off, ha ha!

ISABEL [*rushing to the door*]: *Driven? Off?* Did you say? My heavens. You're right, he's *gone!* Mr Bates, he's *deposited me on your hands and driven away.*

[*She is stunned.*]

Oh, *how funny!* Isn't this *funny!*

[*Laughs wildly, close to sobbing.*]

It's no *surprise* to me, though! All the way down here from Cape

Girardeau, where we stopped for our wedding night, Mr Bates, I had a feeling that the first chance he got to, he would abandon me somewhere!

RALPH: Aw, now, take it easy!

ISABEL: That's what he's done! Put me and my bags in your hands and run away.

RALPH: Aw, now, no! The old boy wouldn't do that, ha ha, for Chrissakes. He just remembered something he had to, had to – go and get at a – drugstore.

ISABEL: If that was the case wouldn't he mention it to me?

RALPH: Aw now, I known that boy a long time and he's always been sort of way out, but never way out that far!

ISABEL: Where is your wife? Where's Mrs Bates, Mr Bates?

RALPH: Oh, she's not here, right now.

ISABEL: I'm SUCH A FOOL!

[*She giggles a little hysterically.*]

Oh, I'm such a *fool!* ... Why didn't I know better, can you answer me that? ... I hope the news of our approach didn't drive your wife away on Christmas eve, Mr Bates ...

RALPH: No, honey.

ISABEL: He brought up everything but the little blue zipper bag which is all I asked faw! ... It had my, all my, it had my – *night* things in it ...

RALPH: Just let me get you a drink. I'm sorry I don't have any egg nog. But I can make a wonderful hot buttered rum. How about a little hot buttered rum?

ISABEL: Thank you, no, I don't drink ...

RALPH: It's never too late to begin to.

ISABEL: No, I don't want liquor.

RALPH: Coffee? Want some hot coffee?

ISABEL: Where is your wife, Mr Bates?

RALPH: Oh, she's – not here now, I'll tell you about that later.

ISABEL: She will be outraged. This is one night of the year when you don't want outside disturbances – on your hands ...

RALPH: I think I know what to give you.

ISABEL: I did expect it but yet I didn't expect it! – I mean it occurred to me, the possibility of it, but I thought I was just being morbid.

RALPH: Aw, now, I know that boy. We been through two wars together, took basic training together and officer's training together. He wouldn't ditch you like that unless he's gone crazy.

ISABEL: George Haverstick is a very sick man, Mr Bates. He was a patient in neurological at Barnes Hospital in Saint Louis, that's how I met him. I was a student nurse there.

[*She is talking quickly, shrilly. She has a prim, severe manner that disguises her prettiness.*]

RALPH: Yeah? What was wrong with him in the hospital, honey?

ISABEL: If we see him again, if he ever comes back to this house, you will *see* what's wrong. *He shakes!* Sometimes it's just barely noticeable, just a constant, slight tremor, you know, a sort of – vibration, like a – like an electric vibration in his muscles or nerves?

RALPH: Aw. That old tremor has come back on him, huh? He had that thing in Korea.

ISABEL: How bad did he have it in Korea, Mr Bates?

RALPH: You know – like a heavy drinker – except he didn't drink heavy.

ISABEL: It's like he had Parkinson's disease but he doesn't have it.

[*She speaks like an outraged spinster, which is quite incongruous to her pretty, child-like appearance.*]

RALPH: What in hell is it then?

ISABEL: THAT is a MYSTERY! He shakes, that's all. He just shakes. Sometimes you'd think that he was shaking to pieces ... Was that a car out front?

[*She goes to the window.*]

No! I've caught a head cold, darn it.

[*Blows her nose.*]

When I met Mr George Haverstick – Excuse me, you're watching TV!

RALPH [*turning off set*]: Naw, I'm not watchin' TV.

ISABEL: I'm so wound up, sitting in silence all day beside my – silent bridegroom, I can't seem to stop talking now, although I – hardly know you. Yes. I met him at Barnes Hospital, the biggest one in

Saint Louis, where I was taking my training as a nurse, he had gone in Barnes instead of the Veterans Hospital because in the Veterans Hospital they couldn't discover any physical cause of this tremor and he thought they just said there wasn't any physical cause in order to avoid having to pay him a physical disability – compensation! I had him as a patient at Barnes Hospital, on the night shift. My, did he keep me running! The little buzzer was never out of his hand. Couldn't sleep under any kind of sedation less than enough to knock an elephant out! – Well, that's where I met George, I was very touched by him, honestly, very, very touched by the boy! I thought he sincerely loved me . . . Yes, I *have* caught a head cold, or am I crying? I guess it's fatigue – exhaustion.

RALPH: You're just going through a period of adjustment.

ISABEL: Of course at Barnes he got the same diagnosis, or lack of diagnosis, that he'd gotten at the Vets Hospital in Korea and Texas and elsewhere, no physical basis for the tremor, perfect physical health, suggested – psychiatry to him! He blew the roof off! You'd think they'd accused him of beating up his grandmother, at least, if not worse! I swear! Mr Bates, I still have sympathy for him, but it wasn't fair of him not to let me know he'd quit his job at the airfield till after our marriage. He gave me that information after the wedding, right after the wedding he told me, right on the bridge, Eads Bridge between Saint Louis and East Saint Louis, he said, 'Little Bit? Take a good look at Saint Louie because it may be your last one!' I'm quoting him exactly, those were his words. I don't know why I didn't say drive me right back . . . Isn't it strange that I didn't say turn around on the other side of this bridge and drive me right back? I gave up student nursing at a great hospital to marry a man not honest enough to let me know he'd given up his job till an hour after the wedding!

RALPH: George is a high-strung boy. But they don't make them any better.

ISABEL: A man's opinion of a man! If they don't make them any better than George Haverstick they ought to stop production!

[RALPH *throws back his head, laughing heartily.*]

No, I mean it, if they don't make them better than a man that would abandon his bride in less than – how many hours? – on the doorstep of a war buddy and drive on without her or any apology to her, if that's the best they make them, I say *don't make them!*

[*There is a pause. She has crouched before the fire again, holding her hands out to the flickering glow.*]

Did George tell you on the phone that he's quit his job?

RALPH [*pouring brandy*]: What job did he quit, honey?

ISABEL: He was a ground mechanic at Lambert's airfield in Saint Louis. I had lost my job too, I hadn't quit, no, I was politely dismissed. My first day in surgery? – I *fainted!* – when the doctor made the incision and I saw the blood, I keeled over . . .

RALPH: That's understandable, honey.

ISABEL: Not in a nurse, not in a girl that had set her heart on nursing, that – how long has he been gone?

RALPH: Just a few minutes, honey. Christmas Eve traffic is heavy and George being George, he may have stopped at a bar on his way back here . . . You'd been going steady how long?

ISABEL: Ever since his discharge from Barnes Hospital. Isn't this suburb called High Point?

RALPH: Yes. High Point over a cavern.

ISABEL: His place was in High Point, too. Another suburb called High Point, spelled Hi dash Point – hyphenated.

RALPH: I guess all fair-sized American cities have got a suburb called High Point, hyphenated or not, but this is the only one I know of that's built on a cavern.

ISABEL [*without really listening to him*]: Cavern?

[*She laughs faintly as if it were a weak joke.*]

Well, I said, George, on the bridge, we're not driving down to Florida in that case. We're going to find you a job; we're going from city to city until you find a new job and I don't care if we cross the Rio Grande, we're not going to stop until you find one! Did I or didn't I make the right decision? In your opinion, Mr Bates.

RALPH: Well. How did he react to it?

ISABEL: Stopped talking and started shaking! So violently I was scared he would drive that funeral car off the road! Ever since then it's been hell! And I am –

[*She springs up from the fireplace chair.*]

– not exactly the spirit of Christmas, am I?

[*She goes to the window to look out; sees nothing but windy snow. There is a low rumble. A picture falls off the wall.*]

What was that?

RALPH: Oh, nothing. The ground just settled a little. We get that all the time here because this suburb, High Point, is built over a great big underground cavern and is sinking into it gradually, an inch or two inches a year. It would cost three thousand dollars to stabilize the foundation of this house even temporarily! But it's not publicly known and we homeowners and the promoters of the project have got together to keep it a secret till we have sold out, in alphabetical order, at a loss but not a complete sacrifice. Collusion, connivance. Disgusting but necessary.

[*She doesn't hear this, murmurs 'What?' as she crosses back to the window at the sound of a car going by.*]

ISABEL: It's funny, I had a hunch he was going to leave me somewhere.

[*She laughs sadly, forlornly, and lets the white window curtains fall together.*]

RALPH: Why don't you take off your coat and sit back down by the fire? That coat keeps the heat off you, honey. That boy's comin' back.

ISABEL: Thank you.

[*She removes her coat.*]

RALPH [*observing with solemn appreciation the perfect neatness of her small body*]: I'm *sure* that boy's coming back. I am now *positive* of it! That's a cute little suit you're wearing. Were you married in that?

ISABEL: Yes, I was married in this travelling suit. Appropriately.

RALPH: You couldn't have looked any prettier in white satin.

[RALPH *is at the bar preparing a snifter of brandy for her. Now he puts a match to it and as it flares up blue, she cries out a little.*]

ISABEL: What is, what are you – ?

RALPH: Something to warm up your insides, little lady.

ISABEL: Well, isn't that sweet of you? Will it burn if I touch it?

RALPH: Naw, naw, naw, take it, take it.

ISABEL: Beautiful. Let me hold it to warm my hands first, before I –

[*He puts the snifter glass of blue-flaming brandy in her hands and they return to the fireplace.*]

I'm not a drinker, I don't think doctors or nurses have any right to be, but I guess *now* – I'm *out* of the nursing profession! *So* ... What a sweet little bar. What a sweet little house. And such a sweet Christmas tree.

RALPH: Yeah. Everything's sweet here. I married a homely girl, honey, but I tried to love her.

[ISABEL *doesn't really hear this remark.*]

ISABEL: I hope your wife didn't take your little boy out because we were coming.

RALPH: I sure did make an effort to love that woman. I almost stopped realizing that she was homely.

ISABEL: So he didn't actually tell you he was going to a drugstore, Mr Bates?

RALPH [*uncomfortably*]: He didn't say so. I just figured he was.

ISABEL: I – well, he's abandoned me here.

RALPH: How long've you known George?

ISABEL: I'm afraid I married a stranger.

RALPH: Everybody does that.

ISABEL: Where did you say your wife was?

RALPH: My wife has quit me.

ISABEL: No! You're joking, aren't you?

RALPH: She walked out on me this evening when I let her know I'd quit my job.

ISABEL [*beginning to listen to him*]: Surely it's just temporary, Mr Bates.

RALPH: Nope. Don't think so. I quit my job and so my wife quit me.

ISABEL: I don't think a woman leaves a man as nice as you, Mr Bates, for such a reason as that.

RALPH: Marriage is an economic arrangement in many ways, let's face it, honey. Also, the situation between us was complicated by the fact that I worked for her father. But that's another story. That's a long other story and you got your mind on George.

ISABEL: I think my pride has been hurt.

RALPH: I told you he's coming back and I'm just as sure of it as I'm sure Dorothea isn't. Or if she does, that she'll find me waiting for her. Ohhhhh, nooooo! I'm cutting out of this High Point over a Cavern on the first military transport I can catch out of Memphis.

ISABEL [*vaguely*]: You don't mean that, Mr Bates, you're talking through your hat, out of hurt feelings, hurt pride.

[*She opens the front door and stands looking out as forlornly as a lost child. She really does have a remarkably cute little figure and* RALPH *takes slow, continual and rather wistful stock of it with his eyes.*]

RALPH: I got what I had comin' to me, that I admit, for marryin' a girl that didn't attract me.

[*He comes up behind her at the door.*]

ISABEL: Did you say didn't attract you?

RALPH: Naw, she didn't attract me in the beginning. She's one year older'n me and I'm no chicken. But I guess I'm not the only man that would marry the only daughter of an old millionaire with diabetes and gallstones and one kidney. Am I?

ISABEL: It's nice out here.

RALPH: But I'm telling you I'm convinced there is no greater assurance of longevity in this world than one kidney, gallstones an' diabetes! That old man has been cheating the undertaker for yea many years. Seems to thrive on one kidney and ...

[*He tosses the beer can down the terrace.*]

Oh, they live on anything – nothing!

ISABEL: Do you always throw beer cans on your front lawn, Mr Bates?

RALPH: Never before in my life. I sure enjoyed it. George is gonna be shocked when he sees me. I sacrificed my youth to –

ISABEL: What?

RALPH: Yep, it's nice out here. I mean, nicer than in there.

ISABEL: You sacrificed your youth?

RALPH: Oh, that. Yeah! I'll tell you more about that unless it bores you.

ISABEL: No.

RALPH: She had fallen into the hands of a psychiatrist when I married this girl. This psychiatrist was charging her father fifty dollars a session to treat her for a condition that he diagnosed as 'psychological frigidity'. She would shiver violently every time she came within touching distance of a possible boy friend. Well – I think the psychiatrist misunderstood her shivers.

ISABEL: She might have shivered because of –

RALPH: That's what I *mean!* Why, the night I met her, I heard a noise like castanets at a distance. I thought some Spanish dancers were about to come on! Ha ha! Then I noticed her teeth – she had buck teeth at that time which were later extracted – were chattering together and her whole body was uncontrollably shaking!

ISABEL: We both married into the shakes! But Mr Bates, I don't think it's very nice of you to ridicule the appearance of your wife.

RALPH: Oh, I'm not!

ISABEL: You WERE!

RALPH: At my suggestion she had the buck teeth extracted. It was like kissing a rock pile before the extractions! I swear!

ISABEL: Now, Mr Bates.

RALPH: This snow almost feels as warm as white ashes out of a – chimney.

ISABEL: Excuse me. I'll get my – sweater.

[*She goes in. He remains on the little paved terrace. When she comes out again in her cardigan, he goes on talking as if there'd been no interruption.*]

RALPH: Yep, her old man was payin' this head-shrinker fifty dollars per session for this condition he diagnosed as 'psychological frigidity'. I cured her of that completely almost overnight. But at thirty-seven, my age, you ain't middle-aged but you're in the shadow of it and it's a spooky shadow. I mean, when you look at *late* middle-aged couples like the McGillicuddys, my absent wife's parents ...

ISABEL: Mr Bates, don't you think I should go downtown and take a hotel room? Even if George comes back, he ought not to find me here like a checked package waiting for him to return with the claim check. Because if you give up your pride, what are you left with, really?

[*She turns and goes back inside. He follows her in. Immediately after they enter, a* NEGRO GIRL *appears on the terrace.*]

Don't you agree, Mr Bates?

[*The* GIRL *rings the doorbell.*]

RALPH: *Here he is now. You see?*

[ISABEL, *who had sunk on to a hassock before the fireplace, now rises tensely as* RALPH *calls out:*]

COME ON IN, LOVER BOY! THAT DOOR AIN'T LOCKED!

[RALPH *opens the door.*]

Oh . . . What can I do fo' you, Susie?

[SUSIE *comes into the room with a sheepish grin.*]

SUSIE: 'Scuse me for comin' to the front door, Mr Bates, but that snow's wet and I got a hole in muh shoe!

RALPH: You alone?

SUSIE: Yes, suh.

RALPH: They sent you for somethin'?

SUSIE: Yes, suh, they sent me faw th' chile's Santie Claus.

RALPH: Aw, they did, huh? Well, you go right back an' tell the McGillicuddys that 'the chile's Santie Claus' is stayin' right here till the chile comes over for it, because I bought it, not them, and I am at least *half* responsible for the 'chile's' existence, *also*. Tell them the chile did not come into the world without a father and it's about time for the chile to acknowledge that fact and for them to acknowledge that fact and – How did you git here, Susie?

SUSIE: Charlie brought me.

RALPH: Who's Charlie?

SUSIE: Charlie's they new *showfer*, Mr Bates.

RALPH: Aw. Well, tell my wife and her folks, the McGillicuddys, that I won't be here tomorrow but 'the chile's Santie Claus' will be here under the tree and say that I said Merry Christmas. Can you remember all that?

SUSIE: Yes, suh.

[*She turns and shouts through the door.*]

Charlie! Don't come up, I'm comin' right down, Charlie!

[*The sound of a Cadillac motor starting is heard below the terrace as*

SUSIE *leaves.* RALPH *looks out of the open door till the car is gone, then slams it shut.*]

RALPH: Dig that, will yuh! Sent a coloured girl over to collect the kid's Christmas! This is typical of the Stuart McGillicuddys. I'd like to have seen Mr Stuart McGillicuddy, the look on his face, when the Western Union messenger give him my message of resignation this afternoon and he was at last exposed to my true opinions of him!

ISABEL: You should have let her take the child's Christmas to it.

RALPH: They'll be over. Don't worry. And – I will be waiting for them with both barrels, man – will I blast 'em! Think of the psychiatrist fees that I saved her fat-head father! I even made her think that she was attractive, and over a five-year period got one pay rise when she give birth to my son which she has turned to a sissy.

[ISABEL *hasn't listened to his speech.*]

ISABEL: I thought that was George at the door ...

RALPH: That's life for you.

ISABEL: What?

RALPH: I said isn't that life for you!

ISABEL: *What* is life for us *all?*

[*She sighs.*]

My philosophy professor at the Baptist college I went to, he said one day, 'We are all of us born, live and die in the shadow of a giant question mark that refers to three questions: Where do we *come* from? *Why? And where, oh where, are we going!*'

RALPH: When did you say you got married?

ISABEL: Yesterday. Yesterday morning.

RALPH: That lately? Well, he'll be back before you can say – Joe Blow.

[*He appreciates her neat figure again.*]

ISABEL: What?

RALPH: Nothing.

ISABEL: Well!

RALPH: D'you like Christmas music?

ISABEL: Everything but 'White Christmas'.

[*As she extends her palms to the imaginary fireplace,* RALPH *is standing a little behind her, still looking her up and down with solemn appreciation.*]

RALPH: Aw, y' don't like 'White Christmas'?

ISABEL: The radio in that car is practically the only thing in it that *works*! We had it on all the time.

[*She gives a little tired laugh.*]

Conversation was impossible, even if there had been a desire to talk! It kept playing 'White Christmas' because it was snowing I guess all the way down here, yesterday and – today . . .

RALPH: A radio in a funeral limousine?

ISABEL: I guess they just played it on the way back from the graveyard. Anyway, once I reached over and turned the volume down. He didn't say anything, he just reached over and turned the volume back up. Isn't it funny how a little thing like that can be so insulting to you? Then I started crying and still haven't stopped! I pretended to be looking out the car window till it got dark.

RALPH: You're just going through a little period of adjustment to each other.

ISABEL: What do you do with a bride left on your doorstep, Mr Bates?

RALPH: Well, I, *ha ha!* – never *had* that experience!

ISABEL: Before? Well, now you're faced with it, I hope you know how to handle it. You know why I know he's left me? He only took in my bags, he left his own in the car, he brought in all of mine except my little blue zipper overnight bag, *that* he kept for some reason. Perhaps he intends to pick up another female companion who could use its contents.

RALPH: Little lady, you're in a bad state of nerves.

ISABEL: Have you ever been so tired that you don't know what you're doing or saying?

RALPH: Yes. Often.

ISABEL: That's my condition, so make allowances for it. Yes, indeed, that *sure* is a mighty *far* drugstore . . .

[*She wanders back to the window, and parts the curtain to peer out.*]

RALPH: He seems gone twice as long because you're thinking about it.

ISABEL: I don't know why I should care except for my overnight bag with my toilet articles in it.

RALPH [*obliquely investigating*]: Where did you spend last night?

ISABEL [*vaguely*]: Where did we spend last night?

RALPH: Yeah. Where did you stop for the night?

ISABEL [*rubbing her forehead and sighing with perplexity*]: In a, in a – oh, a tourist camp called the – Old Man River Motel? Yes, the Old Man River Motel.

RALPH: That's a mistake. The first night ought to be spent in a real fine place regardless of what it cost you. It's so important to get off on the right foot.

[*He has freshened his drink and come around to the front of the bar. She has gone back to the window at the sound of a car.*]

If you get off on the wrong foot, it can take a long time to correct it.

[*She nods in slow confirmation of this opinion.*]

Un-hmmm. Walls are built up between people a hell of a damn sight faster than – broken down ... Y'want me to give you my word that he's coming back? I will, I'll give you my word. Hey.

[*He snaps his fingers.*]

Had he brought me a Christmas present? If not, *that's* what he's doing. *That* explains where he went to.

[*There is a pause. She sits sadly by the fireplace.*]

What went wrong last night?

ISABEL: Let's not talk about that.

RALPH: I don't mean to pry into such a private, intimate thing, but –

ISABEL: No, let's don't! I'll just put it this way and perhaps you will understand me. In spite of my being a student nurse, till discharged – my experience has been limited, Mr Bates. Perhaps it's because I grew up in a small town, an only child, too protected. I wasn't allowed to date till my last year at High and then my father insisted on meeting the boys I went out with and laid down pretty strict rules, such as when to bring me home from parties and so forth. If he smelled liquor on the breath of a boy? At the door? That boy would not enter the door! And that little rule ruled out a goodly number.

RALPH: I bet it did. They should've ate peanuts befo' they called for you, honey.

[*He chuckles, reflectively poking at the fire.*]

That's what we done at the Sisters of Mercy Orphans' Home in Mobile.

ISABEL [*touched*]: Oh. Were you an *orphan*, Mr Bates?

RALPH: Yes, I had that advantage.

[*He slides off the high stool again to poke at the fire. She picks up the antique bellows and fans the flames, crouching beside him.*]

ISABEL: So you were an orphan! People that grow up orphans, don't they value love more?

RALPH: Well, let's put it this way. They get it less easy. To get it, they have to give it: so, yeah, they do value it more.

[*He slides back on to the bar stool. She crouches at the fireplace to fan the fire with the bellows; the flickering light brightens their shy, tender faces.*]

ISABEL: But it's also an advantage to have a parent like my daddy.

[*She's again close to tears.*]

Very strict but devoted. Opposed me going into the nursing profession but I had my heart set on it, I thought I had a vocation, I saw myself as a Florence Nightingale nurse. A lamp in her hand? Establishin' clinics in the – upper Amazon country ...

[*She laughs a little ruefully.*]

Yais, I had heroic daydreams about myself as a dedicated young nurse working side by side with a –

[*She pauses shyly.*]

RALPH: With a dedicated young doctor?

ISABEL: No, the doctor would be older, well, not too old, but – older. I saw myself passing among the pallets, you know, the straw mats, administering to the plague victims in the jungle, exposing myself to contagion ...

[*She exhibits a bit of humour here.*]

RALPH: *Catchin'* it?

ISABEL: Yais, contractin' it eventually *m'self* ...

RALPH: What were the symptoms of it?

ISABEL: A slight blemish appearing on the – hands?

[*She gives him a darting smile.*]

RALPH [*joining in the fantasy with her*]: Which you'd wear gloves to conceal?

ISABEL: Yais, rubber gloves all the time.

RALPH: A crusty-lookin' blemish or more like a fungus?

[*They laugh together.*]

ISABEL: I don't think I – yais, I did, I imagined it being like *scaa-ales*! Like silver fish scales appearing on my hainds and then progressing gradually to the wrists and *fo'*-arms ...

RALPH: And the young doctor discovering you were concealing this condition?

ISABEL: The *youngish middle-aged* doctor, Mr Bates! Yais, discovering I had contracted the plague myself and then a big scene in which she says, Oh, no, you mustn't touch me but he seizes her passionately in his arms, of course, and – exposes himself to contagion.

[RALPH *chuckles heartily, getting off the stool to poke at the fire again. She joins him on the floor to fan the flames with the bellows.*]

ISABEL: And love is stronger than death. You get the picture?

RALPH: Yep, I've seen the picture.

ISABEL: We've had a good laugh together. You're a magician, Ralph, to make me laugh tonight in my present situation. George and I never laugh, we never laugh together. Oh, he makes JOKES, YAIS! But we never have a really genuine laugh together and that's a bad sign, I think, because I don't think a married couple can go through life without laughs together any more than they can without tears.

RALPH: Nope.

[*He removes his shoes.*]

Take your slippers off, honey.

ISABEL: I have the funniest sensation in the back of my head, like –

RALPH: Like a tight rope was coming unknotted?

ISABEL: Exactly! Like a tight rope was being unknotted!

[*He removes her slippers and puts them on the hearth, crosses into the bedroom and comes out with a pair of fluffy pink bedroom slippers. He crouches beside her and feels the sole of her stocking.*]

RALPH: Yep, damp. Take those damp stockings off.

ISABEL: [*unconsciously following the suggestion*]: Does George have a sense of humour? In your opinion? Has he got the ability to laugh at himself and at life and at – human sitations? Outside of off-colour jokes? In your opinion, Mr Bates?

RALPH [*taking the damp stockings from her and hanging them over the footlights*]: Yes. We had some good laughs together, me an' – 'Gawge', ha ha! ...

ISABEL: We never had any together.

RALPH: That's the solemnity of romantic love, little lady, I mean like Romeo and Juliet was not exactly a joke book, ha ha ha!

ISABEL: 'The solemnity of romantic love'! – I wouldn't expect an old war buddy of George's to use an expression like that.

RALPH: Lemme put these on your feet, little lady.

[*She sighs and extends her feet and he slips the soft fleecy pink slippers on them.*]

But you know something? I'm gonna tell you something which isn't out of the joke books either. You got a wonderful boy in your hands, on your hands, they don't make them any better than him and I mean it.

[*He does.*]

ISABEL: I appreciate your loyalty to an old war buddy.

RALPH: Naw, naw, it's not just that.

ISABEL: But if they don't make them any better than George Haverstick, they ought to stop making them, they ought to *cease producing!*

[*She utters a sort of wild, sad laugh which stops as abruptly as it started. Suddenly she observes the bedroom slippers on her feet.*]

What's these, where did they come from?

RALPH: Honey, I just put them on you. Didn't you know?

ISABEL: No! – How strange! – I didn't, I wasn't at all aware of it ...

[*They are both a little embarrassed.*]

Where is your wife, Mr Bates?

RALPH: Honey, I told you she quit me and went home to her folks.

ISABEL: Oh, excuse me, I remember. You told me ...

[*Suddenly the blazing logs make a sharp cracking noise; a spark *apparently has spat out of the grate on to* ISABEL*'s skirt. She gasps and springs up, retreating from the fireplace, and* RALPH *jumps off the bar stool to brush at her skirt. Under the material of the angora wool skirt is the equal and warmer softness of her young body.* RALPH *is abruptly embarrassed, coughs, turns back to the fireplace and picks up copper tongs to shift the position of crackling logs.*

This is a moment between them that must be done just right to avoid misinterpretation. RALPH *would never make a play for the bride of a buddy. What should come out of the moment is not a suggestion that he will or might but that Dotty's body never felt that way. He remembers bodies that did. What comes out of Isabel's reaction is a warm understanding of his warm understanding; just that, nothing more, at all.*]

ISABEL: Thank you. This angora wool is, is – highly inflammable stuff, at least I would – think it – might be . . .

RALPH: Yeah, and I don't want 'Gawge' to come back here and find, a toasted marshmallow bride . . . by my fireplace.

[*They sit down rather self-consciously,* RALPH *on the high stool,* ISABEL *on the low hassock.*]

ISABEL: Yais . . .

RALPH: Huh?

ISABEL: Daddy opposed me going into nursing so much that he didn't speak to me, wouldn't even look at me for a whole week before I took off for Saint Louie.

RALPH: Aw? Tch!

ISABEL: However, at the last moment, just before the train pulled out of the depot, he came stalking up the platform to the coach window with a gift package and an envelope. The package contained flannel nighties and the envelope had in it a list of moral instructions in the form of prayers such as: 'O Heavenly Father, give thy weak daughter strength to –

[*She giggles.*]

– resist the –'

[*She covers her mouth with a hand to suppress a spasm of laughter.*]

Oh, my Lord! Well, you would have to know Daddy to appreciate the –

RALPH: Honey, I reckon I know your daddy. That's what I meant about the orphan's advantage, honey.

[*They laugh together.*]

ISABEL: We sure do have some good laughs together, Mr Bates. Where did I get *these*?

[*She means the bedroom slippers.*]

These aren't mine, where did, how did – ? *Oh – yes*, you –

[*They resume their grave contemplation of the fire.*]

'Heavenly Father, give thy weak daughter the strength of will to resist the lusts of men. Amen.'

[RALPH *chuckles sadly.*]

And I was never tempted to, *not* to, resist them, till – George ...

RALPH: Did George arouse a – ?

ISABEL: I don't suppose another man could see George the way I see him: SAW him. So *handsome?* And so *afflicted?* So afflicted and – *handsome?* With that mysterious *tremor?* With those SHAKES?

RALPH: How did 'Jawge' come on?

ISABEL: Huh? Oh. No. I don't mean he came on like a –

RALPH: Bull? Exactly?

ISABEL: No, no, no, no. It was very strange, very – strange ...

RALPH: What?

ISABEL: He always wanted us to go out on double dates or with a whole bunch of – others. And when we were alone? Together? There was a – funny, oh, a very *odd* — sort of – *timidity*! – between us ... And that, of course is what touched me; oh, that – *touched* me ...

[*There is a pause in the talk.* RALPH *descends from his high perch and passes behind her low hassock with a smile behind her back which is a recognition of the truth of her romantic commitment to George. This is also in the slight, tender pat that he gives to the honey-coloured crown of her head.*]

An' so although I had many strong opportunities to give in to my 'weakness' on, on – week-end dates with young interns and doctors at Barnes? – I was never tempted to do so. But with George –

RALPH: You did? Give in?

ISABEL: Mr Bates, George Haverstick married a virgin, and I can't say for sure that it was my strength of will and not *his* that – deserves the credit . . .

[RALPH *returns to fireplace with beer.*]

RALPH: Yeah, well. Now I'm going to tell you something about that boy that might surprise you after your experience last night at the Old Man River Motel.

[*He opens a beer can.*]

He always bluffs about his ferocious treatment of women, believe me! To hear him talk you'd think he spared them no pity! However, I happen to know he didn't come on as strong with those dolls in Tokyo and Hong Kong and Korea as he liked to pretend to. Because I heard from those dolls . . . He'd just sit up there on a pillow and drink that rice wine with them and teach them *English!* Then come downstairs from there, hitching his belt and shouting, *'Oh, man! Oh, brother!'* – like he'd laid 'em to waste.

ISABEL: That was not his behaviour in the Old Man River Motel. Last night.

RALPH: What went wrong in the Old Man River Motel?

ISABEL: Too many men think that girls in the nursing profession must be – *shock*proof. I'm not, I wasn't – last night . . .

RALPH: Oh. Was he drunk?

ISABEL: He'd been drinking all day in that heaterless retired funeral hack in a snowstorm to keep himself warm. Since I don't drink, I just had to endure it. Then we stopped at the Old Man River Motel, as dreary a place as you could find on this earth! The electric heater in our cabin lit up but gave off no heat! Oh, *George* was comfortable there! Threw off his clothes and sat down in front of the heater as if I were not even present.

RALPH: Aw.

ISABEL: Continuing drinking!

RALPH: Aw.

ISABEL: Then began the courtship, and, oh, what a courtship it was, such tenderness, romance! I finally screamed. I locked myself in the bathroom and didn't come out till he had gotten to bed and then I – slept in a chair . . .

RALPH: You wouldn't –

ISABEL: Mr Bates, I just couldn't! The atmosphere just wasn't right. And he –

[*She covers her face.*]

– I can't tell you more about it just now except that it was a nightmare, him in the bed, pretending to be asleep, and me in the chair pretending to be asleep too and both of us knowing the other one *wasn't* asleep and, and – I can't tell you more about it right now, I just can't tell more than I've told you about it, I –

[*Her sobs become violent and there is a pause.*]

RALPH: Hey! Let me kiss the bride! Huh? Can I kiss the bride?

ISABEL: You're very kind, Mr Bates. I'm sure you were more understanding with your wife when you were going through this –

RALPH: – period of adjustment? Yeah. That's all it is, it's just a little – period of adjustment.

[*He bestows a kiss on her tear-stained cheek and a pat on her head. She squeezes his hand and sinks down again before the fireplace.*]

ISABEL: It isn't as if I'd given him to believe that I was *experienced*! I made it clear that I wasn't. He knows my background and we'd talked at great *length* about my – inhibitions which I know are – *inhibitions*, but – which an understanding husband wouldn't expect his bride to overcome at *once*, in a tourist cabin, after a *long – silent – ride! –* in a *funeral hack* in a *snowstorm* with the *heater not working* in a *shocked condition! –* having just been told that – we were *both* unemployed, and –

RALPH: Little Bit, Little Bit – you had a sleepless night in that motel – why don't you put in a little sack time now. You need it, honey. Take Dotty's bed in there and think about nothing till morning.

ISABEL: You mean you know, now, that George is not coming back?

RALPH: No. I mean that Dotty's not coming back.

ISABEL: I don't think you ever thought that he would come back for me any more than I did.

RALPH: Take Dotty's bed, get some sleep on that foam-rubber mattress while I sit here and watch the Late Late Show on TV.

ISABEL: But, Mister Bates, if your wife does come back here I wouldn't want her to find a stranger in your bedroom.

RALPH: Honey, finding a stranger in a bedroom is far from being the biggest surprise of a lifetime. So you go on in there and lock the door.

ISABEL: Thank you, Mister Bates.

[She enters bedroom.]

I'm only locking the door because of the slight possibility that Mister George Haverstick the Fourth might come back drunk and try to repeat the comedy and tragedy of last night. I hope you realize that.

RALPH: Oh, sure. Good night, sleep tight, honey.

[She locks the bedroom door as RALPH *returns to the fireplace.]*

RALPH *[to himself and the audience]*: What a bitch of a Christmas!

CURTAIN

ACT TWO

No time lapse.

[ISABEL *jumps up as a car is heard stopping out front. She looks wildly at* RALPH, *who gives her a nod and a smile as he crosses to the front door. Snow blows into the living-room as he goes out and shouts:*]

RALPH: HEY!

[ISABEL *catches her breath, waiting.*]

Ha ha!

[ISABEL *expels her breath and sits down.* RALPH, *shouting through snow:*]

Your wife thought she was deserted!

GEORGE [*from a distance*]: *Hey!*

[ISABEL *springs up and rushes to a mirror to wipe away tears. A car door is heard slamming in front of the house.* ISABEL *sits down. She immediately rises, rubbing her hands together, and then sits down again. Then she springs up and starts towards the bedroom. Stops short as* GEORGE *enters.*]

I'm the son of a camel, ha ha! My mother was a camel with two humps, a double hump – dromedary! Ha ha ha!

[GEORGE *and* RALPH *catch each other in a big, rocking hug.* ISABEL *stares, ignored, as the male greetings continue.*]

RALPH: *You ole son of a tail gun!*

GEORGE: *How'sa young squirrel? Ha ha!*

RALPH: *How'sa Texas jack rabbit?*

[*There is a sudden, incongruous stillness. They stare, all three of them,* ISABEL *at* GEORGE, GEORGE *and* RALPH *at each other.* GEORGE *is suddenly embarrassed and says:*]

GEORGE: Well, I see yuh still got yuh dawg.

RALPH: Yeah, m'wife's folks are cat lovers.

GEORGE: You'll get your wife back tomorrow.

RALPH: Hell, I don't want her back.

GEORGE: Y'don't want 'er back?

RALPH: That's right.

GEORGE: Hell, in that case, you won't be able to beat 'er off with a stick, ha ha!

[*His laugh expires as he catches* ISABEL'*s outraged look.*]

Won't be able to beat her away from the door with a stick t'morrow ...

[*They stare at each other brightly, with little chuckles, a constant series of little chuckles,* ISABEL *feels ignored.*]

ISABEL: I doubt that Mr Bates means it.

GEORGE: Didn't you all have a kid of some kind? I don't remember if it was a boy or a girl.

ISABEL: The toys under the tree might give you a clue as to that.

RALPH: Yeah, it's a boy, I guess. Drink?

GEORGE: You bet.

[GEORGE *goes to the bar and starts mixing drinks.*]

ISABEL: How old is your little boy?

RALPH: Three years old and she's awready made him a sissy.

GEORGE: They'll do it ev'ry time, man.

[*He keeps chuckling, as does* RALPH.]

RALPH: I didn't want this kind of a dawg, either. I wanted a Doberman pinscher, a dawg with some guts, not a whiner! But she wanted a poodle and this flop-eared sad sack of a spaniel was a compromise which turned out to be worse'n a poodle, ha, ha! ...

GEORGE: I'll bet yuh dollars to doughnuts your wife and kid'll be back here tomorrow.

RALPH [*in his slow drawl*]: They won't find me here if they do. I'm all packed to go. I would of been gone when you called but I'm waitin' t' git a call from a boy about t' git married. I want him to come over here an' make a cash offer on all this household stuff since I spent too much on Christmas and won't be around to collect my unemployment.

GEORGE: Come along with us. We got a big car out there an' we're as free as a breeze. Ain't that right, Little Bit?

ISABEL: Don't ask me what's right. I don't know! I *do* know, though, that couples with children don't separate at Christmas, and, George, let your friend work out his problems himself. You don't know the situation and don't have any right to interfere in it. And now will you please go get my little blue zipper bag for me? *Please?*

RALPH [*to* GEORGE, *as if she hadn't spoken*]: Naw, I'm just going out to the army airfield a couple miles down the highway and catch the first plane going west.

GEORGE: We'll talk about that.

ISABEL: *George!*

GEORGE: AW, HERE! I forgot to give you your present! After drivin' almost back into Memphis to find a liquor store open.

[*He extends a gift-wrapped magnum of champagne.*]

RALPH: Lover Jesus! Champagne?

GEORGE: Imported and already cold.

RALPH [*glancing briefly at* ISABEL]: Didn't I tell you that he was buyin' me something? She thought you'd deserted her, boy.

ISABEL: *All right, I'll get it myself! I'll go out and get it out of the car myself!*

[*She rushes out into snow, leaving the door open.*

GEORGE *closes the door without apparently noticing her exit.*]

GEORGE: Boy, you an' me have got a lot to talk over.

RALPH: We sure got lots of territory to cover.

GEORGE: So your goddam marriage has cracked up on yuh, has it?

RALPH: How's yours goin'? So far?

GEORGE: We'll talk about it *later*. Discuss it *thoroughly*! *Later!*

RALPH: Y' got married yestiddy mawnin'?

GEORGE: Yeah.

RALPH: How was last night?

GEORGE: We'll talk about *that* later, too.

[ISABEL *rushes into the room in outrage, panting.*]

ISABEL: *I* can't break the lock on that *car*!

GEORGE: Little Bit, I didn't know that you wuh bawn in a barn.

[*He means she left the door open again.*]

ISABEL: I didn't know a lot about you, either!

[GEORGE *closes door.*]

Mr Bates! Mr Bates!

[*He turns towards her with a vague smile.*]

The gentleman I married refuses to get my zipper bag out of the car or unlock the car so I can get it myself.

[*The phone rings.* RALPH *picks it up.*]

RALPH [*in a slow, hoarse drawl, at the phone*]: Aw, hi, Smokey. I'm glad you got my message. Look. I quit Regal Dairy Products and I'm flyin' out of here late tonight or early tomorrow morning and I thought maybe you might like to look over some of my stuff here, the household equipment, and make me a cash offer for it. I'll take less in cash than a cheque since I'm not gonna stop at the Coast, I'm flying straight through to Hong Kong so it would be difficult for me to cash yuh cheque an' of course I expect to make a sacrifice on the stuff here. Hey! Would you like a beaver-skin coat, sheared beaver-skin coat for Gertrude? Aw. I'd let you have if for a, for a – third off! Aw. Well, anyhow, come over right away, Smokey, and make me an offer in cash on as much of this household stuff as you figure that you could use when you git married. O.K.?

[*He hangs up.*]

GEORGE: Hong Kong?

RALPH: Yeah.

GEORGE: Well, how about that! Back to Miss Lotus Blossom in the Pavilion of Joys?

RALPH: I never had it so good. At least not *since*.

ISABEL [*acidly*]: Mr Bates, your character has changed since my gypsy husband appeared! He seems to have had an immediate influence on you, and not a good one. May I wash up in your bathroom?

[*They both look at her with slight, enigmatic smiles.*]

RALPH: What's that, honey?

ISABEL: Will you let me use your bathroom?

RALPH: Aw, sure, honey. I'm sorry you –

GEORGE: Now what's the matter with her?

[*He turns to* ISABEL.]

Now what's the matter with you?

ISABEL: May I talk to you alone? In another room?

RALPH: You all go in the bedroom and straighten things out.

[RALPH *goes out into the snow flurry.* GEORGE *leads* ISABEL *into next room.*]

GEORGE: Now what's the matter with you?

ISABEL: Is this a sample of how I'm going to be treated?

GEORGE: What do you mean? How have I treated you, huh?

ISABEL: I might as well not be present! For all the attention I have been paid since you and your buddy had this tender reunion!

GEORGE: Aren't you being a little unreasonable, honey?

ISABEL: I don't think so. George? If you are unhappy, our marriage can still be annulled. Y'know that, don't you?

GEORGE: You want to get *out* of it, do you?

[RALPH *comes back in with her travelling case. He sets it down and goes to the kitchenette.*]

ISABEL: I don't think it's really very unreasonable of me to want to be treated as if I LIVED! EXISTED!

GEORGE: Will you quit actin' like a spoiled little bitch? I want to tell you something. You're the first woman that ever put me down! Sleepin' las' night in a chair? What kind of basis is that for a happy marriage?

ISABEL: You had to get drunk on a highway! In a heaterless funeral car, after informing me you had just quit your job! Blasting my eardrums, afterwards, with a car radio you wouldn't let me turn down. How was I supposed to react to such kindness? Women are human beings and I am not an exception to that rule, I assure you! I HATED YOU LAST NIGHT AFTER YOU HAD BEEN HATING ME AND TORTURING ME ALL DAY LONG!

[RALPH *comes back into the front room.*]

GEORGE: Torturing you, did you say? WHY DON'T YOU SIMMER DOWN! We ain't ALONE here, y'know!

RALPH [*quietly, from the living room*]: You all are just goin' through a perfectly usual little period of adjustment. That's all it is, I told her –

GEORGE: Aw! You all have been talking?

ISABEL: What did you think we'd been doing while you were gone in that instrument of torture you have for a car?

GEORGE: You've got to simmer down to a lower boiling point, baby.

RALPH [*entering the bedroom*]: Just goin' through a period of adjustment . . .

ISABEL: Adjustment to what, Mr Bates? Humiliation? For the rest of my life? Well, I won't have it! I don't want such an 'adjustment'. I want to – May I –

[*She sobs.*]

– freshen up a little bit in your bathroom before we drive downtown? To check in at a hotel?

RALPH: Sure you can.

GEORGE: I ain't goin' downtown – or checkin' in no hotel.

[*He goes back into the living-room.*]

ISABEL: YOU may do as you *please! I'm* checking in a hotel.

RALPH [*offering her a glass*]: You never finished your drink.

ISABEL: I don't care to, thanks. Too many people think that liquor solves problems, all problems. I think all it does is *confuse* them!

RALPH: I would say that it – *obfuscates* them a little, but –

ISABEL: Does *what* to them, Mr Bates?

RALPH: I work crossword puzzles. I – ha ha! – pick up a lot of long words. Obfuscates means obscures. And problems need obfuscation now and then, honey. I don't mean total or permanent obfuscation, I just mean *temporary* obfuscation, that's all.

[*He is touched by the girl and he is standing close to her, still holding the glass out towards her. He has a fine, simple sweetness and gentleness when he's not 'bugged' by people.*]

D'ya always say *Mister* to men?

ISABEL: Yes, I do till I know them. I had an old-fashioned upbringing and I can't say I regret it. Yes.

[*She is still peering out of the door at her new husband.*]

RALPH: I wish you would say Ralph to me like you *know* me, honey. You got a tension between you, and tensions obfuscate love. Why don't you get that cross look off your face and give him a loving expression? Obfuscate his problems with a sweet smile on your face and –

ISABEL: YOU do that! I'm not in a mood to 'obfuscate' his problems. Mr Bates, I think he'd do better to face them like I'm facing mine, such as the problem of having married a man that seems to dislike me after one day of marriage.

RALPH: Finish this drink and obfuscate that problem because it doesn't exist.

[*He closes the bedroom door. As he comes back to* ISABEL *with the glass,* GEORGE *reopens the door between the two rooms, glares in for a moment and switches the overhead light on, then goes back into the parlour.* RALPH *smiles tolerantly at this show of distrust which is not justified.*]

ISABEL: You have a sweet little bedroom, Mr Bates.

RALPH: I married a *sweet, homely* woman. Almost started to *like* her. I can like *anybody*, but –

ISABEL: Mr Bates? Ralph? This house has a *sweetness* about it!

RALPH: You don't think it's 'tacky'?

ISABEL: No. I think it's – sweet!

RALPH: We got it cheap because this section of town is built right over a cavern.

ISABEL [*without listening*]: What?

RALPH: This High Point suburb is built over an underground cavern and is gradually sinking down in it. You see those cracks in the walls?

ISABEL: Oh . . .

[*She hasn't listened to him or looked.*]

Oh! My little blue bag. May I have it?

RALPH [*through the door*]: She wants a little blue bag.

GEORGE: *Here, give it to her, goddam it!*

[*He tosses the bag into the bedroom.* ISABEL *screams.* RALPH *catches the bag.*]

Now whatcha screamin' faw?

ISABEL: Thank heaven Mr Bates is such a good catch. All my colognes and perfumes are in that bag, including a twenty-five dollar bottle of Vol-de-nuit. Mr Bates, will it be necessary for me to phone the hotel?

GEORGE: Didn't you hear what I said?

ISABEL: Mr Bates! Would you mind phoning some clean, inexpensive hotel to hold a room for us tonight?

GEORGE: I said I'm not gonna check in a hotel tonight!

ISABEL: Reserve a *single* room, please!

RALPH: Sure, sure, honey, I'll do that. Now you just rest an' fresh up an' – Come on, George, let her alone here now, so she can rest an' calm down.

[*He leads* GEORGE *back into the parlour.*]

GEORGE: Look at my hands! Willya look at my hands?

RALPH: What about your hands?

GEORGE: Remember that tremor? Which I had in Korea? Those shakes? Which started in Korea?

RALPH: Aw, is it come back on yuh?

GEORGE: Are you blind, man?

RALPH: Yeah. How's your drink?

GEORGE: She in the bathroom yet?

RALPH: Naw, she's still in the bedroom.

GEORGE: Wait'll she gits in the bathroom so we can talk.

RALPH: What's your drink, ole son?

GEORGE: Beer's fine. Jesus!

RALPH [*at the bar*]: Rough?

GEORGE: Just wait'll she gits in the bathroom so I can tell you about last night.

RALPH: Here.

[*He hands him a beer.*]

GEORGE [*at the bedroom door*]: She's still sittin' there bawling on that bed. Step outside a minute.

[*He goes to the front door and out on to the tiny paved porch. The interior dims as* RALPH *follows him out. For a while they just stand drinking beer with the snow shadows swarming about them.*]

RALPH: Chilly.

GEORGE: I don't feel chilly.

RALPH: *I* do.

[*He pauses.*]

You're not for that little lady in that damn silly little sissy mess of a bedroom!

GEORGE: What's wrong with the bedroom, it looked like a nice little bedroom.

RALPH: A bedroom is just as nice as whoever sleeps in it with you.

GEORGE: I missed that. What was that, now?

[*He rests an arm on Ralph's shoulders.*]

RALPH: How would you like ev'ry time you wint t'bed with your wife, you had to imagine on the bed in the dark that it wasn't her on it with you, in the dark with you, but any one of a list of a thousand or so lovely lays? I done a despicable thing. I married a girl that had no attraction for me excepting I felt sorry for her and her old man's money! I got what I should have gotten: nothing! Just a goddam desk job at Regal Dairy Products, one of her daddy's business operations in Memphis, at eight-five lousy rutten dollars a week! With my background? In the Air Force?

GEORGE: Man, an air record will cut you no ice on the ground. All it leaves you is a – mysterious tremor. Come on back in. I'm freezing to death out here. I'll git her into that bathroom so we can talk.

[*He tosses the beer cans into yard.*]

RALPH: Don't y'know better'n to throw beer cans in a man's front yard?

[*He says this vaguely, glumly, as he follows* GEORGE *back into the cottage and shuts the door behind them.* GEORGE *goes to bedroom.*]

GEORGE [*entering*]: Little Bit, you told me you couldn't wait to get under a good hot shower. There's a good shower in that bathroom. Why don't you go and get under that good hot shower?

ISABEL: I have a lot to think over, George.

GEORGE: Think it over under a good shower in that bathroom, will you? I want to take a bath, too.

ISABEL [*suddenly turning to face him from the bed*]: George, I feel so lonely!

GEORGE: Yeah, and whose fault is that?

ISABEL: I don't know why I suddenly felt so lonely!

[*She sobs again. He regards her coolly from the door.*]

GEORGE: Little Bit, go in the bathroom and take your shower, so I can go take mine, or do you want us to go in and take one together?

[*She rises with a sigh and goes to bathroom door.*]

Naw, I didn't think so.

[*She enters the bathroom. He waits till the shower starts, then returns to the front room.*]

There now, she's in!

[*He shakes both fists in the air with a grimace of torment.*]

Look! I got to get rid of that girl. I got to get rid of her quick. Jesus! You got to help me. I can't stay with that girl.

RALPH: Man, you're married to her.

GEORGE: You're married to one! Where's yours? You son of a tail gun! Don't tell me I'm married to her when we ain't exchanged five remarks with each other since we drove out of Cape Girardeau where she refused to – has she come out of the bathroom? No! – Even *undress*! But huddled up in a chair all night in a blanket, crying? Because she had the misfortune to be my wife?

RALPH: I wouldn't count on it.

GEORGE: On what?

RALPH: Her thinking it's such a misfortune.

GEORGE: I described to you how we passed the night, last night!

RALPH: Is this girl a virgin?

GEORGE: She is a *cast-iron* virgin! And's going to stay one! Determined!

RALPH: I wouldn't count on that.

GEORGE: I would. I count on it. First thing I do tomorrow is pack her on to a plane back to Saint Louie.

RALPH: You must have done something to shock her.

GEORGE: That's the truth, I tried to sleep with her.

RALPH: Maybe you handled the little lady too rough.

GEORGE: Now don't talk to me like a wise old man of the mountain about how to deal with a woman. Who was it had to make dates for who at Big Springs and who was it even had to make arrangements for you with those Tokyo dolls?

RALPH: That's not women, that's gash.

GEORGE: Gash are women.

RALPH: They are used women. You've got a unused woman and got to approach her as one.

GEORGE: She's gonna stay unused as far as I am concerned.

[*He stoops by the Christmas tree.*]

Now what the hell is this thing?

[*He has crouched among the toys under the tree.*]

RALPH: Rocket launcher. Miniature of the rocket-launchin' pad at Cape Canaveral.

GEORGE: No snow! How's it work?

RALPH: Gimme the countdown. I'll show you.

GEORGE: Ten, Nine. Eight. Seven. Six. Five. Four. Three. Two. Oww!

[*The rocket has fired in his face.*]

RALPH: Ain't you got sense enough to stand clear of a rocket launcher? Ha ha! Last week, just last week, I caught the little bugger playin' with a rag doll. Well, I snatched that doll away from him an' pitched it into the fireplace. He tried to pull it out an' burned his hand! Dotty called me a monster! The child screamed 'I hate you!' an' kicked my shins black an' blue! But I'll be damned if any son of Ralph Bates will grow up playin' with dolls. Why, I'll bet you he rides this hawss side-saddle! Naw, a sissy tendency in a boy's got to be nipped in the bud, otherwise the bud will blossom.

GEORGE: I would prefer to have a little girl.

[*He says this wistfully, still rubbing his bruised forehead.*]

Little girls prefer Daddy. Female instinct comes our early in them.

RALPH: I wanted a boy but I'm not sure I got one. However, I got him a real red-blooded boy's Christmas, at no small expense for a man in my income bracket!

[ISABEL *comes out of the bathroom.*]

I like the kid, I mean I – sure would suffer worse than he would if the neighbourhood gang called him 'Sissy!' I'm tolerant. By nature. But if I git partial custody of the kid, even one month in summer, I will correct the sissy tendency in him. Because in this world you got to be what your physical sex is or correct it in Denmark. I mean we got a *man's* world coming up, man! Technical! Terrific! And it's gotta be *fearless! Terrific!*

ISABEL: Mr Bates.

GEORGE [*on his way to the door*]: Whadaya want?

ISABEL: I called for Mistuh Bates.

GEORGE: Mistuh Bates, Mrs Haverstick is anxious to talk to you, suh.

ISABEL: I just want to know if you have called the hotel.

RALPH [*entering*]: Sure, sure, honey. Don't worry about a thing. Everything's gonna be fine.

ISABEL [*she is in a silk robe*]: Thanks, Ralph. You've been awf'ly kind to me. Oh! I helped myself to a little Pepto-Bismol I found in your sweet little bathroom.

RALPH: Aw, that pink stuff? Take it all. I never touch it. It's Dorothea's. She used to get acid stomach.

ISABEL: It's very soothing.

[GEORGE *crosses to the bedroom door, head cocked, somewhat suspicious.*]

RALPH: Well, I cured her of that. I doubt that she's hit that Pepto-Bismol bottle once in the last five years.

ISABEL: I rarely suffer from an upset stomach. Rarely as snow in Memphis!

[*She laughs lightly.*]

But the human stomach is an emotional barometer with some people. Some get headaches, others get upset stomachs.

RALPH: Some even git diarrhoea.

ISABEL: The combination of nervous strain and – Oh! What's this?

[*She picks up a gorgeously robed statue of the infant Jesus.*]

RALPH: Aw, that.

[*He moves farther into the bedroom.* GEORGE *moves closer to the door.*]

That's the Infant of Prague. Prague, Czechoslovakia?

ISABEL: Oh?

RALPH: It was discovered there in the ruins of an old monastery. It has miraculous properties.

ISABEL: Does it?

RALPH: They say that it does. Whoever gives you the Infant of Prague gives you a piece of money to put underneath it for luck. Her father presented this infant to Dorothea so the piece of money was *naturally one penny*. It's s'posed to give you prosperity if you're not prosperous and a child if you're childless. It give us a child but the money is yet to come in, the money's just been goin' out. However, I don't blame the Infant of Prague for that, because –

ISABEL: Mr Bates? Ralph? You know, very often people can be absolutely blind, stupid, and helpless about their own problems and still have a keen intuition about the problems of others?

RALPH: Yeah?

ISABEL: There is such a tender atmosphere in this sweet little house, especially this little bedroom, you can almost – touch it, feel it! I mean you can *breathe* the tender atmosphere in it!

RALPH [*in a slow, sad drawl*]: The colour scheme in this bedroom is battleship grey. And will you notice the cute inscriptions on the twin beds? 'His' on this one, 'Hers' on that one? The linen's marked his and hers, too. Well. The space between the two beds was no-man's-land for a while. Her psychological frigidity was like a, like a – artillery barrage! – between his and hers. I didn't try to break through it the first few nights. Nope. I said to myself, 'Let *her* make the first move.'

ISABEL: *Did she?*

RALPH: What do *you* think?

ISABEL: I think she *did.*

RALPH: *Right you are!*

[*He gives her a little congratulatory pat on the shoulder.*]

GEORGE: What's this heart-to-heart talk goin' on in here?

RALPH [*chuckling*]: Come on out of here, boy. I got something to tell you.

[*He leads* GEORGE *out.*]

GEORGE: What were you up to in there?

RALPH [*whispering loudly*]: Go in there, quick, before she gets dressed, you fool!

GEORGE: I'll be damned if I will!

RALPH: I'll turn the TV on loud.

ISABEL [*calling out*]: I'll be dressed in a jiffy!

RALPH: GO ON! You just got a jiffy!

GEORGE: Yeah, and I've got some pride, too. She put me down last night, first woman ever to put me down in –

RALPH: I know, you told me. GO IN! Lock the door and –

GEORGE: YOU go in! That's what you WANT to do! I never had a girl yet that you didn't want to take over. This time you're welcome. GO IN! GO BACK IN AND BREATHE THE TENDER ATMOSPHERE OF THAT –

RALPH: Jawge? Hey – You're *shakin'*, man, you're shakin' to pieces! What kind of a son of a bitch d'you take me faw?

GEORGE: The kind which you are, which you always have been!

RALPH: She is right about you. You are not well, son . . .

GEORGE: Where d'ya git this 'son' stuff! Don't call me 'son'.

RALPH: Then grow up, will yuh! What's your drink? Same?

GEORGE: Same . . .

RALPH: You're shakin' because you want to go in that bedroom. GO IN! Take the bottle in with you! I'll sit here and watch TV till –

[ISABEL *has put on her travelling suit. She comes into the living-room.*]

Too late *now*!

ISABEL [*in a sweet Texas drawl*]: Mr Bates? Ralph? It breaks my heart to see all those lovely child's toys under the tree and the little boy not here to have his Christmas.

RALPH: He's with his mother.

ISABEL: I know, but his Christmas is here.

RALPH: He's a Mama's boy. He's better off with his Mama.

ISABEL: How are *you* feeling, now, George?

[GEORGE *grunts and turns to the bar.*

ISABEL *makes a despairing gesture to Ralph.*

GEORGE *wheels about abruptly, suspecting some dumb-play.*

ISABEL *laughs lightly and then sighs deeply.*]

GEORGE: I thought you'd set your heart on a single hotel room tonight.

ISABEL: George, you're shaking worse than I've ever seen you.

GEORGE: That's, that's not your problem, that's – *my* problem, not *yours*!

RALPH [*to Isabel*]: Honey? Come here a minute.

[*He whispers something to her.*]

ISABEL: Oh, no. No! Mr Bates, you are confusing the function of a wife with that of a – I feel sorry, I feel very sorry for you not-so-young young men who've depended for love, for tenderness in your lives, on the sort of women available near army camps, in occupied territories! Mr Bates? Ralph?

RALPH: Just take his hand and lead him into the –

ISABEL: RALPH! NO! BELIEVE ME!

RALPH: All right . . .

[*There is a pause.*]

ISABEL: Ralph, why did you quit YOUR job? Did you get the shakes, too?

GEORGE: Don't get bitchy with him.

ISABEL: I WASN'T BEING BITCHY!

RALPH: She wasn't being bitchy. She asked a logical question.

ISABEL: Just a question!

GEORGE: Can't you mind your own business for a change? You got fired too, don't forget! All three of us here is jobless!

ISABEL: I am not forgetting.

[*Primly, with dignity.*]

I am not forgetting a thing, and I have a lot to remember.

GEORGE: Good. I hope you remember it. *Memorize* it!

[*He is getting tight.*]

ISABEL [*sniffing a little*]: I think I caught cold in that car.

GEORGE: Hell, you were born with a cold –

ISABEL: *Stop that!*

GEORGE: In your damn little –

ISABEL: MR BATES, MAKE HIM STOP

Overlapping, barely intelligible

RALPH: Let him blow off some steam.

GEORGE: Incurable cold! You didn't catch it from me.

ISABEL: I wish you had shown this side of your nature before, just a hint, just a clue, so I'd have known what I was in for.

GEORGE: What hint did you give *me*? What clue did *I* have to *your* nature?

ISABEL: Did I disguise my nature?

GEORGE: You sure in hell did!

ISABEL: In what *way*, tell me, please!

GEORGE: You didn't put the freeze on me at Barnes Hospital!

[*To Ralph.*]

She was nurse at Barnes when I went there for those tests. To find out the cause of my shakes. She was my night nurse at Barnes.

ISABEL: Oh, stop! Don't be so crude! How can you be so crude!

GEORGE: She was my night nurse at Barnes and gave me alcohol rubdowns at bedtime.

ISABEL: That was my job. I had to.

GEORGE: Hell, she stroked and petted me with her hands like she had on a pair of silk gloves.

ISABEL: This is insufferable. I am going downtown.

[*She covers her face, sobbing.*]

Just give me carfare downtown.

GEORGE: You remember those dolls with silk gloves on their hands in Tokyo, Ralph? Hell, she could of given them Jap dolls lessons!

ISABEL: I DID NOT TOUCH YOUR BODY EXCEPT AS A NURSE HIRED TO DO IT! YOU KNOW I DIDN'T! I DID NOT TOUCH YOUR BIG OLD LECHEROUS BODY.

GEORGE: How'd you give me a rubdown without touching my body? Huh? How could you give me rubdowns without touching my body? Huh?

ISABEL: Please, please, make him be still. Mr Bates? You believe me? He's making out I seduced him while I was his nurse.

GEORGE: I didn't say that. Don't say I said that. I didn't say that. I said you had soft little fingers and you knew what you were doing. She's say, 'Turn over.' I couldn't turn over. I had to stay on my stomach. I was embarrassed not to.

ISABEL: Ah – I feel nauseated. What filth you have in your mind!

RALPH: Honey? Little lady? Come over and sit here with me. All this will all straighten out. It's going to be all straightened out.

[GEORGE *pours himself a drink. The glass slips out of his shaking fingers.*]

GEORGE: *Worse than ever, worse than ever before!* How could I have kept that job? A ground mechanic with hands that can't hold tools?

ISABEL: Go take your tranquillizers. They're in my zipper bag.

GEORGE: Oh, Jesus!

RALPH [*picking up the dropped glass*]: See, honey? That boy isn't well. Make some allowances for him. You're both nice kids, both of you, wonderful people. And very good-looking people. I'm afraid you're doomed to be happy for a long time together, soon as this little period of adjustment that you're going through right now passes over.

[GEORGE *holds his violently shaking hands in front of him, staring at them fiercely.*

He goes to the bedroom.]

ISABEL: May I call my father, collect?

RALPH: Don't call home, now. Why upset the old people on Christmas Eve?

ISABEL: I'll just say I miss them and want to come home for Christmas.

RALPH: They'll know something's wrong if you go home without your brand-new husband.

ISABEL: Husband! What husband? That man who describes me as a Tokyo whore? Implies that I seduced him in a hospital because I was required to give him alcohol rubdowns at night?

RALPH: All he meant was you excited him, honey.

ISABEL: I assure you that was *not* my intention! I am naturally gentle, I am gentle by nature, and if my touch on his big lecherous body created – *sexual fantasies* in his *mind!* – that's hardly *my* fault, is it?

GEORGE [*returning*]: I am sorry that I upset you.

ISABEL: Will you tell him the truth?

GEORGE: Sure I will. What about?

ISABEL: Did I deliberately excite you in Barnes Hospital?

GEORGE: No. I never said that.

ISABEL: Anybody that heard you would get that impression.

GEORGE: You didn't deliberately do it, you just did it because I was horny for you, that's all, that's all, that's – all . . .

[*He slumps in a chair with a long, despairing sigh. There is a silent pause.*]

ISABEL: I don't blame you alone, George. I blame myself, too. Not for deliberate sexual provocation, but for not realizing before our marriage yesterday that we were – opposite types.

GEORGE [*sadly*]: Yes, opposite types . . .

ISABEL: *I want to talk to my father!*

GEORGE: Talk to him. Call him. I'll pay Ralph the charges.

ISABEL: May I?

RALPH: Sure, honey, call your folks and wish 'em a Merry Christmas.

ISABEL: Thank you. I will if I can stop crying.

RALPH: George? This little girl needs you. Go on, be nice to her, boy.

GEORGE: I need somebody, too. She hasn't got the incurable shakes, *I* have, *I* got 'em! Was *she* nice to *me*? *Last night?*

ISABEL [*tearfully*]: Operator? I want to call long distance, Sweetwater, Texas. Oh-seven-oh-three. No, anybody that answers. It will be Daddy, Mama can't get out of –

[*She sobs.*]

– bed!

[RALPH *makes a sign to George to go over and sit by her.* GEORGE *disregards the suggestion.*]

RALPH: You better hang up and let them call you back. Long distance is very busy on Christmas Eve. Everyone callin' the home folks.

ISABEL: I just hope I stop crying! I don't want Daddy to hear me.

[*She pauses.*]

Poor ole thing. So sweet and faithful to Mama, bedridden with arthritis for seven years, now ... Hello? What? Oh. You'll call me back when you complete the connection, will you, because it's very important, it's really very urgent ...

[*She hangs up. There is silence.*]

RALPH [*finally*]: One bad night in a rutten highway motel and you all are acting like born enemies towards each other!

GEORGE: Don't upset her, she's going to talk to her daddy. And tell him she's married to a stinker.

ISABEL: No, I'm not. I'm going to tell him that I am blissfully happy, married to the kindest man in the world, the second kindest man next to my daddy!

GEORGE: Thanks.

ISABEL: Waits hand and foot on Mama, bedridden with arthritis.

GEORGE: You told Ralph about that.

ISABEL: And has held down a job in a pharmacy all these years ...

GEORGE: Wonderful. I didn't expect to marry a girl in love with her father.

ISABEL: George Haverstick, you are truly a monster!

[*The phone rings.*
She snatches it up.]

What? – DAD! OH, PRECIOUS DADDY!

[*She bursts into violent tears.*]

Can't talk, can't talk, can't talk, can't talk, *can't – talk*!

RALPH: Honey, gi' me the phone!

[*She surrenders it to him.*]

Hello? Hi, Pop, Merry Christmas. No, this isn't George, this is a buddy of his. Isabel wants to talk to you to tell you how happy she is, but she just broke up with emotion. You know how it is, don't you, Pop? Newlyweds? They're naturally full of emotion. They got to go through a little period of adjustment between them. – Fine, yes, she's fine. She'll talk to you soon as she blows her nose. Hey, honey? Your daddy wants to talk to you.

[*She takes the phone, then bursts into violent sobbing again, covering her mouth and handing the phone back to* RALPH.]

Pop? I'll have to talk for her. She's all shook up.

[*He forces the phone back into* ISABEL*'s hand.*]

ISABEL [*choked*]: Dad?

[*She bawls again, covering the mouthpiece.* RALPH *takes the phone back from her.*]

RALPH: Pop? Just talk to her, Pop. She's too shook up to talk back.

[*He forces the phone into her hands again.*]

ISABEL: Dad? How are you, Daddy? Are you? That's wonderful, Daddy. Oh, I'm fine, too. I got married yesterday. Yesterday ... How is Mom? Just the same? Daddy? I may be seeing you soon. Yes. You know I gave up my nursing job at Barnes when I married and so I have lots of free time and I might just suddenly pop in on you – *tomorrow!* – I love you and miss you so much! Good-bye, Merry Christmas, Daddy!

[*She hangs up blindly and goes over to the Christmas tree.*]

I think it's awful your little boy's missing his Christmas. Such a wonderful Christmas. A choo-choo train with depot and tunnel, cowboy outfit, chemical set and a set of alphabet blocks ...

GEORGE: He knows what he got for his kid, you don't have to tell him.

[*There is a pause.*]

ISABEL: Well, now, I feel better, after talking to Daddy.

GEORGE: Does it make you feel uplifted, spiritually?

ISABEL: I feel less lonely. That's all.

GEORGE: I wonder if it would have that effect on me if I called my daddy or mama in Amarillo? That's in Texas, too. Maybe I'd feel less lonely. Huh, Little Bit?

[*She starts out.*]

Just wait a minute. I want to tell you something. In my thirty-four years I've been with a fair share of women and you are the first, you are the first of the lot, that has found me repulsive.

ISABEL: I don't find you 'repulsive', not even your vanity, George silly but not repulsive.

RALPH: Hey, now, you all quit this.

GEORGE: Can you stand there and tell me you find me attractive?

ISABEL: I'm afraid I can't, at this moment.

GEORGE: Well, goddam it, what in hell did you marry me faw?

ISABEL: Mr Bates, your animal is standing by the door as if it wants out. Shall I let it out for you?

RALPH: You two are just goin' through this adjustment period that all young couples go through.

ISABEL: Such a sweet animal! What is this animal's name?

GEORGE: The animal is a dog.

ISABEL: I know it's a dog.

GEORGE: Then why don't you call it a dog!

RALPH: Better put 'er lead on 'er. Her name is Bess.

ISABEL: Shall we take a walk, Bessie? Huh? A nice little run in the snow. See! She does want out. Oh! My coat . . .

RALPH: Here, put on this one, honey.

[*He takes the beaver coat out of the Christmas box under the tree.*]

ISABEL: Oh, what beautiful sheared beaver! It's your wife's Christmas present?

RALPH: It was but it ain't no more.

ISABEL: How soft! Now I know that you love her. You couldn't feel the softness of this fur and not know it was bought as a present for someone you love.

RALPH: Put it on. It's yours. A wedding present to you.

ISABEL: Oh, no I –

RALPH: WILL YOU PLEASE PUT IT ON YUH?

ISABEL: I guess the snow won't hurt it. Come on, Bessie, that's a good lady, come on . . .

[*She goes out.*]

GEORGE: I know of *two* animals that want out and one of them ain't no dawg!

ISABEL [*returning*]: I heard you say that!

GEORGE: Well, good.

ISABEL: If you want out of our marriage, a divorce isn't necessary. We can just get an annulment! So maybe last night was fortunate after all!

[*She stares at him a moment and then goes back out with the dog. As they leave, the dog is barking at something outside.*

GEORGE *comes up beside Ralph and rests an affectionate arm on his shoulders.*

The tempo now becomes very fast.]

RALPH: You old Texas jack rabbit!

GEORGE: You tail-gunner son of a – How you feel?

RALPH: I feel fine!

[*They chuckle shyly together. Then:*

They catch each other in an affectionate bear hug.]

GEORGE: How much money you got?

RALPH: Why?

GEORGE: Remember how we talked about going into something together when we got out of the service? Well, we're out of the service. How much money do you think you can raise?

RALPH: What are *your* assets, Buddy?

GEORGE: I've saved five hundred dollars and can get a thousand for that '52 Caddy.

RALPH: You can't go into no business on as little as that.

GEORGE: You're selling out this house and everything in it, ain't you?

RALPH: I'd have to split it with Dorothea, I reckon.

GEORGE: Look. Let's cut out tomorrow. Let's go to Texas together. We can swing the financing to pick up a piece of ranchland near San Antone and raise us a herd of fine cattle.

RALPH: Why San Antone?

GEORGE: I said near it. It's a beautiful town. A winding river goes through it.

RALPH: Uh-huh. You mentioned 'swing the financing'. How did you – visualize – that?

GEORGE: Noticed my car out there?

RALPH: That funeral limousine?

GEORGE: We cut out of here tomorrow bright and early and drive straight through to West Texas. In West Texas we git us a coloured boy, put a showfer's cap on him an' set him back of the wheel. He drives us up in front of the biggest San Antone bank and there we demand an immediate interview with the president of it. My folks staked out West Texas. The name of the first George Haverstick in West Texas is engraved on the memorial tablet to the Alamo heroes in San Antone! I'm not snowin' you, man! An' they's no better credit card in West Texas than an ancestor's name on that memorial tablet. We will arrive at lunch time an' – invite this bank executive to lunch at the San Antone country club to which I can git us a guest card an' befo' we're in sight of the golf links the financing deal will be swung!

RALPH: Man, a bank president has rode in a awful lot of funeral processions. It's almost one of his main professional duties. He's rode in too many funeral limousines not to know when he's in one. And ain't you afraid that he might, well – notice your shakes?

GEORGE: This little tremor would disappear completely the moment I crossed into Texas!

RALPH: I hope so, man, permanently and completely, but –

GEORGE: Go on. Tear down the project!

RALPH: There's no Ralph Bates, first, second, third, fourth or fifth on that memorial tablet to those – Alamo heroes.

GEORGE: Haven't you blazoned your name in the memory of two wars?

RALPH: Who remembers two wars? Or even one, after some years. There's a great public amnesia about a former war hero.

[*He goes reflectively to the front door.*]

GEORGE: Where you goin'?

RALPH: I'm goin' out to think in this cool night air.

[*He exits on to the paved terrace, switching off the interior lights.* GEORGE *follows gravely.* RALPH *stoops to light up a string of coloured bulbs that cover the arched entrance to the carport.*

It casts a dim rainbow glow on the terrace. Shadowy flakes of snow drift through it.]

Why San Antone? Why cattle? Why not electric equipment?

GEORGE: I know San Antone and cattle!

RALPH: And I know electric equipment.

GEORGE: Yes, you can turn on a set of little Christmas tree lights.

RALPH: I don't want to be your ranch hand!

GEORGE: We'd buy in *equal*.

RALPH: How? One minute you say you'll liquidate all your assets that only appear to be an old funeral car, the next you say we'll drive a bank president out in this funeral car, and you want me to put up all that I realize on the sale of this property here? Your sense of equity is very unequal, and shit-fire anyhow, even if I sell this property, by remote control, from Hong Kong, and Dotty's folks would sure in hell block the transaction – well, look at the cracks in this stucco, y'know how they got there? This Goddam High Point suburb – *listen!* – happens to be built over a great big underground cavern into which it is *sinking*!

GEORGE: *Sinking?*

RALPH: I'm not snowing you, man, this whole community here is gradually sinking, inch by inch by year, into this subterranean cavern and the property owners and the real-estate promoters are in collusion to keep this secret about it: so we can sell out to the next bunch of suckers: DISGUSTING!

GEORGE: Built over a –

RALPH: *Cavern: yes! – a big subterranean cavern*, but so is *your* project, not to mention your *marriage. Cattle! – Cattle?*

GEORGE: The Texas Longhorn isn't just cattle, it's a – dignified beast.

RALPH: Did you say Texas Longhorn? Son, the Texas Longhorn is not only dignified, it is *obsolete*.

GEORGE: Historical, yeah, like the Haversticks of West Texas.

RALPH: The Haversticks of West Texas are not yet obsolete, are they?

GEORGE: I am the last one of 'em an' the prospects of another don't look bright at this moment. But the Texas Longhorn –

[*He exhales.*]

– compared to modern beef cattle such as your Hereford or your Black Angus – it has no carcass value.

RALPH: Well, in that case, why don't you *breed* the Black Angus or the –

GEORGE: I anticipated that question.

RALPH: I hope you're prepared with some answer . . .

GEORGE [*draws on cigarette and flips it away*]: Le' me put it this way. How would you like to breed a herd of noble cattle, a herd that stood for the frontier days of this country! – an' ride to the depot one mawnin' in your station wagon, the name of your ranch stamped on it, to watch these great, dignified beasts being herded on to a string of flatcars, penned in and hauled off to K City packin' houses, Chicago slaughterhouses, the shockin' atrocities which cannot even be thought about without a shudder! – an' wave 'em good-bye as if they was off for a mother-lovin' church picnic?

RALPH: It's a – heart-breakin' pitcher!

[*He chuckles.*]

But I do love a good steak, ha ha! A prime-cut sirloin, however – What would you want to breed this noble herd for? For *kicks*, for – ?

GEORGE: *You* got TV in there, ain't you? Turn on your TV any late afternoon or early evenin' and what do you get – beside the commercials, I mean? A goddam Western, on film. Y'know what I see, outside the camera range? A big painted sign that says 'Haverstick-Bates Ranch' – or 'Bates-Haverstick', you can have top billing! – 'The Last Stand of the Texas Longhorn, a Dignified Beast! We breed cattle for TV Westerns.' We breed us some buffalo, too. The buffalo is also a dignified beast, almost extinct, only thirty thousand head of the buffalo left in this land. We'll increase that number by a sizeable fraction. Hell, we could double that number befo' we –

RALPH: Hang up our boots an' saddles under the – dignified sky of West Texas?

GEORGE [*with feeling*]: There *is* dignity in that sky! There's dignity in the agrarian, the pastoral – way of – existence! A dignity too long lost out of the – American dream –

[*He is shaking a good deal with emotion.*]

– as it used to be in the West Texas-Haverstick days . . .

RALPH: But I want to be dignified, too.

GEORGE: Human dignity's what I'm –

RALPH: I don't want to be caught short by a Texas Longhorn while crossing a pasture one mawnin' in West Texas! Ha ha ha! Naw, I don't want to catch me an ass full of Texas Longhorns before I can jump a fence rail out of that West Texas pasture. I –

GEORGE: SHUT UP! WILLYUH? YOU TV WATCHIN', CANNED-BEER DRINKIN', SPANISH-SUBURBAN-STUCCO-TYPE SON OF – Y'KNOW I THINK BEER IS DOPED? I THINK THEY DOPE IT TO CREATE A NATIONAL TOLERANCE OF THE TV COMMERCIAL! No – No – I'm sorry I come through Memphis . . .

[*He moves away, sadly.*]

I cherished a memory of you –

[CAROLLERS *are heard from a distance.*]

– idolized an old picture of which I was suddenly faced with a, with a – *goddam travesty* of it! – When you opened the door and I was confronted with a – DEFEATED! MIDDLE-AGED! NEGATIVE! LOST! – poor bastard . . .

RALPH: What do you think I saw when I opened that door? A ghostly apparition!

GEORGE: ME?

RALPH: A young man I used to know with an old man's affliction: the palsy!

GEORGE: Thanks! – I appreciate that.

[*Next door the* CAROLLERS *sing: 'Good Rest Ye Merry, Gentlemen, May Nothing Ye Dismay!'*]

Oh, man, oh brother, I sure do appreciate that!

[*He sits down quickly, shaking fiercely, in a metal porch chair, turning it away from Ralph to face the audience.* RALPH *is immediately and truly contrite.*]

Yeah. In addition to those other changes I mentioned in you, you've now exposed another which is the worst of the bunch. You've turned *vicious!*

RALPH: Aw, now –

GEORGE: Yeah, yeah, bitter and vicious! To ridicule an affliction like *mine*, like *this*, is vicious, *vicious!*

[*He holds up his shaky hand.* RALPH *reaches his hand out to take it but doesn't. Instead he drops his hand on George's shoulder.*]

Take that mother-grabbin' hand off my shoulder or I'll break it off you!

RALPH: You ridiculed *my* afflictions.

GEORGE: What afflictions?

RALPH: My life has been an affliction.

[*He says this without self-pity, simply as a matter of fact.*]

GEORGE: Now don't make me cry into this can of Budweiser with that sad story of your childhood in that home for illegitimate orphans.

RALPH: *Foundlings!* Home. I was not illegitimate.

GEORGE: Foundlings are illegitimate.

RALPH: Not – *necessarily* – *always* ...

[*He says this with a humility that might be touching to anyone less absorbed in his own problems than George.* RALPH *looks up at the drift of snow from the dark.*]

No, I meant to live a life in a Spanish-type stucco cottage in a – high point over a cavern, that is an affliction for someone that wanted and dreamed of – *oh, I wish I could be the first man in a moon rocket!* No, not the moon, but Mars, Venus! Hell, I'd like to be transported and transplanted to colonize and fertilize, to be the Adam on a – star in a different *galaxy*, yeah, that far away even! – It's wonderful knowing that such a thing is no longer inconceivable, huh?

GEORGE: You're talking out of character. You're a dedicated conformist, the most earthbound earth man on earth.

RALPH: If you think that about me, you never known me.

GEORGE [*starts off the terrace*]: I'm going walking, alone!

[*He stops abruptly.*]

Naw, if she sees me walking, she'll think I'm out looking for her.

RALPH: Goddam it, why don't you? Intercept her and don't say a word, just stick your hand inside that beaver-skin coat I give her and apply a little soft pressure to her – solar plexus – putting your other arm around her waist, and bring her back here, gently ...

GEORGE: That's what *you* want to do. Go on, *you* intercept her! And bring her back here gently!

RALPH: O.K., I *would* like to do it. But do you think I'd *do* it?

GEORGE: Can you honestly say you wouldn't put the make on her if you thought she'd give in?

RALPH: Nope! I wouldn't do it. And if you don't believe me, git back in that funeral hack and drive to West Texas in it, you – *legitimate* bastard.

GEORGE: Nope, I don't think you would. You're too much of a square.

RALPH: *There's her! There she is!*

GEORGE: Where?

RALPH: Corner. Why's she turning around? She must be lost, go get her. Look. She's joining the carollers!

GEORGE: Good, let her stay with them, and sing! Carols!

RALPH: Naw, I better go get her.

GEORGE: Go and get your *own* wife: leave mine alone!

[RALPH *puts his arm around George's shoulder.*]

And I told you to keep your rutten hand off my shoulder.

RALPH: Break it off me.

GEORGE: What I mean is, the point is – you *chose* your afflictions! Married into them. Mine I didn't choose! It just come on me, mysteriously: my shakes. You wouldn't even be interested in the awful implications of an affliction like mine.

[*He holds up his shaking hand.*]

RALPH: Sure, I'm interested in it, but –

GEORGE: S'pose it never lets up? This thing they can't treat or even find the cause of! S'pose I shake all my life like, like – dice in a crap shooter's fist? – Huh? – I mean at all moments of tension, all times of crisis, I shake! ... Huh? And there's other aspects to it beside the career side. It could affect my love life. Huh? I could start shaking so hard when I started to make out with a girl that I couldn't do it. You know? Couldn't make the scene with her ...

[*There is a slight pause.*]

RALPH: Aw. Was that it?

GEORGE: Was what what?

RALPH: Was that the trouble at the Old Man River Motel, last night, you were scared of impotence with her? Was that the problem?

GEORGE: I don't have that problem. I *never* had that problem.

RALPH: No?

GEORGE: *No!*

[*Tense pause.*]

WHY? Do *you* have that problem?

RALPH: Sometimes. I wasn't excited enough by Dotty to satisfy her, sometimes...

GEORGE: The thought of her old man's money couldn't always excite you?

RALPH: Nope, it couldn't always, that's the truth.

[*He switches off the lights, senselessly, and switches them back on again.*]

Poor ole Dotty. She's got so she always wants it and when I can't give it to her I feel guilty, guilty...

[*He turns the Christmas lights off again, turns them back on again.*]

GEORGE: Well, you know *me.* An Eveready battery, built-in in me.

RALPH [*turning to him with a slow, gentle smile*]: Yeah, I understand, son.

GEORGE: *Don't be so damned understanding!*

RALPH: Well, there she goes – Mrs George Haverstick the Fifth. Look. She's going up to the wrong Spanish-type stucco cottage, there's five almost identical ones in this block.

GEORGE: Don't your dawg know where it lives?

RALPH: Aw, it's a dignified beast. A constant Frigidaire pointer. Points at the Westinghouse Frij an' whines for a handout whenever you enter the kitchen. Knows everyone on the block an' pays calls like a new preacher wherever he thinks –

[*Whistles at dog.*]

– he might be offered a –

[*Whistles.*]

– handout.

[VOICES *down the block, hearty, drunken.*]

You better go git your wife. That Spanish-type stucco cottage is occupied by a bachelor decorator and you know how they destroy wimmen... He is running a sort of a unofficial USO at his house. Service men congregate there.

GEORGE: HAH!

[*He is amused by the picture.*]

RALPH: I got to climb back in a back window because you shut this door and I had put the catch on it.

[*He crosses out the door to the carport as* GEORGE *gazes gravely off.*

The CAROLLERS *are closer. They go into 'God Rest Ye Merry, Gentlemen' again.*

GEORGE *is not inclined to be merry. He glares into the starless air.*

In the bedroom, a windowpane is smashed and RALPH'*s arm reaches through, his fingers groping for the window latch. He finds it, gets the window up and clambers through with some muttered invectives against the hostility of the inanimate objects of the world. As soon as he enters the interior, light and sound inside are brought up. Oddly enough, a TV Western is in progress, approaching the climax of an Indian attack or a cattle stampede. It catches* RALPH'*s attention. He turns gravely to the TV set, for the moment forgetting* GEORGE *outside. Gunfire subsides and the dialogue is brought up loud:*]

DIALOGUE

– Save your ammunition, they'll come back.
– HOW LONG HAVE WE GOT?
– Till sundown. They'll hit us again after dark.
– Let's make a run for it now!
– We'll have to abandon the wagons if we make a run for it. The Rio Grande is at least five miles south of here.
– Mount the women, one woman behind each man on the hawses, unhitch the hawses! Then stampede the cattle. That'll give us a cover while we make our break.
– What is our chances, you think?
– You want a *honest* answer or a *comforting* answer?
– Give me the honest answer.
– The comforting answer would have been fifty-fifty: I'll leave you to imagine the honest answer.
– Rosemary? Come here, a minute. Take this pistol. There's five shots in it. Save the fifth shot for yourself. Now git on this hawss behind me.
– Oh, Buck! I'm so scared!
– *Git up!* O.K. sweetheart?
– Yes!

– Hold on to me tight. Dusty, when I count ten, start the cattle stampede.

[*He starts counting, slowly.*]

GEORGE [*to himself as he paces the terrace*]: Now I don't even want her. If she asked me for it, I wouldn't give it to her, the way I feel now.

[*Sneezes.*]

Catchin' a cold out here! What's he doing in there, the motherless bastard? BATES! REMEMBER ME?

RALPH [*opening the door*]: I thought you'd gone faw your wife.

[RALPH *chuckles and holds the front door open as* GEORGE *withdraws his head from the window and reappears a moment later on the terrace.* RALPH *lets him in.*]

GEORGE: Will you look at that? A Western on Christmas Eve, even! It's a goddam NATIONAL OBSESSIONAL.

RALPH: Yep, a national homesickness in the American heart for the old wild frontiers with the yelping redskin and the covered wagons on fire and –

GEORGE: Will you look at those miserable shorthorn cattle! Those cows, in this corny Western?

[*They both face the TV. There is a pause.*]

RALPH: Yep – an undignified beast. Man? Buddy? I don't have too much confidence in the project of the Dignified West Texas Longhorn Ranch, even now, but I will go along with you. Don't ask me why. I couldn't tell you why, but I will go along with you. Want to shake on it, Buddy?

GEORGE: That champagne ought to be cold now, let's break out that champagne now.

RALPH: It'll be still colder when you've picked up your wife.

GEORGE: I told you my policy, don't interfere with it, huh?

RALPH: Women are vulnerable creatures.

GEORGE: So's a man.

RALPH [*crosses to the kitchenette door*]: I'll open up the champagne while you pick up your wife.

GEORGE: Ralpho? Man?

RALPH: Huh?

GEORGE: Now I know why I come here. You're a *decent square!*

[*The kitchen door swings closed on them;* CAROLLERS *are singing out front. After a moment* ISABEL *appears before the house with the dog. A* LADY CAROLLER *appears on the terrace with a collection plate.*]

ISABEL: Oh – I'm afraid I don't have any money to give you, but –

[*She knocks at the door.*]

Wait! – till they answer the door, I –

[*Raucous voices are heard within.*]

– Some people regard the celebration of the birthday of Jesus as a, as a – sort of a – occasion, excuse for! – just getting drunk and – *disgusting!* I'll probably have to go round the back to get in ...

[*Great howls of hilarity have been coming from the back of the cottage, drowning out* ISABEL*'s efforts to draw attention to the front door.*]

I'm very sorry, I just don't have any money.

[*The* CAROLLER *accepts this in good grace and leaves.*

ISABEL *goes around through the carport. A few seconds later* GEORGE, *in a state of Wild West exuberance, comes charging out of the kitchen with the champagne bottle, shouting:*]

GEORGE: POWDER RIVER, POWWWWW-der RIV-errrr! – a mile wide and –

RALPH: TWO INCHES DEEP!

[*He follows him out as* ISABEL*'s head appears through the open window in the dim bedroom; she lifts the dog through and and hoists herself over the sill.*]

GEORGE: Git me a pitcher with ice and two cans of that Ballantine's ale and I will make us BLACK VELVET!

RALPH: Huh?

GEORGE: Man, you know Black Velvet!

[*He is back in the kitchen.*]

I made it that time in Hong Kong when we had those girls from the –

[RALPH *has gone in behind him. The door swings shut as* ISABEL *picks up the bedside phone in the bedroom.*]

ISABEL: Operator? I want a cab right away, it's an *emergency, yaiss!*

[*Slight pause.*]

Yellow Cab? Checkered! Well, please send a cab right away to – Oh, my goodness, I can't tell you the address, oh, I'll – I'll find out the address and I'll call you right back, right away ...

[*She hangs up with a little stricken cry, followed by convulsive sobs that she stifles forcibly. On the bed, in the pink-shaded lamplight, she looks like a little girl making a first discovery of life's sorrow. Instinctively she reaches out for the Infant of Prague; at the same time, the* CAROLLERS *start singing below the terrace: 'I Wonder as I Wander'. This is a sentimental moment, but not 'sticky'.*]

Little Boy Jesus, so lonesome on your birthday. I know how you feel, *exactly!* –

[*She clasps the infant to her breast, tenderly.*]

– just exactly, because I feel the same way ...

DIMOUT

ACT THREE

No time lapse.

[*The men return with an open, foaming bottle of champagne, and pass it back and forth between them before the fireplace, not noticing that the dog has returned or suspecting* ISABEL'*s presence in the bedroom.*]

GEORGE: I put them in five categories. Those that worship it, those that love it, those that just like it, those that don't like it, those that just tolerate it, those that *don't* tolerate it, those that can't stand it, and, finally, those that not only can't stand it but want to cut it off you.

RALPH [*following him with glasses, chuckling*]: That's more than five categories.

GEORGE: How many did I name?

RALPH: I don't know. I lost count.

GEORGE: Well, you know what I mean. And I have married into that last category. What scares me is that she has had hospital training and is probably able to do a pretty good cutting job. You know what I mean?

RALPH: Ha, ha, yeah. Wel-l-l . . .

[*He sets the glasses down and takes the bottle from* GEORGE. *The little parlour is flickering with firelight.*]

GEORGE: Which class did you marry into? Into the same category?

RALPH: No. She got to like it. More than I did even.

GEORGE: Now you're braggin'.

RALPH: Love is a very difficult – occupation. You got to work at it, man. It ain't a thing every Tom, Dick and Harry has got a true aptitude for. Y'know what I mean? Not every Tom, Dick or Harry understands how to use it. It's not a – offensive weapon. It shouldn't be used like one. Too many guys, they use it like a offensive weapon to beat down a woman with. All right. That rouses resistance. Because a woman has pride, even a woman has pride and resents being raped, and most love-making is rape with these self-regarded – experts! That come downstairs yelling, 'Oh, man, oh, brother!', and hitching their belts up like they'd accomplished something.

GEORGE [*getting the allusion and resentful*]: You mean me?

RALPH: Naw, naw, will yuh listen a minute? I've got ideas on this subject.

GEORGE: A self-regarded expert!

RALPH: You know Goddam right I'm an expert. I know I never had your good looks but made out better.

GEORGE: One man's opinion!

RALPH: Look! Lissen! You got to use – TENDERNESS! – with it, not roughness like raping, snatch-and-grab roughness but true tenderness with it or –

GEORGE: O.K., build yourself up! If that's what you need to!

RALPH: Naw, now, lissen! You know I know what I'm sayin'!

GEORGE: Sure, self-regarded expert!

[*They are both pretty high now.*]

RALPH: I know what went wrong last night at that Cape Girardeau motel as well as if I had seen it all on TV!

GEORGE: What went wrong is that I found myself hitched up with a woman in the 'cut-it-off' category!

[ISABEL *is listening to all this in the bedroom. She stands up and sits down, stands up and sits down, barely able to keep from shouting something.*]

RALPH: Aw, naw, aw, naw. I will tell you what happened. Drink your champagne. What happened, man, is this! You didn't appreciate the natural need for using some tenderness with it. Lacking confidence with it, you wanted to hit her, smash her, clobber her with it. You've got violence in you! That's what made you such a good fighter pilot, the best there was! Sexual violence, that's what gives you the shakes, that's what makes you unstable. That's what made you just sit on the straw mats with the Tokyo dolls, drinking saké with them, teaching them English till it was time to come downstairs and holler, 'Oh, man, oh, brother' like you had laid them to waste!

[*There is a slight pause.* GEORGE *is sweating, flushed.*]

GEORGE: Who in hell ever told you I –

RALPH: I heard it directly from them. You just sat up there drinkin' saké with 'em 'an teachin' 'em English, and then you'd come down shouting, 'Oh, man, oh, brother!' like you had laid 'em to waste.

GEORGE: Which of them told you this story?

RALPH: *Which* of them? ALL! EV'RY ONE!

[*They pause.* ISABEL *sits down on the bed again, raises her hands to either side of her face, slowly shaking her head with a gradual comprehension.*]

GEORGE: Man, at this moment I'd like to bust your face in!

RALPH: I'm tryin' to help you. Don't you know that I am tryin' t' help you?

[*A pause. They look away from each other in solemn reverie for some moments.* ISABEL *rises again from the bed but still doesn't move. After some moments she sits back down. She is crying now.*

RALPH, *continuing gently:*]

You have got this problem.

GEORGE: In Tokyo I never told you –

RALPH: What?

GEORGE: I was choosy. I had a girl on the side. I mean a nice one. One that I wanted to keep to myself, strictly. I didn't want to expose her to a bunch of –

RALPH: Aw, now, man, you don't have to start fabricating some kind of a *Sayonara* fantasy like this!

GEORGE: How about Big Springs, Texas?

RALPH: What about Big Springs, Texas, besides being boring, I mean, what *else* about it?

GEORGE: Plenty. I fixed you up there. You never got nowhere in Big Springs, Texas, till I opened it up for you.

RALPH: Baby, don't be sore.

GEORGE: Sore, I'm not sore. You've done your damndest to make me feel like a phony, but I'm not sore. *You're* sore. Not *me*. *I'm* not sore.

RALPH: You sure are shaking.

GEORGE: Yeah, well, I got this tremor ... Jesus, my goddam voice is got the shakes too! But you know it's the truth, in Big Springs,

Texas, we had the best damn' time you ever had in your life, and I broke the ice there, for you.

RALPH: I don't deny that women naturally like you. Everybody likes you! Don't you know that? People never low-rate you! Don't you know that? I like you. That's for sure. But I hate to see you shaking because of –

GEORGE [*cutting in*]: Look! We're both free now. Like two birds. You're gonna cut out of this High Point over a Cavern. And we'll buy us a piece of ranchland near San Antone and both of us –

RALPH: Yeah, yeah, let's go back to what we wuh tawkin' about. *Tenderness.* With a *woman.*

GEORGE: I don't want to hear a goddam lecture from you about such a thing as that when here you are, night before Christmas, with just a cocker spaniel and presents under a tree, with no one to *take* them from you!

RALPH [*abruptly*]: *Hey!*

GEORGE: *Huh?*

RALPH: Th' *dawg* is back. How *come*?

GEORGE: The dawg come *back*, tha's all . . .

[ISABEL *comes out of the bedroom in coat and hat.*]

ISABEL: Yes, I brought the dog back.

[*A pause, rather long.*]

RALPH: We, uh, we – saw you going up to the wrong – Spanish-type cottage . . .

ISABEL: I haven't discovered the *right* one, Mr Bates.

RALPH: I ain't discovered it either.

GEORGE: What kept you so long in the wrong one?

ISABEL: They invited me in and made me sit down to a lovely buffet supper while they looked up the High Point Bates in the phone book.

[*She pauses.*]

I heard your very enlightening conversation from the bedroom. You're a pair of small boys. Boasting, bragging, showing off to each other . . . I want to call a cab. I'm going downtown, George.

[*He crosses unsteadily to the phone, lifts it and hands it to her with an effort at stateliness.*]

Thank you.

[*To* RALPH.]

Do you know the cab number?

GEORGE: Whacha want, yellow, checkered or what? I'll git it for yuh!

RALPH: Put down th' phone.

ISABEL: I'll get one.

[*She dials the operator.*]

GEORGE: Leave her alone. Let her go downtown. She's free to.

[RALPH *takes the phone from her and puts it back in the cradle.*]

ISABEL: Do I have to walk?

[*She goes to the door, opens it and starts out.*]

There's a car in front of your house, Mr Bates.

RALPH [*rising with sudden energy and rushing to the door*]: YEP! IT'S HER OLD MAN'S CAR! Dorothea's papa, my ex-boss!

ISABEL: Perhaps he'll be kind enough to –

RALPH: Go back in, little lady! Stay in the bedroom till I git through this! Then I'll drive you downtown if you're still determined to go.

[*He has drawn her back in the house.*]

SET DOWN, GEORGE! For Chrissakes. Little lady, will you please wait in the bedroom till I get through this hassle with her old man?

ISABEL: It's all so ridiculous. Yes, all right, I will, but please don't forget your promise to take me downtown right afterwards, Mr Bates!

[*She returns to the bedroom with dignity.* MR *and* MRS MCGILLICUDDY *appear before the house.*

They are a pair of old bulls.]

MRS MCGILLICUDDY: The first thing to discuss is their joint savings account.

[MR MCGILLICUDDY *hammers the knocker on the door.*]

I wish you'd listened to me an' brought your lawyer.

MR MCGILLICUDDY: I can handle that boy. You keep your mouth out of it. Just collect the silver and china and let me handle the talk.

[*He knocks again, violently, dislodging the Christmas wreath attached to the knocker.* MRS MCGILLICUDDY *picks it up.*]

Now what are you gonna do with that Christmas wreath? You gonna crown him with it?

[RALPH *opens the door.*]

RALPH: Well, Mr and Mrs *Mac!*

MR MCGILLICUDDY [*handing him the wreath*]: This come off your knocker.

RALPH: Ha, ha, what a surprise!

MRS MCGILLICUDDY: We've come to pick up some things of Dorothea's.

RALPH: That's O.K. Take out anything that's hers, but don't touch nothing that belongs to us both.

MRS MCGILLICUDDY: We've come with a list of things that belong exclusively to Dorothea!

MR MCGILLICUDDY: Is it true that you called up Emory Sparks at the place you quit your job at and asked him to come over here tonight and make you a cash-on-the-barrel offer for everything in this house?

RALPH: Nope.

MR MCGILLICUDDY: Then how come Emory's fiancée called up Dorothea to give her that information?

MRS MCGILLICUDDY [*impatiently*]: Come on in here, Susie.

[SUSIE *is the coloured maid. She enters with a large laundry basket.*]

Is that the biggest basket you could find?

SUSIE: Yes, ma'am, it's the laundry basket.

MRS MCGILLICUDDY: It isn't the large one. You'll have to make several trips up and down those slippery front steps with that little basket.

MR MCGILLICUDDY: Haven't you got any ice-cream salt?

RALPH: You want to make some ice cream?

MR MCGILLICUDDY: Susie, before you go down those steps with my daughter's china, you'd better collect some clinkers out of the furnace in the basement.

RALPH: How is she going to get clinkers out of an oil-burning furnace?

MR MCGILLICUDDY: Oh, that's right. You burn oil. I forgot about that. Well, Susie, you better tote the basket of china down the terrace. Don't try to make the steps with it.

RALPH: She's not takin' no china out of this house.

MR MCGILLICUDDY: You're not going to sell a goddam thing of my daughter's in this house!

RALPH: All I done was call up Emory Sparks because he's about to get married and invited him over to take a look at this place because I've got to unload it and I can't wait a couple of months to –

MR MCGILLICUDDY: Now, hold on a minute, war hero!

RALPH: I don't like the way you always call me war hero!

MR MCGILLICUDDY: *Why?* Ain't that what you *were*?

GEORGE: You're goddam right he was! I flown over seventy bombing missions with this boy in Korea and before that in the –

MR MCGILLICUDDY: Yes, yes, yes, I know it backwards and forwards, and I know who you are. You are Haverstick, ain't you?

GEORGE: Yeah, you got my name right.

MR MCGILLICUDDY: Well, Haverstick, the war's over and you two bombers are grounded. Now, Susie, go in the kitchen and get that Mixmaster and that new Rôtisserie out in the basket while I collect the silver in that sideboard in there.

RALPH: Susie, don't go in my kitchen. You want to be arrested for trespassing, Susie?

MRS MCGILLICUDDY: Stuart, you'd better call that policeman in here.

RALPH: NO KIDDING!

MRS MCGILLICUDDY: We anticipated that you'd make trouble.

RALPH: How does Dorothea feel about you all doing this?

MR MCGILLICUDDY [*at the door*]: OFFICER! – He's coming.

RALPH: How does Dotty feel? What is her attitude towards this kind of –

[*He is trembling. His voice chokes.* GEORGE *rises and puts a hand on Ralph's shoulder as a young* POLICE OFFICER *enters looking embarrassed.*]

MR MCGILLICUDDY: You know the situation, Lieutenant. We have to remove my daughter's valuables from the house because we've been tipped off this man here, Ralph Bates, is intending to make a quick cash sale of everything in the house and skip out of Memphis tomorrow.

RALPH: THAT'S A GODDAM LIE! WHO TOLD YOU THAT?

MRS MCGILLICUDDY: Emory Sparks's fiancée is Dorothea's good friend! That's how we got the warning. She called to inquire if Dorothea was serious about this matter. How did Dotty feel, how did she FEEL? I'll tell you! SICK AT HER STOMACH! VIOLENTLY SICK AT HER STOMACH.

RALPH: I should think so, goddam it! I should THINK so! She's got many a fault she got from you two, but, hell, she'd never agree to a piece of cheapness like this any more'n she'd believe that story about me callin' –

MR MCGILLICUDDY: How could there be any possible doubt about it when Emory Sparks's fiancée –

RALPH: Will you allow me to speak? I did call Emory Sparks and told him my wife had quit me because I had quit my job, and I merely suggested that he come over and kind of look over the stuff here and see if any of all this goddam electric equipment and so forth would be of any use to him since it isn't to me and since I got to have some financial –

[*He becomes suddenly speechless and breathless.* GEORGE *embraces his shoulder.*]

GEORGE: Now, now, son, this is going to work out. Don't blow a gasket over it.

RALPH: I think you folks had better consider some legal angles of what you're up to here.

MR MCGILLICUDDY [*puffing, red in the face*]: Aw, there's no legal angle about it that I don't know, and if there was, I could cope with that, too. I'm prepared to cope with that trouble. You got no goddam position in this town but what I give you!

RALPH: *Oh!* Uh-huh –

[MRS MCGILLICUDDY *has gone to the bedroom and discovered* ISABEL *in it.*]

MRS MCGILLICUDDY: *Stuart, they have a woman in Dotty's bedroom!*

RALPH: George's wife is in there.

MRS MCGILLICUDDY: How long have you been planning this?

[*She knocks on the bedroom door.*]

Can I come in?

ISABEL: Yes, please.

[MRS MCGILLICUDDY *enters the bedroom.*]

MRS MCGILLICUDDY [*coldly*]: I've come to pick up some things that belong to my daughter.

ISABEL: I told my husband we'd dropped in at the wrong time.

MRS MCGILLICUDDY: May I ask who you are?

ISABEL: I'm Mrs George Haverstick. You probably saw my husband in the front room.

MRS MCGILLICUDDY: Your husband's an old friend of Ralph's, one of his wartime buddies?

ISABEL: Yes, he is, Mrs – I didn't get your name.

MRS MCGILLICUDDY: All I can say is 'Watch out', if he's an old friend of Ralph's!

ISABEL: Why?

MRS MCGILLICUDDY: Birds of a feather, that's all.

[MRS MCGILLICUDDY *opens the closet and starts piling clothes on the bed. In the living-room,* MR MCGILLICUDDY *takes a seat in silence.*]

ISABEL: Are you sure you're doing the right thing?

MRS MCGILLICUDDY [*calling out the door*]: Susie!

SUSIE [*entering*]: Yes, ma'am?

MRS MCGILLICUDDY: Take these clothes of Miss Dotty's out to the car.

[SUSIE *carries out the clothes.*]

ISABEL: I think young people should be given a chance to work things out by themselves.

MRS MCGILLICUDDY: You have no idea at all of the situation. And I'm sure you have your own problems if you have married a friend of my daughter's husband. Is he living on his war record like Ralph Bates is?

ISABEL: He has a distinguished war record and a nervous disability that was a result of seventy-two flying missions in Korea and, and – more than twice that many in –

MRS MCGILLICUDDY: *I'm sick of hearing about past glories! Susie!*

[SUSIE *comes in again*]

Now pick up all Dotty's shoes on the floor of that closet, put 'em in the bottom of the basket, put some paper over them, and then pile her little undies on top of the paper. – Then! If you still have room in the basket, collect some of the china out of the sideboard and cupboards. Be very careful with that. Don't try to carry too much at one time, Susie. That walk and those steps are a hazard.

[*There has been a prolonged silence in the front room during the scene above, which they have been listening to.*]

MR MCGILLICUDDY [*at last*]: Well, you seem to be living the life of Riley. French champagne. Who was the little girl I saw come out and go back in?

RALPH: Mrs George Haverstick.

MR MCGILLICUDDY: That means as much to me as if you said she was a lady from Mars.

RALPH: There's no reason why it should mean anything to you. I just answered your question.

MR MCGILLICUDDY: Why do you feel so superior to me?

RALPH: Aw. Did you notice that?

MR MCGILLICUDDY: From the first time I met you. You have always acted very superior to me for some unknown reason. I'd like to know what it is. You were employed by me till you quit your job today.

RALPH: Does that mean I had to feel inferior to you, Mac?

MR MCGILLICUDDY: You've started calling me 'Mac'?

RALPH: I'm not employed by you, now.

MR MCGILLICUDDY: If there was a war you could be a war hero again, but in a cold war I don't see how you're going to be such a hero. A cold-war hero, ha ha, is not such a hero, at least not in the newspapers.

[*Gathering confidence.*]

Huh? Why don't you answer my question?

RALPH: Which, Mac?

MR MCGILLICUDDY: Why you feel so rutten superior to me.

RALPH: Can I consider that question? For a minute?

MR MCGILLICUDDY: Yeah, consider it, will you? I fail to see anything *special* about you, war hero!

[*He lights a cigar with jerky motions. The two younger men stare at his red, puffy face with intolerant smiles.*]

GEORGE: Let me answer for him. He feels superior to you because you're a big male cow, a spiritual male cow.

RALPH: Shut up, George. Well, Mr Mac? Let me ask you a question. Why did you ask me to marry your daughter?

MR MCGILLICUDDY: DID WHAT? I NEVER! Done any such thing and –

[MRS MCGILLICUDDY *snorts indignantly from the open bedroom door.*]

RALPH: You mean to say you've forgotten that you suggested to me that I marry Dotty?

[MRS MCGILLICUDDY *advances from the bedroom door, bearing a French porcelain clock.*]

MR MCGILLICUDDY: I never forgotten a thing in my adult life, but I never have any such recollections as that. I do remember a conversation I held with you soon after you started to work at Regal Dairy Products an' come to my office to quit because you said you weren't gittin paid well enough an' th' work was monotonous to you.

RALPH: That's right. Five years ago this winter.

MR MCGILLICUDDY: I gave you a fatherly talk. I told you monotony was a part of life. And I said I had an eye on you, which I did at that time.

RALPH: How about the rest of the conversation? In which you said that Dotty was your only child, that you had no son, and Dotty was int'rested in me and if Dotty got married her husband would be the heir to your throne as owner of Regal Dairy an' its subsidiaries such as Royal Ice Cream and Monarch Cheese, huh?

MRS MCGILLICUDDY: HANH!

RALPH: An' you hadn't long for this world because of acute diabetes and so forth and –

MRS MCGILLICUDDY: HANH!

RALPH: And I would be shot right into your shoes when you departed this world? Well, you sure in hell lingered!

MRS MCGILLICUDDY: ARE YOU GOING TO STAND THERE LISTENING TO THIS, STUART? I'M NOT!

MR MCGILLICUDDY: Be still, Mama. I can talk for myself. I did discuss these things with you but how did you arrive at the idea I asked you to marry my daughter?

MRS MCGILLICUDDY: HANH!

[GEORGE *goes to look out of the window as if the scene had ceased to amuse him.*]

RALPH: What other way could it be interpreted, Mac?

[*He is no longer angry.*]

MR MCGILLICUDDY: I offered you a splendid chance in the world which you spit on by your disrespect, your superior – !

RALPH: I respect Dorothea. Always did and still do.

MR MCGILLICUDDY: I'm talkin' about your attitude to me.

RALPH: I know you are. That's all that you care about, not about Dorothea. You don't love Dotty. She let you down by having psychological problems that you brought on her, that you an' Mrs Mac gave her by pushing her socially past her social endowments.

MRS MCGILLICUDDY: WHAT DO YOU MEAN BY THAT?

RALPH: Dotty was never cut out to boost your social position in this city. Which you expected her to. You made her feel inferior all her life.

MRS MCGILLICUDDY: *Me? Me?*

RALPH: Both of yuh. I respected her, though, and sincerely liked her and I married Dotty. Give me credit for that, and provided her with an – offspring. Maybe not much of an offspring, but an offspring, a male one, at least it started a male one. I can't help it if she's turnin' him into a sissy, I –

MRS MCGILLICUDDY: MY GOD, STUART, HOW LONG ARE YOU GONNA STAND THERE AND LISTEN TO THIS WITHOUT –

MR MCGILLICUDDY: *Mama, I told you to keep your mouth outa this!*

RALPH: Yeah, but I MARRIED your baby. Give me credit for that. And provided her with an – offspring!

MRS MCGILLICUDDY: What does he mean by that? That *he* had the baby, not Dotty?

MR MCGILLICUDDY: Mama, I told you to keep your mouth out of this.

MRS MCGILLICUDDY: He talks like he thought he did Dotty a FAVOUR!

RALPH: Now, listen. I don't want to be forced into saying unkind things about Dotty. But you all know damn' well that Dotty was half a year older than me when I married that girl and if I hadn't you would have been stuck with a lonely, unmarried daughter for the rest of your lives!

MRS MCGILLICUDDY: *Oh*, my – GOD!

MR MCGILLICUDDY: Let him talk. I want to hear all, all, all! he has to say about Dotty.

RALPH: You're *going* to hear it, if you stay in my house! I put up a five-year battle between our marriage and your goddam hold on her! You just wouldn't release her! – although I doubt that you wanted her always unmarried.

MRS MCGILLICUDDY: WHAT MAKES YOU THINK SHE WOULD HAVE STAYED UNMARRIED?

RALPH: The indications, past history, when I met her –

MRS MCGILLICUDDY: This is too sickening. I can't stand it, Stuart?

MR MCGILLICUDDY: A bum like you?

RALPH: Don't call *me* a bum!

MR MCGILLICUDDY: What in hell else *are* you? I give you your job which you quit today without warning! Carried you in it despite your indifference to it for – for – for – five –

RALPH: Wait! Like I said. I still respect your daughter, don't want to say anything not kind about her, but let's face facts. Who else but a sucker like me, Ralph Bates, would have married a girl with no looks, a plain, homely girl that probably no one but me had ever felt anything but just – SORRY FOR!

MRS MCGILLICUDDY: OH GOD! STUART, ARE YOU GOING TO STAND THERE AND LET HIM GO ON WITH THAT TALK?

RALPH: HOW IN HELL DO YOU FIGURE HE'S GOING TO STOP ME?

MRS MCGILLICUDDY: OFFICER! CAN'T YOU GET THIS MAN OUT OF HERE?

OFFICER: No, ma'am. I can't arrest him.

RALPH: ARREST ME FOR WHAT, MRS MAC?

GEORGE: That's right, arrest him for what?

MRS MCGILLICUDDY: Stuart? Take out the silver. I don't know where Susie is. We should have come here with your lawyer as well as this – *remarkably – incompetent – policeman!*

MR MCGILLICUDDY: Susie took out the silver.

GEORGE: Naw, she didn't. I got the goddam silver. I'm sitting on it!

[*He sits on silver, then rises and stuffs it under sofa pillow, having been discomforted by the forks.*]

MR MCGILLICUDDY: I guess I'll have to call the Chief of Police, who's a lodge brother of mine, and get a little more police co-operation than we have gotten so far.

OFFICER: O.K., you do that, Mister.

MR MCGILLICUDDY: He'll call you to the phone and give you exact instructions.

OFFICER: That's all right. If he gives 'em, I'll take 'em.

[MRS MCGILLICUDDY *has charged back into the bedroom to collect more things.*]

RALPH: Mr McGillicuddy, you are the worst thing any person can be: mean-minded, small-hearted, and CHEAP! Outstandingly and notoriously cheap! It was almost two months before I could *kiss* Dorothea, sincerely, after meeting her father! That's no crap. It wasn't the homeliness that threw me, it was the association she had in my mind with *you*! It wasn't till I found out she despised you as much as I did that I was able to make real love to Dotty.

MR MCGILLICUDDY: My daughter is *crazy* about me!

RALPH: You're crazy if you *think* so!

[MRS MCGILLICUDDY *comes out of the bedroom.*]

MRS MCGILLICUDDY: All right. All of Dotty's clothes have been taken out. I think we may as well leave now.

MR MCGILLICUDDY: How about the TV? Which I gave Dotty *last* Christmas?

RALPH: You want the TV? O.K.! Here's the TV!

[*He shoves it to the door and pulls the door open.*]

Take the TV out of here – an' git out with it!

MRS MCGILLICUDDY: What is that under the tree? It looks like a new fur coat!

RALPH: That's right. A seven-hundred-and-forty-five-dollar sheared-beaver coat that I'd bought for Dotty for Christmas! – but which I have just now presented to Mrs George Haverstick as her weddin' present.

MR MCGILLICUDDY: The hell you have! How did you git hold of seven hundred and –

RALPH: From my savings account.

MR MCGILLICUDDY: That was a *joint* account!

MRS MCGILLICUDDY: STUART! TAKE THAT COAT! GO ON, PICK UP THAT COAT!

RALPH: By God, if he touches that coat, I'll smash him into next week, and I never hit an old man before in my life.

MRS MCGILLICUDDY: OFFICER! PICK UP THAT COAT!

RALPH: I'll hit any man that tries to pick up that coat!

OFFICER [*putting down the phone, which he has been talking into quietly*]: I talked to my chief. He gave me my instructions. He says not to take any action that might result in publicity, because of Mr Bates having been a very well-known war hero.

MR MCGILLICUDDY: Come on, Mama, I'll just have to refer this whole disgusting business to my lawyer tomorrow, put it all in his hands and get the necessary papers to protect our baby.

MRS MCGILLICUDDY: I just want to say one thing more! Ralph Bates, don't you think for a moment that you are going to escape financial responsibility for the support of your child! Now come on, Stuart! – Isn't it pitiful? All that little boy's Christmas under the tree?

RALPH: Send him over tomorrow to pick it all up. That can go out of the house, the little boy's Christmas can go . . .

[*They all leave.* ISABEL *enters from bedroom.*]

ISABEL: Mr Bates! I don't believe that this is what your wife wanted. I'll also bet you that she is outside in that car and if you would just stick your head out of the window and call her, she would come running in here.

[DOROTHEA *comes on to the paved terrace and knocks at the door.* RALPH *does not move. She knocks again, harder and longer. He starts to rise, sits down again.*]

George, let his wife in the house.

GEORGE: Let's just keep out of this. I reckon he knows what he's doing.

[*A car honks. A* WOMAN'S VOICE *is heard.*]

WOMAN [*off*]: Dorothea! Come back! We'll get the police!

DOROTHEA [*calling at the door*]: Ralph? Ralph? It's Dotty! I want the child's Christmas things!

RALPH: HE'LL GET THEM HERE OR NOWHERE!

DOROTHEA: *I'm not going to leave here without the child's Christmas things!* – Ralph.

RALPH: *Let him come here alone tomorrow morning.*

DOROTHEA: *You can't do that to a child.* – Ralph!

[*The car honks again, long and loud.*]

RALPH [*shouting back*]: Put the kid in a taxi in the morning and I'll let him in to collect his Christmas presents!

MRS MCGILLICUDDY [*appearing behind Dorothea*]: Dorothea! I will not let you humiliate yourself like this! Come away from that door!

DOROTHEA: Mama, stay in the car!

WOMAN: Your father won't wait any longer. He's started the car. He's determined to get the police.

DOROTHEA: RALPH! [*She has removed the door key from her bag.*] I'M COMING IN!

WOMAN: *Dotty, where is your pride!*

[DOROTHEA *enters and slams the door. The* WOMAN *rushes off, crying 'Stuart!'*

DOROTHEA *stares at* RALPH *from the door. He gazes stubbornly at the opposite wall.*]

DOROTHEA: I could tell you'd been drinkin' by your voice. Who are these people you've got staying in the house?

RALPH: Talk about the police! I could get you all arrested for illegal entry!

DOROTHEA: This is your liquor speaking, not you, Ralph.

RALPH: You have abandoned me. You got no right by law to come back into this house and make insulting remarks about my friends.

DOROTHEA: Ralph? Ralph? I know I acted – impetuously this mawnin' . . .

RALPH: Naw, I think you made the correct decision. You realized that you had tied yourself down to a square peg in a round hole that had now popped out of the hole and consequently would be of no further use to you. You were perfectly satisfied for me to remain at that rutten little desk job, tyrannized over by inferior men, for as long as my – heart kept beating.

DOROTHEA: No, Ralph. I wasn't. MY aim for you was your aim. Independence! A business of your own!

RALPH: Not when you were *faced* with it.

DOROTHEA: You sprung it on me at the wrong moment, Ralph. Our savings account is at a very low ebb.

RALPH: Our savings account is all gone, little woman. It went on Christmas, all of it.

[*He pokes at the fire. There is a pause. The fire crackles and flickers.*]

DOROTHEA: *Mama* says you – bought me a *fur coat* for Christmas.

RALPH: Yeah, she took a look at it. Inquired the price. Wanted to take it off with her.

DOROTHEA: You wouldn't have bought me such a beautiful coat if you didn't still care for me, Ralph. You know that, don't you?

RALPH: I made a decision affecting my whole future life. I know it was a big step, but I had the courage to make it.

DOROTHEA: I've always admired your courage.

RALPH: Hah! – I break the news. You walked right out on me, Dotty, takin' my son that you've turned into a sissy. He won't want these boys' toys under that tree. What he'll want is a doll and a – *tea* set.

DOROTHEA: All of these things are a little too old for Ralph Junior but he'll be delighted with them just the same, Ralph.

[*She takes off her cloth coat.*]

I'm going to try on that wonderful-looking beaver.

RALPH: It's not going out of the house, off you or on you, Dotty.

[*She puts on the beaver-skin coat.*]

DOROTHEA: Oh, how lovely, how lovely! Ralph, it *does* prove you love me!

RALPH: It cleaned out our savings account.

DOROTHEA: Both of us have been guilty of impetuous actions. You must've been awfully lonely, inviting a pair of strangers to occupy our bedroom on Christmas Eve.

RALPH: George Haverstick is not any stranger to me. We both of us died in two wars, repeatedly died in two wars and were buried in suburbs named High Point, but his was hyphenated. H-i-hyphen-Point. Mine was spelled out but was built on a cavern for the daughter and grandchild of Mr and Mrs Stuart McGillicuddy. Oh, I told him something which I should have told you five years ago, Dorothea. I married you without love. I married you for –

DOROTHEA: Ralph? Please don't!

RALPH: I married you for your stingy-fisted old papa's promise to –

DOROTHEA: *Ralphie! Don't! I know!*

RALPH: – to make me his Heir Apparent! Assurances, lies! Even broad hints that he would soon kick off!

DOROTHEA: Ralph?

[*She puts her hand over his mouth, beseechingly.*]

Don't you know I know that?

RALPH: Why d'you accept it? If you –

DOROTHEA: I was so –

[*She covers her face.*]

RALPH: Cut it out, have some pride!

DOROTHEA: I *do!*

RALPH: In *what?*

DOROTHEA: In *you!*

RALPH: Oh, for the love of – In me? Why, I'm telling you I'm nothin' better'n a goddam –

DOROTHEA: I know, don't tell me again. I always knew it. – I had my nose done over and my front teeth extracted to look better for you, Ralphie!

RALPH: 'Ralphie!' *Shoot . . .*

[ISABEL *raps discreetly at the bedroom door.*]

Huh? What is it?

ISABEL: I've made some coffee.

DOROTHEA: I *did* improve my appearance, didn't I, Ralph? It was extremely painful.

RALPH: Don't claim you done it for me! Every woman wants to improve on nature any way that she can. Yes! Of course you look better! You think you've won a *argument?*

DOROTHEA: *Me? What* argument? *No!* I've come back *crawling!* – not even embarrassed to do so!

[ISABEL *comes in from the kitchenette with coffee.*]

Oh! Hello. I didn't know you were –

ISABEL: Mrs Bates. I'm Isabel Haverstick. I took the liberty of making some coffee in your sweet little kitchen. Mrs Bates, can I give you some coffee?

DOROTHEA: Thanks, that's awfully sweet of you, Mrs Haverstick. It's nice of you and your husband to drop in on Ralph, but the situation between Ralph and me has changed. I guess I don't have to explain it. You see I've come home. We only have one bedroom and Ralph and I have an awful lot to talk over.

ISABEL: I understand perfectly. George and I are going to go right downtown.

DOROTHEA [*softening*]: You don't have to do that. This sofa lets out to a bed and it's actually more comfortable than the beds in the bedroom. I know, because other times when we've had a falling out, less serious than this time, I have – occupied it.

[*With a little, soft, sad, embarrassed laugh.*]

Of course, I usually called Ralph in before mawnin' ...

ISABEL: Oh, but this is no time for strangers to be here with you!

DOROTHEA [*now really warming*]: You all stay here! I insist! It's really not easy to get a hotel room downtown with so many folks coming into town for Christmas.

ISABEL: Well, if you're sure, if you're absolutely certain our presence wouldn't be inconvenient at all? – I do love this room. The fire is still burning bright – and the Christmas tree is so – pretty.

DOROTHEA: I'll tell my mother and father, they're still outside in the car, to drive home and then we'll all have coffee together.

[*She rushes out in her beaver coat.*]

ISABEL: I like her! She's really nice!

RALPH: She came back for the fur coat.

ISABEL: I think she came back for you.

RALPH: She walked out on me this morning because I had liberated myself from a slave's situation! – and she took the kid with her.

ISABEL: You're just going through a – period of adjustment.

RALPH: We've been married six years.

ISABEL: But all that time you've been under terrible strain, hating what you were doing, and maybe taking it out on your wife, Ralph Bates.

[DOROTHEA *returns.*]

DOROTHEA: All right. I sent them home, much against their objections. I just slammed the car door on them.

RALPH: They comin' back with the police?

DOROTHEA: No. You know they were bluffing.

ISABEL: I think you two should have your coffee alone in your own little bedroom. We'll all get acquainted tomorrow.

DOROTHEA: Ralph?

RALPH [*sadly*]: I don't know. We're living over a cavern . . .

[*He follows* DOROTHEA *into the bedroom. It remains dimly lighted.*]

DOROTHEA: But Mama's took all my things! I forgot to ask them back from her. I'll just have to sleep jay-bird since she took even my nighties.

RALPH: Yes, she was fast and thorough, but didn't get out with that seven-hundred-buck beaver coat.

DOROTHEA: I like your friends. But the girl looks terribly nervous. Well-bred, however, and the boy is certainly very good-looking!

RALPH: Thanks.

[*The bedroom dims out as* DOROTHEA *enters the bathroom. A silence has fallen between the pair in the living-room.*]

ISABEL: Coffee, George?

GEORGE: No, thanks.

ISABEL: Moods change quickly, don't they?

GEORGE: Basic attitudes don't.

ISABEL: Yes, but it takes a long time to form basic attitudes and to know what they are, and meantime you just have to act according to moods.

GEORGE: Is that what you are acting according to, now?

ISABEL: I'm not acting according to anything at all now, I –

[*She sits on a hassock before the fireplace.*]

I don't think she came back just for the coat. Do you?

GEORGE: It's not my business. I don't have any opinion. If that was her reason, Ralph Bates will soon find it out.

ISABEL: Yes...

DOROTHEA [*at the door*]: Excuse me, may I come in?

ISABEL: Oh, please.

DOROTHEA [*entering*]: Mama took all my *things!* Have you got an extra nightie that I could borrow?

ISABEL: Of course I have.

DOROTHEA: I forgot to take anything back...

[ISABEL *opens her overnight bag and extends a gossamer nightgown to Dorothea.*]

Oh! How exquisite! No! – that's your honeymoon nightie. Just give me any old plain one!

ISABEL: Really, I have two of them, exactly alike. Please take it!

DOROTHEA: Are you sure?

ISABEL: I'm positive. You take it!

[*She holds up another.*]

See? The same thing exactly, just a different colour. I gave you the blue one and kept the pink one for me.

DOROTHEA: Oh. Well, thank you so much.

ISABEL: If you'd prefer the pink one – ?

DOROTHEA: I'm delighted with the blue one! Well, g'night, you folks. Sweet dreams.

[*She returns to the dark bedroom.* RALPH *is prone and motionless on the bed. A tiny light spills from the bathroom door.* DOROTHEA *enters the bathroom and closes the door so the bedroom turns pitch-black.*]

GEORGE [*grimly*]: D'ya want me to go outside while you undress?

ISABEL: No, I, I – I'm – just going to take off my *suit.* I – I, I have a *slip* on, I –

[*She gives him a quick, scared look. The removal of her suit is almost panickily self-conscious and awkward.*]

GEORGE: Well. Ralph and I have decided to –

ISABEL [*fearfully*]: *What?*

GEORGE [*finishes his drink, then goes on*]: Ralph and I have decided to go in the cattle business, near San Antone.

ISABEL: Who is going to finance it?

[*She has turned out the lamp.*]

GEORGE: We think we can work it out. We have to be smart, and lucky. Just smart and lucky.

[ISABEL *drops her skirt to her feet and stands before the flickering fireplace in a slip that the light makes transparent.*]

ISABEL: We all have to be smart and lucky. Or unlucky and silly.

[DOROTHEA *comes out of the bathroom. Light from the bathroom brightens the bedroom, where* RALPH *is slowly undressing.*]

RALPH: All right, you're back. But a lot has been discussed and decided on since you cut out of here, Dotty.

DOROTHEA [*picks up something on the dresser*]: Good! What?

RALPH: Please don't rub that Vick's Vap-O-Rub on your chest.

DOROTHEA: I'm *not*! This is Hind's honey-almond cream for *my hands!*

RALPH: Aw.

[*She starts taking off her shoes.*

In the living-room:]

GEORGE: What're you up to?

ISABEL: Up to?

GEORGE: Standin' in front of that fire with that transparent thing on you. You must know it's transparent.

ISABEL: I honestly didn't even think about that.

[ISABEL *crouches by the fire, holding her delicate hands out to its faint flickering glow.*

In the bedroom:]

RALPH: All right. Here it is. George and me are going to cash in every bit of collateral we possess, including the beaver-skin coat and his fifty-two Caddy to buy a piece of ranchland near San Antone.

DOROTHEA: Oh. What are you planning to do on this –

RALPH: – ranch? Breed cattle. Texas Longhorns.

[*A pause.*]

DOROTHEA: I like animals, Ralph.

RALPH: Cocker spaniels.

DOROTHEA: No, I like horses, too. I took equitation at Sonnie Newcomb's. I even learned how to post.

RALPH: Uh-huh.

DOROTHEA: For a little ole Texas girl she sure does have some mighty French taste in nighties!

RALPH: I don't imagine she suffers from psychological frigidity.

DOROTHEA: Honey, I never suffered from that. Did you believe I really suffered from that?

RALPH: When your father proposed to me –

DOROTHEA: Ralph, don't say things like that! Don't, don't humiliate me!

RALPH: Honey, I –

DOROTHEA: PLEASE don't humiliate me by –

RALPH: HONEY!

[*He goes up to her at the dressing table. Sobbing, she presses her head against him.*]

You KNOW I respect you, honey.

ISABEL [*in the other room*]: What an awful, frightening thing it is!

GEORGE: What?

ISABEL: Two people living together, two, two – different worlds! – attempting – existence – together!

[*In the bedroom:*]

RALPH: Honey, will you stop?

DOROTHEA: Respect me, respect me, is that all you can give me when I've loved you so much that sometimes I shake all over at the sight or touch of you? Still? Now? Always?

RALPH: The human heart would never pass the drunk test.

DOROTHEA: Huh?

RALPH: If you took the human heart out of the human body and put a pair of legs on it and told it to walk a straight line, it couldn't do it. It never could pass the drunk test.

DOROTHEA: I love you, baby. And I love animals, too. Hawses, spaniels, longhorns!

RALPH: The Texas longhorn is a – dignified beast.

DOROTHEA: You say that like you thought it was TOO GOOD FOR ME!

RALPH: How do I know that you didn't just come back here for that sheared beaver coat?

[*Living-room:*]

ISABEL: I hope they're getting things ironed out between them.

GEORGE: Why?

ISABEL: They need each other. That's why.

GEORGE: Let's mind our own business, huh?

[*Bedroom:*]

DOROTHEA: You'll just have to WONDER! And WONDER!

[*Living-room:*]

GEORGE: It's a parallel situation. They're going through a period of adjustment just like us.

[*Bedroom:*]

RALPH: All my life, huh?

DOROTHEA: And I'll have to wonder, too, if you love me, Ralph. There's an awful lot of wondering between people.

RALPH: Come on. Turn out the light. Let's go to bed-ville, baby.

DOROTHEA [*turning out the light*]: His or hers?

RALPH: In West Texas we'll get a big one called OURS!

[*In the living-room,* GEORGE *has turned on TV and a chorus is singing 'White Christmas'.*]

GEORGE: Aw. You hate 'White Christmas'.

[*He turns it down.*]

ISABEL: I don't hate it now, baby.

[*He turns it back up, but softly.*
Bedroom:]

DOROTHEA: I'm lookin' *forward* to it. I always wanted a big one, OURS!

RALPH: There's more dignity in it.

DOROTHEA: *Yes!*

[*She giggles breathlessly in the dark.*]

ISABEL [*in the living-room*]: I think they've talked things over and are working things out.

[*Bedroom:*]

RALPH: Yes. It makes it easy to know if – I mean, you don't have to wonder if –

[DOROTHEA *giggles in the dark.*]

That long, long, dangerous walk between 'His' and 'Hers' can be accomplished, or not . . .

[*Living-room:*]

ISABEL: I didn't know until now that the shakes are catching! Why do you keep standing up and sitting back down like a big old jack-in-the-box?

[*A low rumble is heard. It builds. Something falls off a shelf in the kitchenette. Crockery rattles together.*]

WHAT'S THIS!?

GEORGE: Aw, nothin', nothin'.

RALPH [*entering the doorway*]: Well, she jus' slipped again!

DOROTHEA [*appearing behind him*]: Did you all feel that tremor?

ISABEL: Yes, it felt like an earthquake.

DOROTHEA: We get those little tremors all the time because it seems that this suburb is built over a huge underground cavern and is sinking into it, bit by bit. That's the secret of how we could afford to buy this nice little home of ours at such a knockdown price.

ISABEL: It isn't likely to fall in the cavern *tonight*?

DOROTHEA: No. They say it's going to be gradual, about half an inch every year. Do you all mind if I turn on the light a second to see if there's any new cracks?

ISABEL: No, I'll – put on my robe.

[*She does. The room is lighted.*]

DOROTHEA: Yais! Ralph? A *new* one! This one is a jimdandy, all the way 'cross the ceiling! See it, honey? All the way 'cross the ceiling. Well –

[*A pause.*]

We will leave you alone now. I still feel badly about you having to sleep on that folding contraption.

RALPH: Anything I can do? Anything I can –

DOROTHEA: Ralph! Leave them alone. Merry Christmas!

[*She shuts the door.*

Pause. ISABEL *stands before fireplace in the fourth wall.*

Pause.]

GEORGE: Isabel? Little Bit? Marriage is a big step for a man to take, especially when he's – nervous. I'm pretty – nervous.

ISABEL: I know.

GEORGE: For a man with the shakes, especially, it's a – big step to take, it's –

ISABEL: I know what you're trying to tell me.

GEORGE [*taking seat on high stool near fire*]: Do you, honey?

[*He looks up at her quickly, then down.*]

ISABEL: Of course I do. I expect all men are a little bit nervous about the same thing.

GEORGE: What?

ISABEL: About how they'll be at love-making.

GEORGE: Yeah, well, they don't have the shakes. I mean, not all the others have got a nervous tremor like I've got.

ISABEL: Inside or outside, they've all got a nervous tremor of some kind, sweetheart. The world is a big hospital, and I am a nurse in it, George. The whole world's a big hospital, a big neurological ward and I am a student nurse in it. I guess that's still my job! – I love this fire. It feels so good on my skin through this little pink slip. I'm glad she left me the *pink* nightie, tonight.

GEORGE [*huskily*]: Yeah, I'm glad she did, too.

[ISABEL *retires to slip into her nightgown.*]

I wish I had that – little electric buzzer I – had at – Barnes ...

ISABEL: You don't need a buzzer. I'm not way down at the end of a corridor, baby. If you call me, I'll hear you.

[*She returns and hugs her knees, sitting before the fireplace. He rests his head on his cupped hands. She begins to sing softly:*]

'Now the boat goes round the bend,
Good-bye, my lover, good-bye,
It's loaded down with boys and men,
Good-bye, my lover, good-bye.'

RALPH [*in the dark other room*]: She's singin'!

[*Pause.*]

DOROTHEA: Papa said you told him that I was – homely! Did you say that, Ralph? That I was homely?

RALPH: Dotty, you used to be homely but you improved in appearance.

DOROTHEA: You never told me you thought I was homely, Ralph.

RALPH: I just meant you had a off-beat kind of face, honey, but – the rest of you is attractive.

DOROTHEA [*giggles*]: I always knew *I* was homely but you were good enough lookin' to make *up* for it! Baby –

[ISABEL *is singing again, a little forlornly, by the fireplace.*]

ISABEL:

'Bye low, my baby! Bye low, my baby!
Bye low, my baby! Good-bye, my lover, good-bye!'

[GEORGE *whistles softly.*]

Was that for me?

GEORGE: Come here!

ISABEL: No, you come here. It's very nice by the fire.

[*In the other room, as the curtain begins to fall:*]

DOROTHEA: Careful, let me do it! – It isn't mine!

[*She means the borrowed nightgown.*

In the front room, GEORGE *has risen from the bed and is crossing to the fireplace as:*]

THE CURTAIN FALLS

SUMMER AND SMOKE

Who, if I were to cry out, would hear me among the angelic orders?

RILKE

SCENES

Prologue The Fountain

Part One

A SUMMER

Scene I The Same
Scene II The Rectory Interior and Doctor's Office
Scene III The Rectory Interior
Scene IV The Doctor's Office
Scene V The Rectory Interior
Scene VI The Arbour

Part Two

A WINTER

Scene VII The Rectory and Doctor's Office
Scene VIII The Doctor's Office
Scene IX The Rectory and Doctor's Office
Scene X The Fountain
Scene XI The Doctor's Office
Scene XII The Fountain

The entire action of the play takes place in Glorious Hill, Mississippi. The time is the turn of the century through 1916.

THE CAST

The first London production of this play was at the Lyric Theatre, Hammersmith, on Thursday, 22 November 1951, with the following cast:

ALMA WINEMILLER	*Margaret Johnston*
JOHN BUCHANAN	*William Sylvester*
MRS WINEMILLER	*Megs Jenkins*
REV. WINEMILLER	*Allan Jeayes*
PEARL	*Barbara Graley*
DUSTY	*Gaylord Cavallaro*
DR BUCHANAN	*Wensley Pithey*
ROSA GONZALES	*Ingeborg Wells*
NELLIE EWELL	*Sheila Shand Gibbs*
ROGER DOREMUS	*Peter Sallis*
MRS BASSETT	*Joan Young*
VERNON	*Sheldon Allan*
ROSEMARY	*Maria Britnieva*
PAPA GONZALES	*Reginald Dyson*
MR KRAMER	*Harry Towb*

Directed by PETER GLENVILLE

Décor by REECE PEMBERTON

Costumes by WILLIAM CHAPPELL

Original Music composed by PAUL BOWLES

AUTHOR'S PRODUCTION NOTES

As the concept of a design grows out of reading a play I will not do more than indicate what I think are the most essential points.

First of all – *The Sky*.

There must be a great expanse of sky so that the entire action of the play takes place against it. This is true of interior as well as exterior scenes. But in fact there are no really interior scenes, for the walls are omitted or just barely suggested by certain necessary fragments such as might be needed to hang a picture or to contain a door-frame.

During the day scenes the sky should be a pure and intense blue (like the sky of Italy as it is so faithfully represented in the religous paintings of the Renaissance) and costumes should be selected to form a dramatic colour contrast to this intense blue which the figures stand against. (Colour harmonies and other visual effects are tremendously important.)

In the night scenes, the more familiar constellations, such as Orion and the Great Bear and the Pleiades, are clearly projected on the night sky, and above them, splashed across the top of the cyclorama, is the nebulous radiance of the Milky Way. Fleecy cloud forms may also be projected on this cyclorama and made to drift across it.

So much for *The Sky*.

Now we descend to the so-called interior sets of the play. There are two of these 'interior' sets, one being the parlour of an episcopal rectory and the other the home of a doctor next door to the rectory. The architecture of these houses is barely suggested but is of an American Gothic design of the Victorian era. There are no actual doors or windows or walls. Doors and windows are represented by delicate framework of Gothic design. These frames have strings of ivy clinging to them, the leaves of emerald and amber. Sections of wall are used only where they are functionally required. There should be a fragment of wall in back of the rectory sofa, supporting a romantic landscape in a gilt frame. In the doctor's house there should be a section of a wall to support the chart of anatomy. Chirico has used fragmentary walls and interiors in a very evocative way in his painting called *Conversation among the Ruins.* We will deal more specifically with these interiors as we come to them in the course of the play.

Now we come to the main exterior set which is a promontory in a park or public square in the town of Glorious Hill. Situated on this promontory is a fountain in the form of a stone angel, in a gracefully crouching position with wings lifted and her hands held together to form a cup from which water flows, a public drinking fountain. The stone angel of the fountain should probably be elevated so that it appears in the background of the interior scenes as a symbolic figure (Eternity) brooding over the course of the play. *This entire exterior set may be on an upper level, above that of the two fragmentary interiors.* I would like all three units to form an harmonious whole like one complete picture rather than three separate ones. An imaginative designer may solve these plastic problems in a variety of ways and should not feel bound by any of my specific suggestions.

There is one more set, a very small exterior representing an arbour, which we will describe when we reach it.

Everything possible should be done to give an unbroken fluid quality to the sequence of scenes.

There should be no curtain except for the intermission. The other divisions of the play should be accomplished by changes of lighting.

Finally, the matter of music. One basic theme should recur and the points of recurrence have been indicated here and there in the stage directions.

Rome, March 1948

PROLOGUE

In the park near the angel of the fountain. At dusk of an evening in May, in the first few years of this century.

ALMA, *as a child of ten, comes into the scene. She wears a middy blouse and has ribboned braids. She already has the dignity of an adult; there is a quality of extraordinary delicacy and tenderness or spirituality in her, which must set her distinctly apart from other children. She has a habit of holding her hands, one cupped under the other in a way similar to that of receiving the wafer at Holy Communion. This is a habit that will remain with her as an adult. She stands like that in front of the stone angel for a few moments; then bends to drink at the fountain.*

While she is bent at the fountain, JOHN, *as a child, enters. He shoots a pea-shooter at* ALMA*'s bent-over back. She utters a startled cry and whirls about. He laughs.*

JOHN: Hi, preacher's daughter. [*He advances towards her.*] I been looking for you.

ALMA [*hopefully*]: You have?

JOHN: Was it you that put them handkerchiefs on my desk?

[ALMA *smiles uncertainly.*]

Answer up!

ALMA: I put a box of handkerchiefs on your desk.

JOHN: I figured it was you. What was the idea, Miss Priss?

ALMA: You needed them.

JOHN: Trying to make a fool of me?

ALMA: Oh, no!

JOHN: Then what was the idea?

ALMA: You have a bad cold and your nose has been running all week. It spoils your appearance.

JOHN: You don't have to look at me if you don't like my appearance.

ALMA: I like your appearance.

JOHN [*coming closer*]: Is that why you look at me all the time?

ALMA: I – don't!

JOHN: Oh, yeh, you do. You been keeping your eyes on me all the time. Every time I look around I see them cat eyes of yours looking at me. That was the trouble today when Miss Blanchard asked you where the River Amazon was. She asked you twice and you still didn't answer because you w' lookin' at me. What's the idea? What've y' got on y' mind anyhow? Answer up!

ALMA: I was only thinking how handsome you'd be if your face wasn't dirty. You know why your face is dirty? Because you don't use a handkerchief and you wipe your nose on the sleeve of that dirty old sweater.

JOHN [*indignantly*]: Hah!

ALMA: That's why I put the handkerchiefs on your desk and I wrapped them up so nobody would know what they were. It isn't my fault that you opened the box in front of everybody!

JOHN: What did you think I'd do with a strange box on my desk? Just leave it there till it exploded or something? Sure I opened it up. I didn't expect to find no – *handkerchiefs*! – in it . . .

ALMA [*in a shy trembling voice*]: I'm sorry that you were embarrassed. I honestly am awfully sorry that you were embarrassed. Because I wouldn't embarrass you for the world!

JOHN: Don't flatter yourself that I was embarrassed. I don't embarrass that easy.

ALMA: It was stupid and cruel of those girls to laugh.

JOHN: Hah!

ALMA: They should all realize that you don't have a mother to take care of such things for you. It was a pleasure to me to be able to do something for you, only I didn't want you to know it was me who did it.

JOHN: Hee-haw! Ho-hum! Take 'em back! [*He snatches out the box and thrusts it towards her.*]

ALMA: *Please* keep them.

JOHN: What do I want with them?

[ALMA *stares at* JOHN *helplessly. He tosses the box to the ground and goes up to the fountain and drinks. Something in her face mollifies him and he sits down at the base of the fountain with a manner that does not preclude a more friendly relation. The dusk gathers deeper.*]

JOHN: Does she have a name?

ALMA: Yes, I found out she does. It's carved in the base, but its' all worn away so you can't make it out with your eyes.

JOHN: Then how do you know it?

ALMA: You have to read it with your fingers. I did and it gave me cold shivers! *You* read it and see if it doesn't give *you* cold shivers. Go on! Read it with your fingers!

JOHN: Why don't you tell me and save the trouble?

ALMA: I'm not going to tell you.

[JOHN *grins indulgently and turns to the pediment, crouching before it and running his fingers along the worn inscription.*]

JOHN: E?

ALMA: Yes, E is the first letter!

JOHN: T?

ALMA: Yes!

JOHN: E?

ALMA: E!

JOHN: K?

ALMA: No, no, not K! – R!

[*He slowly straightens up.*]

JOHN: Eternity?

ALMA: *Eternity!* – Didn't it give you the cold shivers?

JOHN: Nahh.

ALMA: Well, it did me!

JOHN: Because you're a preacher's daughter. Eternity. What is eternity?

ALMA [*in a hushed wondering voice*]: It's something that goes on and on when life and death and time and everything else is all through with.

JOHN: There's no such thing.

ALMA: There is. It's what people's souls live in when they have left their bodies. My name is Alma and Alma is Spanish for soul. Did you know that?

JOHN: Hee-haw! Ho-hum! Have you ever seen a dead person?

ALMA: No.

JOHN: I have. They made me go in the room when my mother was dying and she caught hold of my hand and wouldn't let me go – and so I screamed and hit her.

ALMA: Oh, you didn't do that.

JOHN [*sombrely*]: Uh-huh. She didn't look like my mother. Her face was all ugly and yellow and – terrible – bad-smelling! And so I hit her to make her let go of my hand. They told me that I was a devil!

ALMA: You didn't know what you were doing.

JOHN: My dad is a doctor.

ALMA: I know.

JOHN: He wants to send me to college to study to be a doctor but I wouldn't be a doctor for the world. And have to go in a room and watch people dying! ... Jesus.

ALMA: You'll change your mind about that.

JOHN: Oh, no, I won't. I'd rather *be* a devil, like they called me and go to South America on a boat! ... Give me one of them handkerchiefs.

[ALMA *brings them eagerly and humbly to the fountain.* JOHN *takes one out and wets it at the fountain and scrubs his face with it.*]

Is my face clean enough to suit you now?

ALMA: Yes! – Beautiful!

JOHN: *What!*

ALMA: I said 'Beautiful'!

JOHN: Well – let's – kiss each other.

ALMA *turns away.*]

Come on, let's just try it!

[JOHN *seizes her shoulders and gives her a quick rough kiss. She stands amazed, with one hand cupping the other.*

The voice of a child in the distance calls: 'Johnny! Johnny!'

JOHN *suddenly snatches at* ALMA*'s hair-ribbon, jerks it loose and then runs off with a mocking laugh.*

Hurt and bewildered, ALMA *turns back to the stone angel, for comfort. She crouches at the pediment and touches the inscription with her fingers. The scene dims out with music.*

PART ONE: A SUMMER

SCENE I

Before the curtain rises a band is heard playing a patriotic anthem, punctuated with the crackle of fireworks.

The scene is the same as for the Prologue. It is the evening of 4 July in a year shortly before the First World War. There is a band concert and a display of fireworks in the park. During the scene the light changes from faded sunlight to dusk. Sections of roof, steeples, weather-vanes, should have a metallic surface that catches the mellow light on the back-drop; when dusk has fallen the stars should be visible.

As the curtain rises, the REV. *and* MRS WINEMILLER *come in and sit on the bench near the fountain.*

MRS WINEMILLER *was a spoiled and selfish girl who evaded responsibilities of later life by slipping into a state of perverse childishness. She is known as* MR WINEMILLER*'s 'Cross'.*

MR WINEMILLER [*suddenly rising*]: There is Alma, getting on the bandstand!

[MRS WINEMILLER *is dreamily munching popcorn.*]

AN ANNOUNCER'S VOICE [*at a distance*]: The Glorious Hill Orchestra brings you Miss Alma Winemiller, The Nightingale of the Delta, singing ... 'La Golondrina'.

MR WINEMILLER [*sitting back down again*]: This is going to provoke a lot of criticism.

[*The song commences. The voice is not particularly strong, but it has great purity and emotion.* JOHN BUCHANAN *comes along. He is now a Promethean figure, brilliantly and restlessly alive in a stagnant society. The excess of his power has not yet found a channel. If it remains without one, it will burn him up. At present he is unmarked by the dissipations in which he relieves his demoniac unrest; he has the fresh and shining look of an epic hero. He walks leisurely before the*

WINEMILLERS' *bench, negligently touching the crown of his hat but not glancing at them; climbs the steps to the base of the fountain, then turns and looks in the direction of the singer. A look of interest touched with irony appears on his face.*

A couple, strolling in the park, pass behind the fountain.]

THE GIRL: Look who's by the fountain!

THE MAN: Bright as a new silver dollar!

JOHN: Hi, Dusty! Hi, Pearl!

THE MAN: How'd you make out in that floating crap game?

JOHN: I floated with it as far as Vicksburg, then sank.

THE GIRL: Everybody's been calling: 'Johnny, Johnny – where's Johnny?'

[JOHN'S *father,* DR BUCHANAN, *comes on from right, as the* REV. *and* MRS WINEMILLER *move off the scene to left, towards the band music.* DR BUCHANAN *is an elderly man whose age shows in his slow and stiff movements. He walks with a cane.* JOHN *sees him coming, but pretends not to and starts to walk off.*]

DR BUCHANAN: *John!*

JOHN: Oh! Hi, Dad...

[*The men stare at each other for a long tense moment. Finally* JOHN *speaks awkwardly.*]

I – uh – meant to wire you but I must've forgot. I got tied up in Vicksburg Saturday and just now got back to town ... I haven't been to the house yet ... Is – everything – O.K.?

DR BUCHANAN [*hoarsely with mounting fury*]: I left you in charge of my practice for the week-end. While I was gone, what happened?

JOHN: Oh Dad, you know what happened.

DR BUCHANAN: Yes, I know what happened. A woman died of a haemorrhage...

JOHN: It was a terminal case of –

DR BUCHANAN: Be quiet, God damn you!

[JOHN *turns away.*]

Stay here! And listen to me. There is no room in the medical profession for wasters – drunkards – lechers!

JOHN: All right, then, let me out of it!

DR BUCHANAN: You were never in it! A medical diploma don't make you a doctor. No doctor fit to be called one would show that sort of – criminal irresponsibility towards his –

JOHN [*shouting*]: *Then let me out of it!*

DR BUCHANAN: I've sent your things to the Alhambra Hotel. [*Starts to go.*]

JOHN: Dad! I was with the old lady from seven till three in the morning. When she – lapsed into coma, I went out for some air. I saw the death of my mother, and ever since then I've had a dread of it that makes me unsuitable material for a doctor. I'm made for the science of medicine but not the practice of it.

DR BUCHANAN: I need you here, for a while. Pick up your things at the Alhambra Hotel, John – and bring them back to the house.

JOHN: – Yes, sir . . .

DR BUCHANAN: I have to call on a patient. [*Nods slightly and goes off upper right.*]

[JOHN *looks after him with a faint, affectionate smile, then sits down on the steps with an air of relief, handkerchief to forehead, and a whistle of relief.*

MRS WINEMILLER *comes in from left, followed by her husband.*]

MRS WINEMILLER: Where is the ice-cream man?

MR WINEMILLER: Mother, hush! [*Just then the song ends. There is applause. Then the band strikes up the Santiago Waltz. He sees his daughter approaching.*] Here we are, Alma!

[ALMA WINEMILLER *enters.* ALMA *had an adult quality as a child, and now, in her middle twenties, there is something prematurely spinsterish about her. An excessive propriety and self-consciousness is apparent in her nervous laughter; her voice and gestures belong to years of church entertainments, to the position of hostess in a rectory. People her own age regard her as rather quaintly and humorously affected. She has grown up mostly in the company of her elders. Her true nature is still hidden even from herself. She is dressed in pale yellow and carries a yellow silk parasol.*

As ALMA *passes in front of the fountain,* JOHN *slaps his hands resoundingly together a few times. She catches her breath in a slight laughing sound, makes as if to retreat, with a startled 'Oh', but then goes quickly to her parents. The applause from the crowd continues.*]

MR WINEMILLER: They seem to want to hear you sing again, Alma.

[ALMA *turns nervously about, touching her throat and her chest.* JOHN *grins, applauding by the fountain. When the applause dies out,* ALMA *sinks faintly on the bench.*]

ALMA: Open my bag, Father. My fingers have frozen stiff! [*She draws a deep laboured breath.*] I don't know what came over me – absolute panic! Never, never again, it isn't worth it – the tortures that I go through!

MR WINEMILLER [*anxiously*]: You're having one of your nervous attacks?

ALMA: My heart's beating so! It seemed to be in my *throat* the whole time I was singing!

[JOHN *laughs audibly from the fountain.*]

Was it noticeable, Father?

MR WINEMILLER: You sang extremely well, Alma. But you know how I feel about this, it was contrary to my wishes and I cannot imagine why you wanted to do it, especially since it seemed to upset you so.

ALMA: I don't see how anyone could object to my singing at a patriotic occasion. If I had just sung well! But I barely got through it. At one point I thought that I wouldn't. The words flew out of my mind. Did you notice the pause? Blind panic! They really never came back, but I went on singing – I think I must have been improvising the lyric! Whew! Is there a handkerchief in it?

MRS WINEMILLER [*suddenly*]: Where is the ice-cream man?

ALMA [*rubbing her fingers together*]: Circulation is slowly coming back . . .

MR WINEMILLER: Sit back quietly and take a deep breath, Alma.

ALMA: Yes, my handkerchief – now . . .

MRS WINEMILLER: Where is the ice-cream man?

MR WINEMILLER: Mother, there isn't any ice-cream man.

ALMA: No, there isn't any ice-cream man, Mother. But on the way home Mr Doremus and I will stop by the drug store and pick up a pint of ice-cream.

MR WINEMILLER: Are you intending to stay here?

ALMA: Until the concert is over. I promised Roger I'd wait for him.

MR WINEMILLER: I suppose you have noticed who is by the fountain?

ALMA: *Shhh!*

MR WINEMILLER: Hadn't you better wait on a different bench?

ALMA: This is where Roger will meet me.

MR WINEMILLER: Well, Mother, we'll run along now.

[MRS WINEMILLER *has started vaguely towards the fountain,* MR WINEMILLER *firmly restraining her.*]

This way, this way, Mother! [*He takes arm and leads her off.*]

MRS WINEMILLER [*calling back, in a childish voice*]: Strawberry, Alma. Chocolate, chocolate and strawberry mixed! Not vanilla!

ALMA [*faintly*]: Yes, yes, Mother – vanilla . . .

MRS WINEMILLER [*furiously*]: I said *not* vanilla. [*Shouting.*] Strawberry!

MR WINEMILLER [*fiercely*]: Mother! We're attracting attention. [*He propels her forcibly away.*]

[JOHN *laughs by the fountain.* ALMA *moves her parasol so that it shields her face from him. She leans back, closing her eyes.* JOHN *notices a firecracker by the fountain. He leans over negligently to pick it up. He grins and lights it and tosses it towards* ALMA*'s bench. When it goes off she springs up with a shocked cry, letting the parasol drop.*]

JOHN [*jumping up as if outraged*]: Hey! Hey, you!

[*He looks off to right.* ALMA *sinks back weakly on the bench.* JOHN *solicitously advances.*]

Are you all right?

ALMA: I can't seem to – catch my breath! Who threw it?

JOHN: Some little rascal.

ALMA: Where?

JOHN: He ran away quick when I hollered!

ALMA: There ought to be an ordinance passed in this town forbidding firecrackers.

JOHN: Dad and I treated fifteen kids for burns the last couple of days. I think you need a little restorative, don't you? [*He takes out a flask.*] Here!

ALMA: What is it?

JOHN: Apple-jack brandy.

ALMA: No thank you.

JOHN: Liquid dynamite.

ALMA: I'm sure.

[JOHN *laughs and returns it to his pocket. He remains looking down at* ALMA *with one foot on the end of her bench. His steady, smiling look into her face is disconcerting her.*

In ALMA*'s voice and manner there is a delicacy and elegance, a kind of 'airiness', which is really natural to her, as it is, in a less marked degree, to many Southern girls. Her gestures and mannerisms are a bit exaggerated but in a graceful way. It is understandable that she might be accused of 'putting on airs' and being 'affected' by the other young people of the town. She seems to belong to a more elegant age, such as the eighteenth century in France. Out of nervousness and self-consciousness she has a habit of prefacing and concluding her remarks with a little breathless laugh. This will be indicated at points, but should be used more freely than indicated; however, the characterization must never be stressed to the point of making her at all ludicrous in a less sympathetic way.*]

ALMA: You're – home for the summer?

[JOHN *gives an affirmative grunt.*]

Summer is not the pleasantest time of year to renew an acquaintance with Glorious Hill – is it?

[JOHN *gives an indefinite grunt.* ALMA *laughs airily.*]

The Gulf wind has failed us this year, disappointed us dreadfully this summer. We used to be able to rely on the Gulf wind to cool the nights off for us, but this summer has been an exceptional season.

[JOHN *continues to grin disconcertingly down at* ALMA; *she shows her discomfiture in flurried gestures.*]

JOHN [*slowly*]: Are you – disturbed about something?

ALMA: That firecracker was a shock.

JOHN: You should be over that shock by now.

ALMA: I don't get over shocks quickly.

JOHN: I see you don't.

ALMA: You're planning to stay here and take over some of your father's medical practice?

JOHN: I haven't made up my mind about anything yet.

ALMA: I hope so, we all hope so. Your father was telling me that you have succeeded in isolating the germ of that fever epidemic that's broken out at Lyon.

JOHN: Finding something to kill it is more of a trick.

ALMA: You'll do that! He's so positive that you will. He says that you made a special study of bacter ... bacter ...

JOHN: Bacteriology!

ALMA: Yes! At Johns Hopkins! That's in Boston, isn't it?

JOHN: No. Baltimore.

ALMA: Oh, Baltimore. Baltimore, Maryland. Such a beautiful combination of names. And bacteriology – isn't that something you do with a microscope?

JOHN: Well – partly ...

ALMA: I've looked through a telescope, but never a microscope. What ... what do you – see?

JOHN: A – universe, Miss Alma.

ALMA: What kind of a universe?

JOHN: Pretty much the same kind that you saw through the lens of a telescope – a mysterious one ...

ALMA: Oh, yes ...

JOHN: Part anarchy – and part order!

ALMA: The footprints of God!

JOHN: But not God.

ALMA [*ecstatically*]: To be a doctor! And deal with these mysteries under the microscope lens ... I think it is more religious than being a priest! There is so much suffering in the world it actually makes one sick to think about it, and most of us are so helpless to relieve it ... But a physician! Oh, my! With his magnificent gifts and training what a joy it must be to know that he is equipped and appointed to bring relief to all of this fearful suffering – and fear! And it's an expanding profession; it's a profession that is continually widening its horizons. So many diseases have already come under scientific control but the commencement is just – beginning! I mean there is so much more that is yet to be done, such as mental afflictions to be brought under control ... And with your father's example to inspire you! Oh, my!

JOHN: I didn't know you had so many ideas about the medical profession.

ALMA: Well, I am a great admirer of your father, as well as a patient. It's such a comfort knowing that he's right next door, within arm's reach as it were!

JOHN: Why? Do you have fits? . . .

ALMA: Fits? [*She throws back her head with a peal of gay laughter.*] Why no, but I do have attacks! – of nervous heart trouble. Which can be so alarming that I run straight to your father!

JOHN: At two or three in the morning?

ALMA: Yes, as late as that, even . . . occasionally. He's very patient with me.

JOHN: But does you no good?

ALMA: He always reassures me.

JOHN: Temporarily?

ALMA: Yes . . .

JOHN: Don't you want more than that?

ALMA: What?

JOHN: It's none of my business.

ALMA: What were you going to say?

JOHN: You're Dad's patient. But I have an idea . . .

ALMA: Please go on!

[JOHN *laughs a little.*]

Now you have to go on! You can't leave me up in the air! What were you going to tell me?

JOHN: Only that I suspect you need something more than a little temporary reassurance.

ALMA: *Why?* You think it's more serious than . . . ?

JOHN: You're swallowing air, Miss Alma.

ALMA: I'm what?

JOHN: You're swallowing air, Miss Alma.

ALMA: I'm swallowing air?

JOHN: Yes, you swallow air when you laugh or talk. It's a little trick that hysterical women get into.

ALMA [*uncertainly*]: Ha-ha . . . !

JOHN: You swallow air and it presses on your heart and gives you palpitations. That isn't serious in itself but it's a symptom of something that is. Shall I tell frankly?

ALMA: Yes!

JOHN: Well, what I think you have is a *doppelganger*! You have a *doppelganger* and the *doppelganger* is badly irritated.

ALMA: Oh, my goodness! I have an irritated *doppelganger*! [*She tries to laugh, but is definitely uneasy.*] How awful that sounds! What exactly *is* it?

JOHN: It's none of *my* business. You are not *my* patient.

ALMA: But that's downright wicked of you! To tell me I have something awful-sounding as that, and then refuse to let me know what it is! [*She tries to laugh again, unsuccessfully.*]

JOHN: I shouldn't have said anything! I'm not your doctor ...

ALMA: Just how did you arrive at this – diagnosis of my case? [*She laughs.*] But of course you're teasing me. Aren't you? ... There, the Gulf wind is stirring! He's actually moving the leaves of the palmetto! And listen to them complaining ...

[*As if brought in by this courier from the tropics,* ROSA GONZALES *enters and crosses to the fountain. Her indolent walk produces a sound and an atmosphere like the Gulf wind on the palmettos, a whispering of silk and a slight rattle of metallic ornaments. She is dressed in an almost outrageous finery, with lustrous feathers on her hat, greenish blue, a cascade of them, also diamond and emerald earrings.*

JOHN [*sharply*]: *Who is that?*

ALMA: I'm surprised that you don't know.

JOHN: I've been away quite a while.

ALMA: That's the Gonzales girl ... Her father's the owner of the gambling casino on Moon Lake.

[ROSA *drinks at the fountain and wanders leisurely off.*]

She smiled at you, didn't she?

JOHN: I thought she did.

ALMA: I hope that you have a strong character.

[JOHN *places a foot on the end of the bench.*]

JOHN: Solid rock.

ALMA [*nervously*]: The pyrotechnical display is going to be brilliant.

JOHN: The what?

ALMA: The fireworks.

JOHN: Aw!

ALMA: I suppose you've lost touch with most of your *old* friends here.

JOHN: [*laconically*]: Yeah.

ALMA: You must make some *new* ones! I belong to a little group that meets every ten days. I think you'd enjoy them, too. They're young people with – intellectual and artistic interests ...

JOHN [*sadly*]: Aw, I see ... intellectual ...

ALMA: You must come! – sometime – I'm going to remind you of it ...

JOHN: Thanks. Do you mind if I sit down?

ALMA: Why, certainly not, there's room enough for two! Neither of us are – terribly large in diameter! [*She laughs shrilly.*]

[*A girl's voice is heard calling: 'Good-bye, Nellie!' and another answers: 'Good-bye!'* NELLIE EWELL *enters – a girl of sixteen with a radiantly fresh healthy quality.*]

Here comes someone much nicer! One of my adorable little vocal pupils, the youngest and prettiest one with the least gift for music.

JOHN: I know that one.

ALMA: Hello, there, Nellie dear!

NELLIE: Oh, Miss Alma, your singing was so beautiful it made me cry.

ALMA: It's sweet of you to fib so. I sang terribly.

NELLIE: You're just being modest, Miss Alma. Hello, Dr John! Dr John!

JOHN: Yeah?

NELLIE: That book you gave me is too full of long words.

JOHN: Look 'em up in the dictionary, Nellie.

NELLIE: I did, but you know how dictionaries are. You look up one long word and it gives you another long word and you look up that long word and it gives you the long word you looked up in the first place.

[JOHN *laughs.*]

I'm coming over tomorrow for you to explain it all to me. [*She laughs and goes off.*]

ALMA: What book is she talking about?

JOHN: A book I gave her about the facts of nature. She came over to the office and told me her mother wouldn't tell her anything and she had to know because she'd fallen in love.

ALMA: Why the precocious little – imp! [*She laughs.*]

JOHN: What sort of a mother has she?

ALMA: Mrs Ewell's the merry widow of Glorious Hill. They say that she goes to the depot to meet every train in order to make the acquaintance of travelling salesmen. Of course she is ostracized by all but a few of her own type of women in town, which is terribly hard for Nellie. It isn't fair to the child. Father didn't want me to take her as a pupil because of her mother's reputation, but I feel that one has a duty to perform towards children in such – circumstances ... And I always say that life is such a mysteriously complicated thing that no one should really presume to judge and condemn the behaviour of anyone else!

[*There is a faraway 'puff' and a burst of golden light over their heads. Both look up. There is a long-drawn 'Ahhh ...' from the invisible crowd. This is an effect that will be repeated at intervals during the scene.*]

There goes the first skyrocket! Oh, look at it burst into a million stars!

[JOHN *leans way back to look up and allow his knees to spread wide apart so that one of them is in contact with* ALMA'*s. The effect upon her is curiously disturbing.*]

JOHN [*after a moment*]: Do you have a chill?

ALMA: Why, no! – no. Why?

JOHN: You're shaking.

ALMA: Am I?

JOHN: Don't you feel it?

ALMA: I have a touch of malaria lingering on.

JOHN: You have malaria?

ALMA: Never severely, never really severely. I just have touches of it that come and go. [*She laughs airily.*]

JOHN [*with a gentle grin*]: Why do you laugh that way?

ALMA: What way?

[JOHN *imitates her laugh.* ALMA *laughs again in embarrassment.*]

JOHN: Yeah. That way.

ALMA: I do declare, you haven't changed in the slightest. It used to delight you to embarrass me and it still does!

JOHN: I guess I shouldn't tell you this, but I heard an imitation of you at a party.

ALMA: Imitation? Of what?

JOHN: You.

ALMA: I? – I? Why, *what* did they imitate?

JOHN: You singing at a wedding.

ALMA: My voice?

JOHN: Your gestures and facial expression! Some people have got the idea you're a little bit affected.

ALMA: How mystifying!

JOHN: No, I shouldn't have told you. You're upset about it.

ALMA: I'm not in the least upset, I am just mystified. Who gave this imitation at this party you spoke of?

JOHN [*grinning*]: I don't think she'd want that told.

ALMA: Oh, it was a *she* then?

JOHN: You don't think a man could do it?

ALMA: No, and I don't think a lady would do it either!

JOHN: I didn't think it would have made you so mad, or I wouldn't have brought it up.

ALMA: Oh, I'm not mad. I'm just mystified and amazed, as I always am by unprovoked malice in people. These people who call me affected and give these unkind imitations of me – I wonder if they stop to think that my circumstances are somewhat different from theirs? My father and I have a certain – cross – to bear!

JOHN: What cross?

ALMA: Living next door to us, you should know what cross.

JOHN: Mrs Winemiller?

ALMA: Almost immediately after my father was ordained into the Ministry she started slipping back into her childhood to escape the responsibilities of a rectory. I had to take over those responsibilities at an early age, and that may have made me seem strange to some of my more critical contemporaries.

[*Another rocket goes up. Another 'Ahhh ...' from the crowd.*]

JOHN: You ought to go out with young people.

ALMA: I am not a recluse. I don't fly around here and there giving imitations of other people at parties. But I am not a recluse by any manner of means.

JOHN: I have seen you in the public library and the park, but only two or three times have I seen you out with a boy and it was always someone like this Roger Doremus.

ALMA: I'm afraid that you and I move in different circles. If I wished to be as outspoken as you are, which is sometimes just an excuse for being rude – I might say that I've yet to see you in the company of a – well, a – reputable young woman. And the pity of it is that you are preparing to be a doctor. You're intending to practise your father's profession here in Glorious Hill. [*She catches her breath in a sob.*] While he is devoting himself to the fever at Lyon you drive your automobile at a reckless pace from one disorderly roadhouse to another! And you – a gifted young doctor – *Magna cum Laude!* [*She turns aside, touching her eyelids with a handkerchief.*] You know what I call it? I call it a *desecration*!

[ALMA *sobs uncontrollably. Then she springs up from the bench.* JOHN *catches her hand.*]

JOHN: You're not going to run off, are you?

ALMA: Singing in public always – always upsets me! – Let go of my hand.

[JOHN *holds on to it, grinning up at* ALMA *in the deepening dusk. The stars are coming out in the cyclorama with its leisurely floating cloud-forms. In the distance the band is playing 'La Golondrina'.*]

Please let go of my hand.

JOHN: Don't run off mad.

ALMA: Let's not make a spectacle of ourselves.

JOHN: Then sit back down.

[*A skyrocket goes up. The crowd 'Ahhh . . . s'.*]

ALMA: You threw that firecracker and started a conversation just in order to tease me as you did as a child. You came to this bench in order to embarrass me and to hurt my feelings with the report of that vicious – imitation! No, let go of my hand so I can leave, now. You've succeeded in your purpose. I *was* hurt! I *did* make a fool of myself as you intended! So let me go now!

JOHN: You're attracting attention! Don't you know that I really *like* you, Miss Alma?

ALMA: No, you don't.

[*Another skyrocket.*]

JOHN: Sure I do. A lot. Sometimes when I come home late at night I look over at the rectory. I see something white at the window. Could that be you, Miss Alma? Or, is it your *doppelganger*, looking out of the window that faces my way?

ALMA: Enough about *doppelganger* – whatever that is!

JOHN: There goes a nice one, roman candle they call it!

[*This time the explosion is in back of them. A roman candle shoots up puffs of rainbow-coloured light in back of the stone angel of the fountain. They turn in profile to watch it.*]

JOHN [*counting the puffs of light*]: Four – five – six – that's all? No – seven!

[*There is a pause.* ALMA *sits down slowly.*]

ALMA [*vaguely*]: Dear me ... [*She fans herself.*]

JOHN: How about going riding?

ALMA [*too eagerly*]: When ... now?

[ROSA GONZALES *has wandered up to the fountain again.* JOHN'*s attention drifts steadily towards her and away from* ALMA.]

JOHN [*too carelessly*]: Oh ... some afternoon.

ALMA: Would you observe the speed limit?

JOHN: Strictly with you, Miss Alma.

ALMA: Why then, I'd be glad to – John.

[JOHN *has risen from the bench and crosses to the fountain.*]

JOHN: And wear a hat with a plume!

ALMA: I don't have a hat with a plume!

JOHN: Get one!

[*Another skyrocket goes up, and there is another long 'Ahhh ...' from the crowd.* JOHN *saunters up to the fountain.* ROSA *has lingered beside it. As he passes her he whispers something. She laughs and moves leisurely off.* JOHN *takes a quick drink at the fountain, then follows* ROSA, *calling back 'good night' to* ALMA. *There is a sound of laughter in the distance.* ALMA *sits motionless for a moment, then touches a small white handkerchief to her lips and nostrils.* MR DOREMUS *comes in, carrying a French horn case. He is a small man, somewhat like a sparrow.*]

ROGER: *Whew!* Golly! Moses! – Well, how did it go, Miss Alma?

ALMA: How did – what – go?

ROGER [*annoyed*]: My solo on the French horn.

ALMA [*slowly, without thinking*]: I paid no attention to it. [*She rises slowly and takes his arm.*] I'll have to hang on your arm – I'm feeling so dizzy!

[*The scene dims out. There is a final skyrocket and a last 'Ahhh ...' from the crowd in the distance. Music is heard, and there is light on the angel.*]

SCENE II

The Winemillers' parlour.

MRS WINEMILLER *enters from the inside door. She is carrying her parasol, from the folds of which she removes a hat with billowing white plumes. Looking in the mirror, she places the hat on her head.*

MRS WINEMILLER:

If I wore a tall hat in a sunny room,
I would sweep the ceiling with a cavalier's plume!

If I wore a velvet cloak along the esplanade
I'd fascinate an officer in red and gold brocade!

If I spoke behind a fan on a white verandah
I would shock a simple heart with my heartless candour!
Ha ha ha ha!

[*The telephone rings.* MRS WINEMILLER *snatches off the hat, hides it under the centre table, and quickly sits at the table and works on her picture puzzle. The telephone goes on ringing.* ALMA *comes in to answer it.*]

ALMA: Hello ... Yes, Mr Gillam ... She did? ... Are you sure? ... How shocking! ...

[MRS WINEMILLER *now retrieves the hat and puts it on.*]

Thank you, Mr Gillam ... the hat is here.

[MR WINEMILLER *comes in through the inside door. He is distracted.*]

MR WINEMILLER: Alma! Alma, your mother ... !

ALMA: I know, Father, Mr Gillam just phoned. He told me she picked up a white plumed hat and he pretended not to notice in order to save you the embarrassment, so I – I told him to just charge it to us.

MR WINEMILLER: That hat looks much too expensive.

ALMA: It's fourteen dollars. You pay six of it, Father, and I'll pay eight.

MR WINEMILLER: What an insufferable cross we have to bear.

[*He retires despairingly from the room, through the inner door.*]

ALMA: I have a thousand and one things to do before my club meeting tonight, so you work quietly on your picture puzzle or I shall take the hat back, plume and all.

MRS WINEMILLER [*throwing pieces of the puzzle on the floor*]: The pieces don't fit!

[ALMA *picks up the pieces and puts them on the table.*]

The pieces don't fit!

[ALMA *stands for a moment looking at the hat. She reaches for the phone, then puts it down. Then she picks it up again, and asks for 'ELM 362'. The telephone across the way in the doctor's office rings and that part of the scene lights up.* JOHN *comes in.*]

JOHN [*answering the phone*]: Hello

ALMA: John! [*She fans herself rapidly with a palm leaf clutched in her free hand and puts on a brilliant, strained smile as if she were actually in his presence.*]

JOHN [*sitting on the desk and, during the conversation, mixing a bromo*]: Miss Alma?

ALMA: You recognized my voice?

JOHN: I recognized your laugh.

ALMA: Ha-ha! How are you, you stranger you?

JOHN: I'm pretty well, Miss Alma. How're you doing?

ALMA: Surviving, just surviving! Isn't it fearful?

JOHN: Uh-huh.

ALMA: You seem unusually laconic. Or perhaps I should say more than usually laconic.

JOHN: I was at Moon Lake Casino last night and I'm just recovering from it.

ALMA: Well, sir, I have a bone to pick with you!

JOHN: What's that, Miss Alma? [*He drains the glass of bromo.*]

ALMA: The time of our last conversation on the Fourth of July, you said you were going to take me riding in your automobile.

JOHN: Aw. Did I say that?

ALMA: Yes indeed you did, sir! And all these hot afternoons I've been breathlessly waiting and hoping that you would remember that promise. But now I know how insincere you are. Ha-ha!

MRS WINEMILLER: Ha ha ha!

ALMA: Time and again the four-wheeled phenomenon flashes by the rectory and I have yet to put my – my quaking foot in it.

MRS WINEMILLER: Quaking foot in it. Ha-ha! Four-wheeled phenomenon.

JOHN: What was that, Miss Alma! I didn't understand you.

ALMA: I was just reprimanding you, sir! Castigating you verbally! Ha-ha!

JOHN: What about, Miss Alma?

ALMA: Never mind. I know how busy you are.

MRS WINEMILLER: She's busy.

ALMA [*whispers*]: Mother, *hush*!

JOHN: I'm afraid we have a bad connection.

ALMA: I hate telephones. I don't know why, but they always make me laugh as if someone were poking me in the ribs! I swear to goodness they do!

JOHN: Why don't you just go to your window and I'll go to mine and we can holler across?

ALMA: The yard's so wide I'm afraid it would crack my voice! And I've got to sing at somebody's wedding tomorrow.

JOHN: You're going to sing at a wedding?

ALMA: Yes. 'The Voice that Breathed o'er Eden!' And I'm as hoarse as a frog! [*Another gale of laughter almost shakes her off her feet.*]

JOHN: Better come over and let me give you a gargle.

ALMA: Nasty gargles – I hate them!

MRS WINEMILLER [*mockingly*]: Nasty gargles – I hate them!

ALMA: Mother, shhh! – please! As you no doubt have gathered, there is some interference at this end of the line! What I wanted to say is –

you remember my mentioning that little club I belong to?

JOHN: Aw! Aw, yes! Those cultural meetings!

ALMA: Oh, now, don't call it that. It's just a little informal gathering every Wednesday and we talk about the new books and read things out loud to each other!

JOHN: Serve any refreshments?

ALMA: Yes, we serve refreshments!

JOHN: Any liquid refreshments?

ALMA: Both liquid and solid refreshments.

JOHN: Is this an invitation?

ALMA: Didn't I promise I'd ask you? It's going to be tonight! – at eight at my house, at the rectory, so all you'll have to do is cross the yard!

JOHN: I'll try to make it, Miss Alma.

ALMA: Don't say try as if it required some Herculean effort! All you have to do is ...

JOHN: Cross the yard! Uh-huh – reserve me a seat by the punchbowl.

ALMA: That gives me an idea! We *will* have punch, fruit punch, with claret in it. Do you like claret?

JOHN: I just dote on claret.

ALMA: Now you're being sarcastic! Ha-ha-ha!

JOHN: Excuse me, Miss Alma, but Dad's got to use this phone.

ALMA: I won't hang up till you've said you'll come without fail!

JOHN: I'll be there, Miss Alma. You can count on it.

ALMA: Au revoir, then! Until eight.

JOHN: G'bye, Miss Alma.

[JOHN *hangs up with an incredulous grin.* ALMA *remains holding the phone with a dazed smile until the office interior has dimmed slowly out.*]

MRS WINEMILLER: Alma's in love, Alma's in lo-ove!

ALMA [*sharply*]: Mother, you are wearing out my patience.

[NELLIE *rings the bell.* ALMA *answers it.*]

Oh, it's you, Nellie. Go straight to the piano, Nellie, and practise your scales while I go find the punchbowl for my club meeting.

[ALMA *leads* NELLIE *to the piano, then exits through the inner door.* NELLIE *sings a scale.* MRS WINEMILLER *imitates her. During the imitation* ALMA *re-enters with the punchbowl and crosses to the love seat.*]

ALMA: Mother, you're interrupting the lesson.

NELLIE: Oh, Miss Alma, I don't feel like taking a lesson today.

ALMA: Frankly, Nellie, I don't understand why you wanted to take vocal lessons at all.

NELLIE [*cheerfully*]: I don't have a voice, Miss Alma?

ALMA: Yes, you do have a voice but your voice is better for – speaking.

NELLIE: Don't you know why I took lessons?

ALMA: I'm afraid I don't.

NELLIE: I had a crush on you!

ALMA: On *me*?

NELLIE: You know what crushes are?

ALMA: Oh, yes, but – why on me?

NELLIE: Because you've been nice to me in spite of Mother's reputation.

ALMA: – Both of us – have – mothers . . .

NELLIE: Yes, but yours doesn't go to the depot at midnight to meet the travelling salesman that get off the Cannonball Express!

ALMA: No . . . Mine doesn't do *that*!

DUSTY [*off*]: Johnny!

NELLIE: Anyway, I had a crush on you. Those were the days when I had crushes on girls, but those days are over with now and I – have crushes on – *boys* . . .

ALMA: I hope that you will be sensible about them.

DUSTY [*off*]: Johnny!

ALMA: What are you doing at the window, Nellie?

NELLIE: Watching someone I have a *terrible* crush on!

ALMA: Someone – next door?

NELLIE: You know who – Dr Johnny, Junior. You know, I thought I'd always hate men. Loathe and despise them. But now, oh, I think he's the wonderfullest person in all the world. Don't you think so?

ALMA: In appearance perhaps, but his character is weak. Where do you see him? [*She catches* MRS WINEMILLER'*s eye.*]

NELLIE: He isn't dressed, so I think it must be his bedroom.

ALMA: Please come away from the window.

NELLIE: He's brushing his hair.

ALMA: Nellie, come away from that window.

DUSTY [*off*] Johnny! Johnny!

NELLIE: Someone's calling him.

ALMA: Yes, these people who shout his name in front of his house are of such a character that the old doctor cannot permit them to come inside the door. And when they have brought him home at night, left him sprawling on the front steps, sometimes at daybreak – it takes two people, his father and the old cook, one pushing and one pulling, to get him upstairs to bed.

A GIRL'S VOICE [*off*]: Johnny! Johnny!

NELLIE: They're calling again. There he is. He's getting into his shirt.

ALMA: Nellie, don't look out the window and have us caught spying.

MRS WINEMILLER [*suddenly*]: Show Nellie how *you* spy on him! Oh, she's a good one at spying. She stands behind the curtain and *peeks* around it, and ...

ALMA [*frantically*]: *Mother!*

MRS WINEMILLER: She spies on him. Whenever he comes in at night she rushes downstairs to watch him out of this window!

ALMA [*interrupting her*]: Be still!

MRS WINEMILLER [*going right on*]: She called him just now and had a fit on the telephone!

[*The old lady cackles derisively.* ALMA *snatches her cigarette from her and crushes it under her foot.*]

ALMA: Nellie, Nellie, please go.

NELLIE [*with a startled giggle*]: All right, Miss Alma, I'm going. [*She crosses quickly to the door, looking back once with a grin.*] Good night, Mrs Winemiller!

[NELLIE *goes out, up the fountain steps.* MRS WINEMILLER *goes outside the door.*

MRS WINEMILLER: Alma's in love! Alma's in lo-ove!

[ALMA *drags* MRS WINEMILLER *inside and forces her on to the fender seat.*]

ALMA: If ever I hear you say such a thing again, if ever you dare to repeat such a thing in my presence or anybody else's – then it will be the last straw! You understand me? Yes, you undersantd me! You act like a child, but you have the devil in you. And God will punish you – yes! I'll punish you too. I'll take your cigarettes from you and give you no more. I'll give you no ice-cream either. Because I'm tired of your malice, yes. I'm tired of your malice and your self-indulgence. People wonder why I'm tied down here! They pity me – think of me as an old maid already! In spite of I'm young. Still young! It's you – it's you, you've taken my youth away from me! I wouldn't say that – I'd try not even to think of it – if you were just kind, just simple! But I could spread my life out like a rug for you to step on and you'd step on it, and not even say 'Thank you, Alma!' Which is what you've done always – and now you dare to tell a disgusting lie about me – in front of that girl!

MRS WINEMILLER: What lie, what lie do you mean?

ALMA [*seizing the hat from* MRS WINEMILLER'*s head*]: Give me that hat, Mother. It goes back.

MRS WINEMILLER [*lunges at the hat*]: *Fight! Fight!*

[ALMA *snatches at the plumed hat.* MRS WINEMILLER *snatches, too. The hat is torn between them.*]

ALMA: Upstairs, Mother!

MRS WINEMILLER [*retreats to the inner door*]: Can I have some ice-cream?

ALMA: Upstairs, Mother

[MRS WINEMILLER *goes.*]

A hat with a plume.

SCENE III

Inside the rectory.

The meeting is in progress, having just opened with the reading of the minutes by ALMA. *She stands before the green plush sofa and the others. This group includes* MR DOREMUS, VERNON, *a willowy young man with an open collar and Byronic locks, the widow* BASSETT, *and a wistful older girl with a long neck and thick-lensed glasses.*

ALMA [*reading*]: Our last meeting which fell on July fourteenth ...

MRS BASSETT: Bastille Day!

ALMA: Pardon me?

MRS BASSETT: It fell on Bastille Day! But, honey, that was the meeting before last.

ALMA: You're perfectly right. I seem to be on the wrong page ... [*She drops the papers.*]

MRS BASSETT: Butterfingers!

ALMA: Here we are! July twenty-fifth! Correct?

MRS BASSETT: Correct!

[*A little ripple of laughter goes about the circle.*]

ALMA [*continuing*]: It was debated whether or not we ought to suspend operations for the remainder of the summer as the departure of several members engaged in the teaching profession for their summer vacations ...

MRS BASSETT: Lucky people!

ALMA: ... had substantially contracted our little circle.

MRS BASSETT: Decimated our ranks!

[*There is another ripple of laughter.*

JOHN *appears outside the door-frame and rings the bell.*]

ALMA [*with agitation*]: Is that – is that – the doorbell?

MRS BASSETT: It sure did sound like it to me.

ALMA: Excuse me a moment. I think it may be ...

[ALMA *crosses to the door-frame and makes the gesture of opening the door.* JOHN *steps in, immaculately groomed and shining, his white linen coat over his arm and a white Panama hat in his hand. He is a startling contrast to the other male company, who seem to be outcasts of a state in which he is a prominent citizen.*]

ALMA [*shrilly*]: Yes, it is – our guest of honour! Everbody, this is Dr John Buchanan, Junior.

JOHN [*easily glancing about the assemblage*]: Hello, everybody. [*To* ALMA] Did I miss much?

ROSEMARY: Good evening.

MRS BASSETT: Why, Dr John!

ALMA: Not a thing! Just the minutes – I'll put you on the sofa. Next to me.

MRS BASSETT: I never thought he'd show up. Congratulations, Miss Alma.

[ALMA *laughs breathlessly and makes an uncertain gesture.* JOHN *settles gingerly on the sofa. They all stare at him with a curious sort of greediness.*]

ALMA: Well, now! we are completely assembled!

MRS BASSETT [*eagerly*]: Vernon has his verse play with him tonight!

ALMA [*uneasily*]: Is that right, Vernon?

[*Obviously it is.* VERNON *has a pile of papers eight inches thick on his knees. He raises them timidly with downcast eyes.*]

ROGER [*quickly*]: We decided to put that off till cooler weather. Miss Rosemary is supposed to read us a paper tonight on William Blake.

MRS BASSETT: Those dead poets can keep!

[JOHN *laughs.*]

ALMA [*excitedly jumping up*]: Mrs Bassett, everybody! This is the way I feel about the verse play. It's too important a thing to read under any but ideal circumstances. Not only atmospheric – on some cool evening with music planned to go with it! – but everyone present so that nobody will miss it! Why don't we . . .

ROGER: Why don't we take a standing vote on the matter?

ALMA: Good, good, perfect!

ROGER: All in favour of putting the verse play off till cooler weather, stand up!

[*Everybody rises but* ROSEMARY *and* MRS BASSETT. ROSEMARY *starts vaguely to rise, but* MRS BASSETT *jerks her arm.*]

ROSEMARY: Was this a vote?

ROGER: Now, Mrs Bassett, no rough tactics, please!

ALMA: Has everybody got fans? John, you haven't got one!

[ALMA *looks about for a fan for* JOHN. *Not seeing one, she takes* ROGER'*s out of his hand and gives it to* JOHN. ROGER *is nonplussed.* ROSEMARY *gets up with her paper.*]

ROSEMARY: The poet – William Blake was born in 1757. Visionary he was, but certainly not demented.

MRS BASSETT: Insane, insane; that man was a mad fanatic!

[MRS BASSETT *squints her eyes tight shut and thrusts her thumbs into her ears. The reactions range from indignant to conciliatory.*]

ROGER: Now, Mrs Bassett!

MRS BASSETT: This is a free country. I can speak my opinion. And I have *read up* on him. Go on, Rosemary. I wasn't criticizing your paper.

[*But* ROSEMARY *sits down, hurt.*]

ALMA: Mrs Bassett is only joking, Rosemary.

ROSEMARY: No, I don't want to read it if she feels that strongly about it.

MRS BASSETT: Not a bit, don't be silly! I just don't see why we should encourage the writings of people like that who have already gone into a drunkard's grave!

VERNON: Drunkard's?

VARIOUS VOICES [*exclaiming*]: Did he? I never heard that about him. Is that true?

ALMA: Mrs Bassett is mistaken about that. Mrs Bassett, you have confused Blake with someone else.

MRS BASSETT [*positively*]: Oh, no, don't tell me. I've read up on him and know what I'm talking about. He travelled around with a Frenchman who took a shot at him and landed them both in jail! Brussels, Brussels!

ROGER [*gaily*]: Brussels sprouts!

MRS BASSETT: That's where it happened, fired a gun at him in a drunken stupor, and later one of them died of T.B. in the gutter! All right. I'm finished. I won't say anything more. Go on with your paper, Rosemary. There's nothing like contact with culture!

[ALMA *gets up.*]

ALMA: Before Rosemary reads her paper on Blake, I think it would be a good idea, since some of us aren't acquainted with his work, to preface the critical and biographical comments with a reading of once of his loveliest lyric poems.

ROGER: Oh yes, Miss Alma.

[*Exclamations from others*].

ROSEMARY: I'm not going to read anything at all! Not I!

ALMA: Then let me read it then. [*She takes a paper from* ROSEMARY.] ... This is called 'Love's Secret'.

[ALMA *clears her throat and waits for a hush to settle.* ROSEMARY *looks stonily at the carpet.* MRS BASSETT *looks at the ceiling.* JOHN *coughs.*]

Never seek to tell thy love,
Love that never told can be,
For the gentle wind doth move
Silently, invisibly.
I told my love, I told my love,
I told him all my heart.
Trembling, cold in ghastly fear
Did my love depart.
No sooner had he gone from me
Than a stranger passing by,
Silently, invisibly,
Took him with a sigh!

[*There are various effusions and enthusiastic applause.*]

MRS BASSETT: Honey, you're right. That isn't the man I meant. I was thinking about the one who wrote about 'the bought red lips'. Who was it that wrote about the 'bought red lips'?

[JOHN *has risen abruptly. He signals to* ALMA *and points to his watch. He starts to leave.*]

ALMA [*springing up*]: *John!*

JOHN [*calling back*]: I have to call on a patient! Excuse me, everybody.

ALMA: Oh, John!

[ALMA *calls after him so sharply that the group is startled into silence.*]

ROSEMARY [*interpreting this as a cue to read her paper*]: 'The poet, William Blake, was born in 1757 ...'

[ALMA *suddenly rushes to the door and goes out after* JOHN.]

ROGER: Of poor but honest parents.

MRS BASSETT: No supercilious comments out of you, sir. Go on, Rosemary. [*She speaks loudly.*] She has such a beautiful *voice*!

[ALMA *returns inside, looking stunned.*]

ALMA: Please excuse the interruption, Rosemary. Dr Buchanan had to call on a patient.

MRS BASSETT [*archly*]: I bet I know who the patient was. Ha-ha! That Gonzales girl whose father owns Moon Lake Casino and goes everywhere with two pistols strapped on his belt. Johnny Buchanan will get himself shot in that crowd!

ALMA: Why, Mrs Bassett, what gave you such an idea? I don't think that John even knows that Gonzales girl!

MRS BASSETT: He knows her, all right. In the biblical sense of the word, if you'll excuse me!

ALMA: No, I will not excuse you! A thing like that is inexcusable!

MRS BASSETT: Have you fallen for him, Miss Alma? Miss Alma has fallen for the young doctor! They tell me he has lots of new lady patients!

ALMA: Stop it! [*She stamps her foot furiously and crushes the palm leaf fan between her clenched hands.*] I won't have malicious talk here! You drove him away from the meeting after I'd bragged so much about how bright and interesting you all were! You put your worst foot forward and simpered and chattered and carried on like idiots, idiots! What am I saying? I – I – please excuse me! [*She rushes out of the inner door.*]

ROGER: I move that the meeting adjourn.

MRS BASSETT: I second the motion.

ROSEMARY: I don't understand – what happened?

MRS BASSETT: Poor Miss Alma! I'm afraid she's going just like her mother.

ROSEMARY: What a meeting!

[*They all go out.*

After a moment ALMA *re-enters with a tray of refreshments, looks about the deserted interior and bursts into hysterical laughter.*

The light dims out.]

SCENE IV

In the doctor's office.

JOHN *has a wound on his arm which he is bandaging with* ROSA'*s assistance.*

JOHN: Hold that end. Wrap it around. Pull it tight.

[*There is a knock at the door. They look up silently. The knock is repeated.*]

I better answer before they wake up the old man.

[JOHN *goes out. A few moments later he returns, followed by* ALMA. *He is rolling down his sleeve to conceal the bandage.* ALMA *stops short at the sight of* ROSA.]

Wait outside, Rosa. In the hall. But be quiet!

[ROSA *gives* ALMA *a challenging look as she withdraws from the lighted area.* JOHN *explains about* ROSA.]

Miss Alma, a little emergency case.

ALMA: The patient you had to call on.

[JOHN *grins.*]

I want to see your father.

JOHN: He's asleep. Anything I can do?

ALMA: No, I think not. I have to see your father.

JOHN: It's 2 a.m., Miss Alma.

ALMA: I know, I'm afraid I'll have to see him.

JOHN: What's the trouble?

[*The voice of* JOHN'*s* FATHER *is heard, calling from above.*]

DR BUCHANAN: John! What's going on down there?

JOHN [*at the door*]: Nothing much, Dad. Somebody got cut in a fight.

DR BUCHANAN: I'm coming down.

JOHN: No. Don't! Stay in bed!

[JOHN *rolls up his sleeve to show* ALMA *the bandaged wound. She gasps and touches her lips.*]

I've patched him up, Dad. You sleep! [*He executes the gesture of closing a door quietly on the hall.*]

ALMA: You've been in a brawl with that – woman!

[JOHN *nods and rolls the sleeve back down.* ALMA *sinks faintly into a chair.*]

JOHN: Is your *doppelganger* cutting up again?

ALMA: It's your father I want to talk to.

JOHN: Be reasonable, Miss Alma. You're not that sick.

ALMA: Do you suppose I would come here at two o'clock in the morning if I were not seriously ill?

JOHN: It's no telling what you would do in a state of hysteria. [*He puts some powders in a glass of water.*] Toss that down, Miss Alma.

ALMA: What is it?

JOHN: A couple of little white tablets dissolved in water.

ALMA: What kind of tablets?

JOHN: You don't trust me?

ALMA: You are not in any condition to inspire much confidence.

[JOHN *laughs softly.* ALMA *looks at him helplessly for a moment, then bursts into tears. He draws up a chair beside hers and puts his arm gently about her shoulders.*]

I seem to be all to pieces.

JOHN: The intellectual meeting wore you out.

ALMA: You made a quick escape from it.

JOHN: I don't like meetings. The only meetings I like are between two people.

ALMA: Such as between yourself and the lady outside?

JOHN: Or between you and me.

ALMA [*nervously*]: Where is the medicine?

JOHN: Oh. You've decided to take it?

ALMA: Yes, if you . . .

[ALMA *sips and chokes.* JOHN *gives her his handkerchief. She touches her lips with it.*]

JOHN: Bitter?

ALMA: Awfully bitter.

JOHN: It'll make you sleepy.

ALMA: I do hope so. I wasn't able to sleep.

JOHN: And you felt panicky?

ALMA: Yes. I felt walled in.

JOHN: You started hearing your heart?

ALMA: Yes, like a drum!

JOHN: It scared you?

ALMA: It always does.

JOHN: Sure. I know.

ALMA: I don't think I will be able to get through the summer.

JOHN: You'll get through it, Miss Alma.

ALMA: How?

JOHN: One day will come after another and one night will come after another till sooner or later the summer will be all through with and then it will be fall, and you will be saying, I don't see how I'm going to get through the fall.

ALMA: Oh . . .

JOHN: That's right. Draw a deep breath!

ALMA: Ah . . .

JOHN: Good. Now draw another!

ALMA: Ah . . .

JOHN: Better? Better?

ALMA: A little.

JOHN: Soon you'll be much better. [*He takes out a big silver watch and holds her wrist.*] Did y'know that time is one side of the four-dimensional continuum we're caught in?

ALMA: What?

JOHN: Did you know space is curved, that it turns back on to itself like a soap-bubble, adrift in something that's even less than space? [*He laughs a little as he replaces the watch.*]

ROSA [*faintly from outside*]: Johnny!

JOHN [*looking up as if the cry came from there*]: Did you know that the Magellanic clouds are a hundred thousand light years away from the earth? No?

[ALMA *shakes her head slightly.*]

That's something to think about when you worry over your heart, that little red fist that's got to keep knocking, knocking against the big black door.

ROSA [*more distinctly*]: Johnny! [*She opens the door a crack.*]

JOHN: Calla de la boca [*The door closes and he speaks to* ALMA.] There's nothing wrong with your heart but a little functional disturbance, like I told you before. You want me to check it?

[ALMA *nods mutely.* JOHN *picks up his stethoscope.*]

ALMA: The lady outside, I hate to keep her waiting.

JOHN: Rosa doesn't mind waiting. Unbutton your blouse.

ALMA: Unbutton . . . ?

JOHN: The blouse.

ALMA: Hadn't I better – better come back in the morning, when your father will be able to . . . ?

JOHN: Just as you please, Miss Alma.

[ALMA *hesitates. Then begins to unbutton her blouse. Her fingers fumble.*]

Fingers won't work?

ALMA [*breathlessly*]: They are just as if frozen!

JOHN [*smiling*]: Let me. [*He leans over her.*] Little pearl buttons . . .

ALMA: If your father discovered that woman in the house . . .

JOHN: He won't discover it.

ALMA: It would distress him terribly.

JOHN: Are you going to tell him?

ALMA: Certainly not!

[JOHN *laughs and applies the stethoscope to her chest.*]

JOHN: Breathe! . . . Out! . . . Breathe! . . . Out!

ALMA: Ah . . .

JOHN: Um-hmmm . . .

ALMA: What do you hear?

JOHN: Just a little voice saying: 'Miss Alma is lonesome!'

[ALMA *rises and turns her back to him.*]

ALMA: If your idea of helping a patient is to ridicule and insult . . .

JOHN: My idea of helping you is to tell you the truth.

[ALMA *looks up at* JOHN. *He lifts her hand from the chair arm.*]

What is this stone?

ALMA: A topaz.

JOHN: Beautiful stone . . . Fingers still frozen?

ALMA: A little.

[JOHN *lifts her hand to his mouth and blows his breath on* ALMA'*s fingers.*]

JOHN: I'm a poor excuse for a doctor, I'm much too selfish. But let's try to think about you.

ALMA: Why should you bother about me? [*She sits down*].

JOHN: You know I like you and I think you're worth a lot of consideration.

ALMA: Why?

JOHN: Because you have a lot of feeling in your heart, and that's a rare thing. It makes you too easily hurt. Did I hurt you tonight?

ALMA: You hurt me when you sprang up from the sofa and rushed from the rectory in such – in such mad haste that you left your coat behind you!

JOHN: I'll pick up the coat sometime.

ALMA: The time of our last conversation you said you would take me riding in your automobile sometime, but you forgot to.

JOHN: I didn't forget. Many's the time I've looked across at the rectory and wondered if it would be worth trying, you and me ...

ALMA: You decided it wasn't?

JOHN: I went there tonight, but it wasn't you and me ... Fingers warm now?

ALMA: Those tablets work quickly. I'm already feeling drowsy. [*She leans back with her eyes nearly shut.*] I'm beginning to feel almost like a water lily. A water lily on a Chinese lagoon.

[*A heavy iron bell strikes three.*]

ROSA: *Johnny!*

[ALMA *starts to rise.*]

ALMA: I *must* go.

JOHN: I will call for you Saturday night at eight o'clock.

ALMA: What?

JOHN: I'll give you this box of tablets but watch how you take them. Never more than one or two at a time.

ALMA: Didn't you say something else a moment ago?

JOHN: I said I would call for you at the rectory Saturday night.

ALMA: Oh ...

JOHN: Is that all right?

[ALMA *nods speechlessly. She remains with the box nesting in the palm of her hand as if not knowing it was there.* JOHN *gently closes her fingers on the box.*]

ALMA: Oh! [*She laughs faintly.*]

ROSA [*outside*]: *Johnny!*

JOHN: Do you think you can find your way home, Miss Alma?

*[*ROSA *steps back into the office with a challenging look.* ALMA *catches her breath sharply and goes out of the side door.*

JOHN *reaches above him and turns out the light. He crosses to* ROSA *by the anatomy chart and takes her roughly in his arms. The light lingers on the chart as the interior dims out.]*

SCENE V

In the rectory.

Before the light comes up a soprano voice is heard singing 'From the Land of the Sky Blue Waters'.

As the curtain rises, ALMA *gets up from the piano.* MR *and* MRS WINEMILLER, *also, are in the lighted room.*

ALMA: What time is it, Father?

[MR WINEMILLER *goes on writing. She raises her voice.]*

What time is it, Father?

MR WINEMILLER: Five of eight. I'm working on my sermon.

ALMA: Why don't you work in the study?

MR WINEMILLER: The study is suffocating. So don't disturb me.

ALMA: Would there be any chance of getting Mother upstairs if someone should call?

MR WINEMILLER: Are you expecting a caller?

ALMA: Not expecting. There is just a chance of it.

MR WINEMILLER: Whom are you expecting?

ALMA: I said I wasn't expecting anyone, that there was just a possibility . . .

MR WINEMILLER: Mr Doremus? I thought that this was his evening with his mother?

ALMA: Yes, it is his evening with his mother.

MR WINEMILLER: Then who is coming here, Alma?

ALMA: Probably no one. Probably no one at all.

MR WINEMILLER: This is all very mysterious.

MRS WINEMILLER: That tall boy next door is coming to see her, that's who's coming to see her.

ALMA: If you will go upstairs, Mother, I'll call the drug store and ask them to deliver a pint of fresh peach ice-cream.

MRS WINEMILLER: I'll go upstairs when I'm ready – good and ready, and you can put that in your pipe and smoke it, Miss Winemiller!

[MRS WINEMILLER *lights a cigarette.* MR WINEMILLER *turns slowly away with a profound sigh.*]

ALMA: I may as well tell you who might call, so that if he calls there will not be any unpleasantness about it. Young Dr John Buchanan said he might call.

MRS WINEMILLER: See!

MR WINEMILLER: You can't be serious.

MRS WINEMILLER: Didn't I tell you?

ALMA: Well, I am.

MR WINEMILLER: That young man might come here?

ALMA: He asked me if he might and I said, yes, if he wished to. But it is now after eight so it doesn't look like he's coming.

MR WINEMILLER: If he does come you will go upstairs to your room and I will receive him.

ALMA: If he does come I'll do no such thing, Father.

MR WINEMILLER: You must be out of your mind.

ALMA: I'll receive him myself. You may retire to your study and Mother upstairs. But if he comes I'll receive him. I don't judge people by the tongues of gossips. I happen to know that he has been grossly misjudged and misrepresented by old busy-bodies who're envious of his youth and brilliance and charm!

MR WINEMILLER: If you're not out of your senses, then I'm out of mine.

ALMA: I daresay we're all a bit peculiar, Father ...

MR WINEMILLER: Well, I have had one almost insufferable cross to bear and perhaps I can bear another. But if you think I'm retiring into my study when this young man comes, probably with a whisky bottle in one hand and a pair of dice in the other, you have another think coming. I'll sit right here and look at him until he leaves. [*He turns back to his sermon.*]

[*A whistle is heard outside the open door.*]

ALMA [*speaking quickly*]: As a matter of fact I think I'll walk down to the drug store and call for the ice-cream myself. [*She crosses to the door, snatching up her hat, gloves and veil.*]

MRS WINEMILLER: There she goes to him! Ha-ha!

[ALMA *rushes out.*]

MR WINEMILLER [*looking up*]: Alma! Alma!

MRS WINEMILLER: Ha-ha-haaaaa!

MR WINEMILLER: Where is Alma? – Alma! [*He rushes through the door.*] Alma!

MRS WINEMILLER: Ha-ha! Who got fooled? Who got fooled! Ha-haaaa! Insufferable cross yourself, you old – windbag . . .

THE CURTAIN COMES DOWN

SCENE VI

A delicately suggested arbour, enclosing a table and two chairs. Over the table is suspended a torn paper lantern. This tiny set may be placed way downstage in front of the two interiors, which should be darkened out, as in the fountain scenes. In the background, as it is throughout the play, the angel of the fountain is dimly visible.

Music from the nearby pavilion of the casino can be used when suitable for background.

JOHN*'s voice is audible before he and* ALMA *enter.*

JOHN [*from the darkness*]: I don't understand why we can't go in the casino.

ALMA: You do understand. You're just pretending not to.

JOHN: Give me one reason.

ALMA [*coming into the arbour*]: I am a minister's daughter.

JOHN: That's no reason. [*He follows her in. He wears a white linen suit, carrying the coat over his arm.*]

ALMA: You're a doctor. That's a better reason. You can't any more afford to be seen in such places than I can – less!

JOHN [*bellowing*]: Dusty!

DUSTY [*from the darkness*]: Coming!

JOHN: What are you fishing in that pocketbook for?

ALMA: Nothing.

JOHN: What have you got there?

ALMA: Let go!

JOHN: Those sleeping tablets I gave you?

ALMA: Yes.

JOHN: What for?

ALMA: I need one.

JOHN: *Now?*

ALMA: Yes.

JOHN: Why?

ALMA: Why? Because I nearly died of heart failure in your automobile. What possessed you to drive like that? A demon?

[DUSTY *enters*].

JOHN: A bottle of vino rosso.

DUSTY: Sure. [*He withdraws.*]

JOHN: Hey! Tell Shorty I want to hear the 'Yellow Dog Blues'.

ALMA: Please give me back my tablets.

JOHN: You want to turn into a dope-fiend taking this stuff? I said take one when you need one.

ALMA: I need one now.

JOHN: Sit down and stop swallowing air.

[DUSTY *returns with a tall wine bottle and two thin-stemmed glasses.*]

When does the cock-fight start?

DUSTY: 'Bout ten o'clock, Dr Johnny.

ALMA: When does *what start*?

JOHN: They have a cock-fight here every Saturday night. Ever seen one?

ALMA: Perhaps in some earlier incarnation of mine.

JOHN: When you wore a brass ring in your nose?

ALMA: Then maybe I went to exhibitions like that.

JOHN: You're going to see one tonight.

ALMA: Oh, no, I'm not.

JOHN: That's what we came here for.

ALMA: I didn't think such exhibitions were legal.

JOHN: This is Moon Lake Casino where anything goes.

ALMA: And you're a frequent patron?

JOHN: I'd say constant.

ALMA: Then I'm afraid you must be serious about giving up your medical career.

JOHN: You bet I am. A doctor's life is walled in by sickness and misery and death.

ALMA: I am distressed to hear it. Have you told your father?

JOHN: He won't be told. It was to be – demonstrated.

ALMA: Last night I heard the phone ringing in your office again and again. No one answered. It was agonizing. I shut my bedroom window so that I wouldn't hear it, but I still heard it . . .

JOHN: I heard it too. Screaming at me all night. I haven't answered his phone since he left, Miss Alma. [*He pours wine.*]

ALMA: May I be so presumptuous as to inquire what you'll do when you quit?

JOHN: You may be so presumptuous as to inquire.

ALMA: But you won't tell me?

JOHN: I haven't made up my mind, but I've been thinking of South America lately.

ALMA [*sadly*]: Oh . . .

JOHN: I've heard that cantinas are lots more fun than saloons, and señoritas are caviar among females.

ALMA: Dorothy Sykes' brother went to South America and was never heard of again. It takes a strong character to survive in the tropics. Otherwise its a quagmire.

JOHN: You think my character's weak?

ALMA: I think you're confused, just awfully, awfully confused, as confused as I am – but in a different way . . .

JOHN [*stretching out his legs*]: Hee-haw, ho-hum.

ALMA: You used to say that as a child – to signify your disgust!

JOHN [*grinning*]: Did I?

ALMA [*sharply*]: Don't sit like that!

JOHN: Why not?

ALMA: You look so indolent and worthless.

JOHN: Maybe I am.

ALMA: If you must go somewhere, why don't you choose a place with a bracing climate?

JOHN: Parts of South America are as cool as a cucumber.

ALMA: I never knew that.

JOHN: Well, now you do.

ALMA: Those Latins all dream in the sun – and indulge their senses.

JOHN: Well, it's yet to be proven that anyone on this earth is crowned with so much glory as the one that uses his senses to get all he can in the way of – satisfaction.

ALMA: Self-satisfaction?

JOHN: What other kind is there?

ALMA: I will answer that question by asking you one. Have you ever seen, or looked at a picture of, a Gothic cathedral?

JOHN: Gothic cathedrals? What about them?

ALMA: How everything reaches up, how everything seems to be straining for something out of the reach of stone – or human – fingers? ... The immense stained windows, the great arched doors that are five or six times the height of the tallest man – the vaulted ceiling and all the delicate spires – all reaching up to something beyond attainment! To me – well, that is the secret, the principle back of existence – the everlasting struggle and aspiration for more than our human limits have placed in our reach ... Who was that said that – oh, so beautiful thing! – 'All of us are in the gutter, but some of us are looking at the stars!'

JOHN: Mr Oscar Wilde.

ALMA [*somewhat taken aback*]: Well, regardless of who said it, it's still true. Some of us are looking at the stars! [*She looks up raptly and places her hand over his.*]

JOHN: It's no fun holding hands with gloves on, Miss Alma.

ALMA: That's easily remedied. I'll just take the gloves off.

[*Music is heard.*]

JOHN: Christ! [*He rises abruptly and lights a cigarette.*] Rosa Gonzales is dancing in the Casino.

ALMA: You *are* unhappy. You hate me for depriving you of the company inside. Well, you'll escape by and by. You'll drive me home and come back out by yourself ... I've only gone out with three young men at all seriously, and with each one there was a desert between us.

JOHN: What do you mean by a desert?

ALMA: Oh – wide, wide stretches of uninhabitable ground.

JOHN: Maybe you made it that way by being stand-offish.

ALMA: I made quite an effort with one or two of them.

JOHN: What kind of an effort?

ALMA: Oh, I – tried to entertain them the first few times. I would play and sing for them in the rectory parlour.

JOHN: With your father in the next room and the door half open?

ALMA: I don't think that was the trouble.

JOHN: What was the trouble?

ALMA: I – I didn't have my heart in it. [*She laughs uncertainly.*] A silence would fall between us. You know, a silence?

JOHN: Yes, I know a silence.

ALMA: I'd try to talk and he'd try to talk and neither would make a go of it.

JOHN: The silence would fall?

ALMA: Yes, the enormous silence.

JOHN: Then you'd go back to the piano?

ALMA: I'd twist my ring. Sometimes I twisted it so hard that the band cut my finger! He'd glance at his watch and we'd both know that the useless undertaking had come to a close . . .

JOHN: You'd call it quits?

ALMA: Quits is – what we'd call it . . . One or two times I was rather sorry about.

JOHN: But you didn't have your heart in it?

ALMA: None of them really engaged my serious feelings.

JOHN: You do have serious feelings – of that kind?

ALMA: Doesn't everyone – sometimes?

JOHN: Some women are cold. Some women are what is called frigid.

ALMA: Do I give that impression!

JOHN: Under the surface you have a lot of excitement, a great deal more than any other woman I have met. So much that you have to carry these sleeping pills with you. The question is why? [*He leans over and lifts her veil.*]

ALMA: What are you doing that for?

JOHN: So that I won't get your veil in my mouth when I kiss you.

ALMA [*faintly*]: Do you want to do that?

JOHN [*gently*]: Miss Alma. [*He takes her arms and draws her to her feet.*] Oh, Miss Alma, Miss Alma! [*He kisses her.*]

ALMA [*in a low, shaken voice*]: Not 'Miss' any more. Just Alma.

JOHN [*grinning gently*]: 'Miss' suits you better, Miss Alma.

[JOHN *kisses* ALMA *again. She hesitantly touches his shoulders, but not quite to push him away. He speaks softly to her.*]

Is it so hard to forget you're a preacher's daughter?

ALMA: There is no reason for me to forget that I am a minister's daughter. A minister's daughter's no different from any other young lady who tries to remember that she *is* a lady.

JOHN: This lady stuff, is that so important?

ALMA: Not to the sort of girls that you may be used to bringing to Moon Lake Casino. But suppose that some day ... [*she crosses out of the arbour and faces away from him*] suppose that some day you – *married* ... The woman that you selected to be your wife, and not only your wife but – the mother of your children! [*She catches her breath at the thought.*] Wouldn't you want that woman to be a lady? Wouldn't you want her to be somebody that you, as her husband, and they as her precious children – could look up to with very deep respect?

[*There is a pause.*]

JOHN: There's other things between a man and a woman besides respect. Did you know that, Miss Alma?

ALMA: Yes ...

JOHN: There's such a thing as intimate relations.

ALMA: Thank you for telling me that. So plainly.

JOHN: It may strike you as unpleasant. But it does have a good deal to do with – connubial felicity, as you'd call it. There are some women that just give in to a man as a sort of obligation imposed on them by the – cruelty of nature! [*He finishes his glass and pours another.*] And there you are.

ALMA: There *I* am?

JOHN: I'm speaking generally.

ALMA: Oh.

[*Hoarse shouts go up from the Casino.*]

JOHN: The cock-fight has started!

ALMA: Since you have spoken so plainly, I'll speak plainly, too. There are some women who turn a possibly beautiful thing into something no better than the coupling of beasts! – but love is what you bring to it.

JOHN: You're right about that.

ALMA: Some people bring just their bodies. But there are some people, there are some women, John – who can bring their hearts to it, also – who can bring their souls to it!

JOHN [*derisively*]: Souls again, huh? – those Gothic cathedrals you dream of!

[*There is another hoarse prolonged shout from the Casino.*]

Your name is Alma and Alma is Spanish for soul. Sometime I'd like to show you a chart of the human anatomy that I have in the office. It shows what our insides are like, and maybe you can show me where the beautiful soul is located on the chart. [*He drains the wine bottle.*] Let's go watch the cock-fight.

ALMA: No!

[*There is a pause.*]

JOHN: I know something else we could do. There are rooms above the Casino . . .

ALMA [*her back stiffening*]: I'd heard that you made suggestions like that to girls that you go out with, but I refused to believe such stories were true. What made you think I might be amenable to such a suggestion?

JOHN: I counted your pulse in the office the night you ran out because you weren't able to sleep.

ALMA: The night I was ill and went to your father for help.

JOHN: It was me you went to.

ALMA: It was your father, and you wouldn't call your father.

JOHN: Fingers frozen stiff when I . . .

ALMA [*rising*]: Oh! I want to go home. But I won't go with you. I will go in a taxi! [*She wheels about hysterically.*] Boy! Boy! Call a taxi!

JOHN: I'll call one for you, Miss Alma. – Taxi! Taxi!

[*He goes out of the arbour.*]

ALMA [*wildly*]: *You're not a gentleman!*

JOHN [*from the darkness*]: Taxi!

ALMA: *You're not a gentleman!*

[*As he disappears she makes a sound in her throat like a hurt animal. The light fades out of the arbour and comes up more distinctly on the stone angel of the fountain.*]

JOHN [*off*]: Taxi!

END OF PART ONE

PART TWO: A WINTER

SCENE VII

The sky and the southern constellations, almost imperceptibly moving with the earth's motion, appear on the great cyclorama.

The rectory interior is lighted first disclosing ALMA *and* ROGER DOREMUS *seated on the green plush sofa under the romantic landscape in its heavy gilt frame. On a tiny table beside them is a cut-glass pitcher of lemonade with cherries and orange slices in it, like a little aquarium of tropical fish.* ROGER *is entertaining* ALMA *with a collection of photographs and postcards, mementoes of his mother's trip to the Orient. He is enthusiastic about them and describes them in phrases his mother must have assimilated from a sedulous study of literature provided by Cook's Tours.* ALMA *is less enthusiastic; she is preoccupied with the sounds of a wild party going on next door at the doctor's home. At present there is Mexican music with shouts and stamping.*

Only the immediate area of the sofa is clearly lighted; the fountain is faintly etched in light and the night sky walls the interior.

ROGER: And this is Ceylon, the Pearl of the Orient!

ALMA: And who is this fat young lady?

ROGER: That is Mother in a hunting costume.

ALMA: The hunting costume makes her figure seem bulky. What was your mother hunting?

ROGER [*gaily*]: Heaven knows what she was hunting! But she found Papa.

ALMA: Oh, she met your father on this Oriental tour?

ROGER: Ha-ha! – yes . . . He was returning from India with dysentery and they met on the boat.

ALMA [*distastefully*]: Oh . . .

ROGER: And here she is on top of a ruined temple!

ALMA: How did she get up there?

ROGER: Climbed up, I suppose.

ALMA: What an active woman.

ROGER: Oh yes, active – is no word for it! Here she is on an elephant's back in Burma.

ALMA: Ah!

ROGER: You're looking at it upside down, Miss Alma!

ALMA: Deliberately – to tease you.

[*The doorbell rings.*]

Perhaps that's your mother coming to fetch you home.

ROGER: It's only ten-fifteen. I never leave till ten-thirty.

[MRS BASSETT *comes in.*]

ALMA: Mrs Bassett!

MRS BASSETT: I was just wondering who I could turn to when I saw the rectory light and I thought to myself, Grace Bassett, you trot yourself right over there and talk to Mr Winemiller!

ALMA: Father has retired.

MRS BASSETT: Oh, what a pity. [*She sees* ROGER.] Hello, Roger! . . . I saw that fall your mother took this morning. I saw her come skipping out of the Delta Planters' Bank and I thought to myself, now isn't that remarkable, a woman of her age and weight so light on her feet? And just at that very moment – *down she went*! I swear to goodness I thought she had broken her hip! Was she bruised much?

ROGER: Just shaken up, Mrs Bassett.

MRS BASSETT: Oh, how lucky! She certainly must be made out of India rubber! [*She turns to Alma.*] Alma – Alma, if it is not too late for human intervention, your father's the one right person to call up old Dr Buchanan at the fever clinic at Lyon and let him know!

ALMA: About – what?

MRS BASSETT: You must be stone-deaf if you haven't noticed what's been going on next door since the old doctor left to fight the epidemic. One continual orgy!

ALMA: These people who clouded his name outside have come indoors.

MRS BASSETT: Well, not five minutes ago a friend of mine who works at the County Courthouse called to inform me that young Dr John and Rosa Gonzales have taken a licence out and are going to be married tomorrow!

ALMA: Are you – quite certain?

MRS BASSETT: Certain? I'm always certain before I speak!

ALMA: Why would he – do such a thing?

MRS BASSETT: August madness! They say it has something to do with the falling stars. Of course, it might also have something to do with the fact that he lost two or three thousand dollars at the casino which he can't pay except by giving himself to Gonzales' daughter. [*She turns to* ALMA.] Alma, what are you doing with that picture puzzle?

ALMA [*with a faint, hysterical laugh*]: The pieces don't fit!

MRS BASSETT [*to* ROGER]: I shouldn't have opened my mouth.

ALMA: Will both of you please go!

[ROGER *goes out.*]

MRS BASSETT: I knew this was going to upset you. Good night, Alma.

[MRS BASSETT *leaves. Flamenco music is heard from the doctor's house, stamping and hand clapping. The lights come up in his office, where the phone is ringing.* JOHN *enters and stares at the phone, a magnum of champagne in his hand. The ring is repeated again and again.*

ALMA, *in the rectory, crosses to her telephone.*]

ALMA: Long distance, please . . . Please get me the fever clinic at Lyon . . . I want to speak to Dr Buchanan, Senior.

[*In the opposite interior* JOHN *reaches for the phone. But* ROSA, *entering behind him, intercepts him and holds the receiver down with her jewelled fingers.*]

JOHN: You don't think I ought to answer this 'frantic appeal'?

ROSA: No frantic appeal except mine.

[ROSA *leans back across the desk. Music. Torrid embrace. Rectory dims out completely. John's phone rings again.* ROSA *keeps her hand on it.*

JOHN: Maybe someone is bleeding.

ROSA: *You* are bleeding. A little. There is blood on your face.

JOHN: Whenever I leave you I have a little blood on me. You never make love without biting or scratching a little. Why is that?

ROSA: – Because I know I can't hold you.

JOHN: You're doing a better job of it than anyone else. A lot better than Father and his flock of grey people.

ROSA: I hold you for one summer.

[*Guitar: Flamenco. Quick transition.*]

There, now, they play the flamenco! Olé! Olé!

JOHN: Olé! Dance, Rosa!

ROSA [*ecstatically*]: I will dance if you hold your eyes on my body as if your eyes are your hands!

JOHN: I have my eyes on your body.

[ROSA *dances slowly about* JOHN.]

ROSA: Tomorrow we leave here together?

JOHN: Yes, we make a 'voy-age'! – We sail out of Galveston. I have the tickets.

ROSA: Two pieces of paper that you can tear in two.

JOHN: No, we make a vay-aaaage! How do you say it in Spanish?

ROSA: *Viaggio!*

JOHN: *Viaggio!* – over the Gulf, and under the little islands and still further south, and further and further and further, until at night we can see the gold cross in the sky ...

ROSA: And then what happens?

JOHN: Oh, then we stop. We stop at some – tropical port – to pick up a letter.

ROSA: What letter, Johnny, a letter saying 'Come home'?

JOHN: No. A letter containing a fat cheque from Papa Gonzales.

ROSA: Oh, from Papa?

JOHN: Yes, we'll live on that fat remittance of your papa. Sure. What else? Not long ago that idea would have disgusted me. But something this summer has made it acceptable to me, and not just acceptable. No, more than that. – Necessary! – Has anyone ever slid downhill as fast as I have this summer? Like a greased pig! And yet every evening I put on a clean white suit. I have a dozen. Six in the closet, five in the wash, and one on me! And when I shave in the morning, I don't see a sign of depravity in my face. But all this summer I've spent the days remembering the nights, and anticipating the next one.

[*The phone rings again.* JOHN *stares at it as* ROSA *takes the receiver off the hook.*]

– Dance, Rosa! Why don't you dance?

[ROSA *starts to dance. Suddenly weeping, she throws herself to the floor beside* JOHN.]

ROSA: I can't dance any more.

[*The voice of* GONZALES *is heard, bellowing, in the next room.*]

GONZALES: *The sky is the limit!*

[JOHN *is sobered.*]

JOHN: Why does your father want me for a son-in-law?

ROSA [*sobbing*]: *I want you – I, I want you!*

JOHN [*raising her from the floor*]: Why do you?

ROSA [*clinging to him*]: Maybe because – I was born in Piedras Negras, and grew up in a one-room house with a dirt floor, and all of us had to sleep in that one room, five Mexicans and three geese and a little game-cock named Pepe! Ha-ha! [*She laughs hysterically.*] Pepe was a good fighter! That's how Papa began to make money, winning bets on Pepe! Ha-ha! We all slept in the one room. And in the night, I would hear the love-making. Papa would grunt like a pig to show his passion. I thought to myself, how dirty it was, love making, and how dirty it was to be Mexicans and all have to sleep in one room with a dirt floor and not smell good because there was not any bathtub!

[*The accordion continues.*]

JOHN: What has that got to do with ... ?

ROSA: Me wanting you? You're tall! You smell good! And, oh, I'm so glad that you never grunt like a pig to show your passion! [*She embraces him convulsively.*] Ah, but *quien sabe*! Something might happen tonight, and I'll wind up with some dark little friend of Papa's.

GONZALES [*imperiously*]: Rosa! Rosa!

ROSA: Si, si, Papa, aqui estoy!

GONZALES [*entering unsteadily*]: The gold beads ... [*He fingers a necklace of gold beads that* ROSA *is wearing.*] Johnny ... [*He staggers up to* JOHN *and catches him in a drunken embrace.*] Listen! When my girl Rosa was little she see a string a gold bead and she want those gold bead so bad that she cry all night for it. I don' have money to buy a string a gold bead so next day I go for a ride up to Eagle Pass and I walk in a dry good store and I say to the man: 'Please give me a string a gold bead.' He say: 'Show me the money,' and I say: 'Here is the money!' And I reach down to my belt and I pull out – not the money – but this! [*He pulls out a revolver.*] Now – now I have money, but I still have this! [*Laughing.*] She got the gold bead. Anything that she want I get for her with this [*he pulls out a roll of bills*] or this! [*He waves the revolver.*]

JOHN [*pushing* GONZALES *away*]: Keep your stinking breath out of my face, Gonzales!

ROSA: Dejalo, dejalo, Papa!

GONZALES [*moving unsteadily to the couch, with* ROSA *supporting him*]: Le doy la tierra y si la tierra no basta – le doy el cielo! [*He collapses on to the couch.*] The sky is the limit!

ROSA [*to* JOHN]: Let him stay there. Come on back to the party.

[ROSA *leaves the room.* JOHN *goes over to the window facing the rectory and looks across. The light comes up in the rectory living-room as* ALMA *enters, dressed in a robe. She goes to the window and looks across at the doctor's house. As* ALMA *and* JOHN *stand at the windows looking towards each other through the darkness music is heard. Slowly, as if drawn by the music,* JOHN *walks out of his house and crosses over to the rectory.* ALMA *remains motionless at the window until* JOHN *enters the room, behind her. The music dies away and there is a murmur of wind. She slowly turns to face* JOHN.]

JOHN: I took the open door for an invitation. The Gulf wind is blowing tonight ... cools things off a little. But my head's on fire ...

[ALMA *says nothing.* JOHN *moves a few steps towards her.*]

The silence?

[ALMA *sinks on to the love seat, closing her eyes.*]

Yes, the enormous silence [*He goes over to her.*] I will go in a minute, but first I want you to put your hands on my face ... [*He crouches beside her.*] Eternity and Miss Alma have such cool hands.

[JOHN *buries his face in* ALMA*'s lap. The attitude suggests a stone Pietà.* ALMA*'s eyes remain closed.*

On the other side of the stage DR BUCHANAN *enters his house and the light builds a little as he looks around in the door of his office. The love-theme music fades out and the Mexican music comes up strongly, with a definitely ominous quality, as* ROSA *enters the office from the other side.*]

ROSA: Johnny! [*She catches sight of* DR BUCHANAN *and checks herself in surprise.*] Oh! I thought you were Johnny! ... But you are Johnny's father ... I'm Rosa Gonzales!

DR BUCHANAN: I know who you are. What's going on in my house?

ROSA [*nervously*]: John's giving a party because we're leaving tomorrow. [*Defiantly.*] Yes! Together! I hope you like the idea, but if you don't, it don't matter, because *we* like the idea and my father likes the idea.

DR BUCHANAN: You scum, get out of my house!

GONZALES [*drunkenly, sitting up on the couch*]: The sky is the limit.

[DR BUCHANAN *turns to* GONZALES *and raises his silver-headed cane in a threatening gesture.*]

DR BUCHANAN: Get your – swine out of – my house! [*He strikes* GONZALES *with his cane.*] And you, get out of here, do you hear me? And you there, all of you there, corrupting my home with your drinking and lecherous women.

[*A woman screams off-stage.*]

Get out, get out!

GONZALES [*staggering up from the couch in pain and surprise*]: Aieeeee!

ROSA [*breathlessly, backing against the anatomy chart*]: No! No, Papa!

DR BUCHANAN [*striking at the chest of the bull-like man with his cane*]: Get your swine out, I said! Get them out of my house!

[DR BUCHANAN *repeats the blow. The drunken* GONZALES *roars with pain and surprise. He backs up and reaches under his coat.*]

ROSA [*wildly and despairingly*]: No, no, no, no, no, no!

[ROSA *covers her face against the anatomy chart. A revolver is fired. There is a burst of light. The cane drops. The music stops short. Everything dims out but a spot of light on* ROSA *standing against the anatomy chart with closed eyes and her face twisted like that of a tragic mask.*]

[*Senselessly*] Aaaaaahhhhhh . . . Aaaaaahhhhhh . . .

[*The theme music is started faintly and light disappears from everything but the wings of the stone angel.*]

SCENE VIII

The doctor's office.

The stone angel is dimly visible above.

JOHN *is seated in a hunched position at the table.* ALMA *enters with a coffee tray. The sounds of a prayer come through the inner door.*

MR WINEMILLER:

'Oh, God, to whom all hearts are open
And from whom no secrets are hid,
Help this, Thy servant, in his hour of need,
And if it be Thy will, O Lord, take him unto Thyself,
Granting him the peace of life everlasting. . . .'

JOHN: What is that mumbo-jumbo your father is spouting in there?

ALMA: A prayer.

JOHN: Tell him to quit. We don't want that worn-out magic.

ALMA: You may not want it, but it's not a question of what you want any more. I've made you some coffee.

JOHN: I don't want any.

ALMA: Lean back and let me wash your face off, John. [*She presses a towel to the red marks on his face.*] It's such a fine face, a fine and sensitive face, a face that has power in it that shouldn't be wasted.

JOHN: Never mind that. [*He pushes her hand away.*]

ALMA: You have to go in to see him.

JOHN: I couldn't. He wouldn't want me.

ALMA: This happened because of his devotion to you.

JOHN: It happened because some meddlesome Mattie called him back here tonight. Who was it did that?

ALMA: I did.

JOHN: It *was* you then!

ALMA: I phoned him at the fever clinic in Lyon as soon as I learned what you were planning to do. I told him to come here and stop it.

JOHN: You brought him here to be shot.

ALMA: You can't put the blame on anything but your weakness.

JOHN: *You* call me weak?

ALMA: Sometimes it takes a tragedy like this to make a weak person strong.

JOHN: You – white-blooded spinster! You so right people, pious pompous mumblers, preachers and preacher's daughters, all muffled up in a lot of worn-out magic! And I was supposed to minister to your neurosis, give you tablets for sleeping and tonics to give you the strength to go on mumbling your worn-out mumbo-jumbo!

ALMA: Call me whatever you want, but don't let your father hear your drunken shouting. [*She tries to break away from him.*]

JOHN: Stay here! I want to look at something. [*He turns her about.*] This chart of anatomy, look!

ALMA: I've seen it before. [*She turns away.*]

JOHN: You've never dared to look at it.

ALMA: Why should I?

JOHN: You're scared to.

ALMA: You must be out of your senses.

JOHN: You talk about weakness but can't even look at a picture of human insides.

ALMA: They're not important.

JOHN: That's your mistake. You think you're stuffed with rose-leaves. Turn around and look at it, it may do you good!

ALMA: How can you behave like this with your father dying and you so . . .

JOHN: Hold still! Now listen here to the anatomy lecture. You see this chart? It's a picture of a – a picture of a – tree – with three birds in it. This top bird is the brain. The bird is hungry. He's hungry for something called Truth. He doesn't get much, he's never satisfied with it, he keeps on shaking his cold and weak little wings and saying: 'Cheep! Cheep!' – This bird underneath is the belly. He's hungry, too, but he's the practical bird, just hungry for food! – And down here's the lowest bird – or maybe, the highest, who knows? – Yes, take a look at him, too; he's hungry, too, hungry as both the others and twice as lonesome! – What's he hungry for? Love! – There they all are on the chart! Three birds, three hungry little birds in one tall, withering tree! – Yes, a withering tree they can't fly out of! – Well – I've fed the birds, I've fed all three of those birds as much as I was able. You've fed none of them, nothing! – Well – maybe the middle bird, the practical one, the belly, a little – watery subsistence. – But love? Or Truth? Nothing – nothing but hand-me-down notions – attitudes – poses! And two of the birds in your tree are going to die of starvation before the tree falls down – or gets blown over! That's what I had to tell you, and – now you can go! The anatomy lecture is over.

ALMA: So that is your high conception of human desires. What you have here is not the anatomy of a beast, but a man. And I – I reject your opinion of where love is, and the kind of truth you believe the brain to be seeking! – There is something not shown on the chart.

JOHN: You mean the part that Alma is Spanish for, do you?

ALMA: Yes, that's not shown on the anatomy chart! But it's there, just the same, yes, there! Somewhere, not seen, but there. And it's *that* that I loved you with – that! Not what you mention! – Yes, did love you with, John, did nearly *die* of when you hurt me!

[JOHN *turns slowly to her and speaks gently.*]

JOHN: I wouldn't have made love to you.

ALMA [*uncomprehendingly*]: What?

JOHN: The night at the casino – I wouldn't have made love to you. Even if you had consented to go upstairs. I couldn't have made love to you.

[ALMA *stares at* JOHN *as if anticipating some unbearable hurt.*]

Yes, yes! Isn't that funny? I'm more afraid of your soul than you're afraid of my body. You'd have been as safe as the angel of the fountain – because I wouldn't feel *decent* enough to touch you ...

MR WINEMILLER [*off*]: Alma!

[MR WINEMILLER *comes in.*]

He's resting more easily now.

ALMA: Oh ...

[ALMA *nods her head.* JOHN *reaches for his coffee cup.*]

It's cold. I'll heat it.

JOHN: It's all right.

MR WINEMILLER: Alma, Dr John wants you.

ALMA: I . . .

MR WINEMILLER: He asked if you would sing for him.

ALMA: I – couldn't – now.

JOHN: Go in and sing to him, Miss Alma!

[MR WINEMILLER *withdraws through the outer door.* ALMA *looks back at* JOHN *hunched over the coffee cup. He doesn't return her look. She passes into the blurred orange space beyond the inner door, leaving it slightly open. After a few moments her voice rises softly within, singing.* JOHN *suddenly rises. He crosses to the door, shoves it slowly open and enters.*]

[*Softly and with deep tenderness*] Father?

[*The light dims out in the house, but lingers on the stone angel.*]

SCENE IX

The cyclorama is the faint blue of a late afternoon in autumn. There is band music – a Sousa march – in the distance. As it grows somewhat louder, ALMA *enters the rectory interior in a dressing-gown and with her hair hanging loose. She looks as if she had been through a long illness, the intensity drained, her pale face listless. She crosses to the window frame, but the parade is not in sight, so she returns weakly to the sofa and sits down, closing her eyes with exhaustion.*

The REV. *and* MRS WINEMILLER *enter the outer door frame of the rectory, a grotesque-looking couple.*

MRS WINEMILLER *has on her plumed hat, at a rakish angle, and a brilliant scarf about her throat. Her face wears a roguish smile that suggests a musical-comedy pirate. One hand holds the minister's arm and with the other she is holding an ice-cream cone.*

MR WINEMILLER: Now you may let go of my arm, if you please! She was on her worst behaviour. Stopped in front of the White Star Pharmacy on Front Street and stood there like a mule; wouldn't budge till I bought her an ice-cream cone. I had it wrapped in tissue paper because she had promised me that she wouldn't eat it until we got home. The moment I gave it to her she tore off the paper and walked home licking it every step of the way! – just – just to humiliate me!

[MRS WINEMILLER *offers* MR WINEMILLER *the half-eaten cone, saying: 'Lick?'*]

No, thank you!

ALMA: Now, now children.

[MR WINEMILLER*'s irritation shifts to* ALMA.]

MR WINEMILLER: Alma! Why don't you get dressed? It hurts me to see you sitting around like this, day in, day out, like an invalid when there is nothing particularly wrong with you. I can't read your mind. You may have had some kind of disappointment, but you must not make it an excuse for acting as if the world had come to an end.

ALMA: I have made the beds and washed the breakfast dishes and phoned the market and sent the laundry out and peeled the potatoes and shelled the peas and set the table for lunch. What more do you want?

MR WINEMILLER [*sharply*]: I want you to either get dressed or stay in your room.

[ALMA *rises indifferently, then her father speaks suddenly.*]

At night you get dressed. Don't you? Yes, I heard you slipping out of the house at two in the morning. And that was not the first time.

ALMA: I don't sleep well. Sometimes I have to get up and walk for a while before I am able to sleep.

MR WINEMILLER: What am I going to tell people who ask about you?

ALMA: Tell them I've changed and you're waiting to see in what way.

[*The band music becomes a little louder.*]

MR WINEMILLER: Are you going to stay like this indefinitely?

ALMA: Not indefinitely, but you may wish that I had.

MR WINEMILLER: Stop twisting that ring! Whenever I look at you you're twisting that ring. Give me that ring! I'm going to take that ring off your finger!

[MR WINEMILLER *catches* ALMA'S *wrist. She breaks roughly away from him.*]

MRS WINEMILLER [*joyfully*]: Fight! Fight!

MR WINEMILLER: Oh, I give up!

ALMA: That's better. [*She suddenly crosses to the window as the band music gets louder.*] Is there a parade in town?

MRS WINEMILLER: Ha-ha – yes! They met him at the station with a great big silver loving-cup!

ALMA: Who? Who did they ...?

MRS WINEMILLER: That boy next door, the one you watched all the time!

ALMA: Is that true, Father?

MR WINEMILLER [*unfolding his newspaper*]: Haven't you looked at the papers?

ALMA: No, not lately.

MR WINEMILLER [*wiping his eyeglasses*]: These people are grasshoppers, just as likely to jump one way as another. He's finished the work his father started, stamped out the fever and gotten all of the glory. Well, that's how it is in this world. Years of devotion and sacrifice are overlooked an' forgotten while some young an' lucky walks off with the honours!

[ALMA *has crossed slowly to the window. The sun brightens and falls in a shaft through the frame.*]

ALMA [*suddenly crying out*]: *There he is!*

[JOHN *appears on ramp upper left. Raises the silver loving-cup over his head in a sort of salute. Spot of light on him as the rectory begins to dim out.*]

ALMA: So much has changed – so – quickly ...

[JOHN *enters the office, puts the cup down on the desk, looks at it, then starts to take off his coat down right.* NELLIE *enters through the inner door, carrying a book. She bangs the book down on the desk.* JOHN *turns and sees her.*]

JOHN: So *you're* the young lady Miss Burke said was waiting for me!

NELLIE: Yes, I'm the young lady – waiting for you!

JOHN: High heels, feathers, and paint!

NELLIE: Not paint!

JOHN: Natural colour?

NELLIE: Excitement.

JOHN: Over what?

NELLIE: Everything! You! You here! Didn't you see me at the depot? I shouted and waved my arm off! I'm home for Thanksgiving.

JOHN: From where?

NELLIE: Sophie Newcomb's.

[JOHN *remains staring at* NELLIE, *unbelieving. At last she draws a book from under her arm.*]

Here is that nasty book you gave me last summer when I was pretending such ignorance of things?

JOHN: Only pretending?

NELLIE: Yes.

[JOHN *ignores the book.* NELLIE *tosses it on the table.*]

... Well?

[JOHN *laughs uneasily and sits on the table.*]

Shall I go now, or will you look at my tongue? [*She crosses to him, sticking out her tongue.*]

JOHN: Red as a berry!

NELLIE: Peppermint drops! Will you have one? [*She holds out a bag.*]

JOHN: Thanks.

[NELLIE *giggles as* JOHN *takes one.*]

What's the joke, Nellie?

NELLIE: They make your mouth so sweet!

JOHN: So?

NELLIE: I always take one when I hope to be kissed.

JOHN [*after a pause*]: Suppose I took you up on that?

NELLIE: I'm not scared. Are you?

[JOHN *gives* NELLIE *a quick kiss. She clings to him, raising her hand to press his head against her own. He breaks free after a moment and turns the light back on.*]

JOHN [*considerably impressed*]: Where did you learn such tricks?

NELLIE: I've been away to school. But they didn't teach me to love.

JOHN: Who are you to be using that long word?

NELLIE: That isn't a long word!

JOHN: No? [*He turns away from her.*] Run along, Nellie, before we get into trouble.

NELLIE: Who's afraid of trouble, you or me?

JOHN: I am. Run along! Hear me?

NELLIE: Oh, I'll go. But I'll be back for Christmas! [*She laughs and runs out.*] So long!

JOHN: So long!

[*He whistles and wipes his forehead with a handkerchief.*]

SCENE X

An afternoon in December. At the fountain in the park. It is very windy. ALMA *enters upper left. She looks at the angel, drops on her knees to feel the lettering at its base.*

MRS BASSETT *enters down left – against the wind – followed by* ROSEMARY.

MRS BASSETT [*starts to speak off-stage*]: Such wind, such wind!

ROSEMARY: Why, Miss Alma!

MRS BASSETT: Alma, it's been a coon's age since I've seen you.

ALMA: I saw you at the public library last Monday.

MRS BASSETT: I didn't see *you*.

ALMA: I was not visible. I have what they call 'stack permission'.

ROSEMARY: I must feed the birdies! Here, birdies! [*Opens bag and holds out breadcrumbs.*]

MRS BASSETT: Oh, what's that?

ALMA: I am allowed to browse among the shelves. I was browsing among the shelves when I heard you talking about me with the librarian.

ROSEMARY: Here, birds, here, birds!

ALMA: Mrs Bassett, something you said isn't true. I haven't been going out lately, I haven't been very well, but – I am not – as you put it – 'going the way Mother went'.

ROSEMARY [*off*]: Here, birdies, birdies, birds!

MRS BASSETT: Why, Miss Alma, who ever said that you were!

ALMA: YOU did, Mrs Bassett.

MRS BASSETT: Whatever I said was meant kindly out of genuine – affection and – concern! Oh, Alma, Alma, everybody loves you, nobody in Glorious Hill would speak unkindly of you! You ought to start coming to the little club meetings again, we've missed you so. At the last meeting Vernon read his verse play.

ALMA: Oh. – How was it received?

MRS BASSETT: Maliciously! Spitefully and vindictively torn to pieces like children tear wings off butterflies!

ROSEMARY: Here, birdies!

MRS BASSETT: But Vernon rose above it! There's nothing you can't rise above if you keep your courage!

NELLIE [*off*]: Merry Christmas! [*Laugh.*] I said – Merry Christmas!

MRS BASSETT: I see that Ewell girl coming and I don't want to meet her! Rosemary? Shall we go now?

ROSEMARY: We might as well. There's nothing but crows in the square and I'm not going to feed them. All the little birds have blown away. [*She goes off down right.*]

MRS BASSETT [*to* ALMA]: Merry Christmas! Merry Christmas!

ALMA [*as* MRS BASSETT *goes*]: Merry Christmas! [*Goes off down left.*]

[NELLIE *enters down left.*]

NELLIE: Miss Alma! Oh, there you are!

ALMA: Why, Nellie . . . Nellie Ewell!

NELLIE: I was by the rectory. Just popped in for a second; the holidays are so short that every minute is precious. They told me you'd gone to the park.

ALMA: This is the first walk I've taken in quite a while.

NELLIE: You've been ill!

ALMA: Not ill, just not very well. How you've grown up, Nellie.

NELLIE: It's just my clothes. Since I went off to Sophie Newcomb, I've picked out my own clothes, Miss Alma. When Mother had jurisdiction over my wardrobe, she tried to keep me looking like a child!

ALMA: Your voice is grown-up, too.

NELLIE: They're teaching me diction, Miss Alma. I'm learning to talk like you, long A's and everything, such as 'cahn't' and 'bahth' and 'lahf' instead of 'laugh'. Yesterday I slipped. I said I 'lahfed and lahfed till I nearly died laughing'. Johnny was so amused at me!

ALMA: Johnny?

NELLIE: Your next-door neighbour!

ALMA: Oh! I'm sure it must be a very fashionable school.

NELLIE: Oh yes, they're preparing us to be young ladies in society. What a pity there's no society here to be a young lady in . . . at least not for me, with Mother's reputation!

ALMA: You'll find other fields to conquer.

NELLIE: What's this I hear about *you*?

ALMA: I have no idea, Nellie.

NELLIE: That you've quit teaching singing and gone into retirement.

ALMA: Naturally I had to stop teaching while I was ill and as for retiring from the world . . . it's more a case of the world retiring from me.

NELLIE: I know somebody whose feelings you've hurt badly.

ALMA: Why, who could that be, Nellie?

NELLIE: Somebody who regards you as an angel!

ALMA: I can't think who might hold me in such esteem.

NELLIE: Somebody who says that you refused to see him.

ALMA: I saw nobody. For several months. The long summer wore me out so.

NELLIE: Well, anyhow, I'm going to give you your present. [*She hands her a small package from the basket.*]

ALMA: Nellie, you shouldn't have given me anything.

NELLIE: I'd like to know why not?

ALMA: I didn't expect it.

NELLIE: After the trouble you took with my horrible voice?

ALMA: It's very sweet of you, Nellie.

NELLIE: Open it!

ALMA: Now?

NELLIE: Why, sure.

ALMA: It's so prettily wrapped I hate to undo it.

NELLIE: I love to wrap presents and since it was for you, I did a specially dainty job of it.

ALMA [*winding the ribbon about her fingers*]: I'm going to save this ribbon. I'm going to keep this lovely paper too, with the silver stars on it. And the sprig of holly . . .

NELLIE: Let me pin it on your jacket, Alma.

ALMA: Yes, do. I hardly realized that Christmas was coming . . . [*She unfolds the paper, revealing a lace handkerchief and a card.*] What an exquisite handkerchief.

[*Card drops to the floor.*]

NELLIE: I hate to give people handkerchiefs, it's so unimaginative.

ALMA: I love to get them.

NELLIE: It comes from Maison Blanche!

ALMA: Oh, does it really?

NELLIE: Smell it!

ALMA: Sachet *Roses*! Well, I'm just more touched and pleased than I can possibly tell you!

NELLIE: The card!

NELLIE: You dropped it. [*She snatches up the card and hands it to* ALMA.]

ALMA: Oh, how clumsy of me! Thank you, Nellie. 'Joyeux Noël . . . to Alma . . . from Nellie and . . . [*She looks up slowly.*] John?'

NELLIE: He helped me wrap presents last night and when we came to yours we started talking about you. Your ears must have burned!

[*The wind blows loudly.* ALMA *bends stiffly forward.*]

ALMA: You mean you – spoke well of me?

NELLIE: 'Well of'! We raved, simply raved! Oh, he told me the influence you'd had on him!

ALMA: Influence?

NELLIE: He told me about the wonderful talks he'd had with you last summer when he was so mixed up and how you inspired him and you more than anyone else was responsible for his pulling himself together, after his father was killed, and he told me about . . .

[ALMA *rises stiffly from the bench.*]

Where are you going, Miss Alma?

ALMA: To drink at the fountain.

NELLIE: He told me about how you came in the house that night like an angel of mercy!

ALMA [*laughing harshly by the fountain*]: This is the only angel in

Glorious Hill. [*She bends to drink.*] Her body is stone and her blood is mineral water.

[*The wind is louder.*]

NELLIE: How penetrating the wind is!

ALMA: I'm going home, Nellie. You run along and deliver your presents now ... [*She starts away.*]

NELLIE: But wait till I've told you the wonderfullest thing I ...

ALMA: I'm going home now. Good-bye.

NELLIE: Oh – Good-bye, Miss Alma.[*She snatches up her festive basket and rushes in the other direction with a shrill giggle as the wind pulls at her skirt.*]

THE LIGHTS DIM OUT

SCENE XI

An hour later. In JOHN*'s office.*

The interior is framed by the traceries of Victorian architecture and there is one irregular section of wall supporting the anatomy chart. Otherwise the stage is open to the cyclorama.

In the background mellow golden light touches the vane of a steeple [*a gilded weathercock*]. *Also the wings of the stone angel. A singing wind rises and falls throughout the scene.*

JOHN *is seated at a white enamelled table examining a slide through a microscope.*

A bell tolls the hour of five as ALMA *comes hesitantly in. She wears a russet suit and a matching hat with a plume. The light changes, the sun disappearing behind a cloud, fading from the steeple and the stone angel till the bell stops tolling. Then it brighten again.*

ALMA: No greetings? No greetings at all?

JOHN: Hello, Miss Alma.

ALMA [*speaking with animation to control her panic.*]: How white it is here, such glacial brilliance! [*She covers her eyes, laughing.*]

JOHN: New equipment.

ALMA: Everything new but the chart.

JOHN: The human anatomy's always the same old thing.

ALMA: And such a tiresome one! I've been plagued with sore throats.

JOHN: Everyone has here lately. These Southern homes are all improperly heated. Open grates aren't enough.

ALMA: They burn the front of you while your back is freezing!

JOHN: Then you go into another room and get chilled off.

ALMA: Yes, yes, chilled to the bone.

JOHN: But it never gets quite cold enough to convince the damn fools that a furnace is necessary so they go on building without them.

[*There is the sound of wind.*]

ALMA: Such a strange afternoon.

JOHN: Is it? I haven't been out.

ALMA: The Gulf wind is blowing big, white – what do they call them? cumulus? – clouds over! Ha-ha! It seemed determined to take the plume off my hat, like that fox terrier we had once named Jacob snatched the plume off a hat and dashed around and around the back yard with it like a trophy!

JOHN: I remember Jacob. What happened to him?

ALMA: Oh, Jacob. Jacob was such a mischievous thief. We had to send him out to some friends in the country. Yes, he ended his days as – a country squire! The tales of his exploits ...

JOHN: Sit down, Miss Alma.

ALMA: If I'm disturbing you ...?

JOHN: No – I called the rectory when I heard you were sick. Your father told me you wouldn't see a doctor.

ALMA: I needed a rest, that was all ... You were out of town mostly ...

JOHN: I was mostly in Lyon, finishing up Dad's work in the fever clinic.

ALMA: Covering yourself with sudden glory!

JOHN: Redeeming myself with good works.

ALMA: It's rather late to tell you how happy I am, and also how proud. I almost feel as your father might have felt – if ... And – are you – happy now, John?

JOHN [*uncomfortably, not looking at her*]: I've settled with life on fairly acceptable terms. Isn't that all a reasonable person can ask for?

ALMA: He can ask for much more than that. He can ask for the coming true of his most improbable dreams.

JOHN: It's best not to ask for too much.

ALMA: I disagree with you. I say, ask for all, but be prepared to get nothing! [*She springs up and crosses to the window. She continues.*] No, I haven't been well. I've thought many times of something you told me last summer, that I have a *doppelganger*. I looked that up and I found that it means another person inside me, another self, and I don't know whether to thank you or not for making me conscious of it! – I haven't been well ... For a while I thought I was dying, that that was the change that was coming.

JOHN: When did you have that feeling?

ALMA: August. September. But now the Gulf wind has blown that feeling away like a cloud of smoke, and I know now I'm not dying, that it isn't going to turn out to be that simple ...

JOHN: Have you been anxious about your heart again? [*He retreats to a professional manner and takes out a silver watch, putting his fingers on her wrist.*]

ALMA: And now the stethoscope?

[JOHN *removes the stethoscope from the table and starts to loosen* ALMA*'s jacket. She looks down at his bent head. Slowly, involuntarily, her gloved hands lift and descend on the crown of his head. He gets up awkwardly. She suddenly leans towards him and presses her mouth to his.*]

Why don't you say something? Has the cat got your tongue?

JOHN: Miss Alma, what can I say?

ALMA: You've gone back to calling me 'Miss Alma' again.

JOHN: We never really got past that point with each other.

ALMA: Oh, yes, we did. We were so close that we almost breathed together!

JOHN [*with embarrassment*]: I didn't know that.

ALMA: No? Well, I did, I knew it. [*Her hand touches his face tenderly.*] You shave more carefully now? You don't have those little razor cuts on your chin that you dusted with gardenia talcum ...

JOHN: I shave more carefully now.

ALMA: So that explains it!

[ALMA's *fingers remain on his face, moving gently up and down it like a blind person reading Braille. He is intensely embarrassed and gently removes her hands from him.*]

Is it – impossible now?

JOHN: I don't think I know what you mean.

ALMA: You know what I mean, all right! So be honest with me. One time I said 'no' to something. You may remember the time, and all that demented howling from the cock-fight? But now I have changed my mind, or the girl who said 'no', she doesn't exist any more, she died last summer – suffocated in smoke from something on fire inside her. No, she doesn't live now, but she left me her ring – You see? This one you admired, the topaz ring set in pearls ... And she said to me when she slipped this ring on my finger – 'Remember I died empty-handed, and so make sure that your hands have *something in them*!' [*She drops her gloves. She clasps his head again in her hands.*] I said, 'But what about pride?' – She said, 'Forget about pride whenever it stands between you and what you must have!'

[JOHN *takes hold of* ALMA's *wrists.*]

And then I said, 'But what if he doesn't want me?' I don't know what she said then. I'm not sure whether she said anything or not – her lips stopped moving – yes, I think she stopped breathing!

[JOHN *gently removes* ALMA's *craving hands from his face.*]

No?

[JOHN *shakes his head in dumb suffering.*]

Then the answer is 'no'!

JOHN [*forcing himself to speak*]: I have a respect for the truth, and I have a respect for you – so I'd better speak honestly if you want me to speak.

[ALMA *nods slightly.*]

You've won the argument that we had between us.

ALMA: What – argument?

JOHN: The one about the chart.

ALMA: Oh – the chart! [*She turns from him and wanders across to the chart. She gazes up at it with closed eyes, and her hands clasped in front of her.*]

JOHN: It shows that we're not a package of rose leaves, that every interior inch of us is taken up with something ugly and functional and no room seems to be left for anything else in there.

ALMA: No . . .

JOHN: But I've come around to your way of thinking, that something else is in there, an immaterial something – as thin as smoke – which all of those ugly machines combine to produce and that's their whole reason for being. It can't be seen so it can't be shown on the chart. But it's there, just the same, and knowing it's there – why, then the whole thing – this – this unfathomable experience of ours – takes on a new value, like some – some wildly romantic work in a laboratory! Don't you see?

[*The wind comes up very loud, almost like a choir of voices. Both of them turn slightly,* ALMA *raising a hand to her plumed head as if she were outdoors.*]

ALMA: Yes, I see! Now that you no longer want it to be otherwise you're willing to believe that a spiritual bond can exist between us two!

JOHN: Can't you believe that I am sincere about it?

ALMA: Maybe you are. But I don't want to be talked to like some incurably sick patient you have to comfort. [*A harsh and strong note comes into her voice.*] Oh, I suppose I am sick, one of those weak and divided people who slip like shadows among you solid strong ones. But sometimes, out of necessity, we shadowy people take on a strength of our own. I have that now. You needn't try to deceive me.

JOHN: I wasn't.

ALMA: You needn't try to comfort me. I haven't come here on any but equal terms. You said, let's talk truthfully. Well, let's do! Unsparingly, truthfully, even shamelessly, then! It's no longer a secret that I love you. It never was. I loved you as long ago as the time I asked you to read the stone angel's name with your fingers. Yes, I remember the long afternoons of our childhood, when I had to stay indoors to practise my music – and heard your playmates calling you, 'Johnny, Johnny!' How it went through me, just to hear your name called! And how I – rushed to the window to watch you jump the porch railing! I stood at a distance, half-way down the block, only to keep in sight of your torn red sweater, racing about the vacant lot you played in. Yes, it had begun that early, this affliction of love, and has never let go of me since, but kept on growing. I've lived next door to you all the days of my life, a weak and divided person who stood in adoring awe of your singleness, of your strength. And that is my story! Now I wish *you* would tell *me* – why didn't it happen between us? Why did I fail? Why did you come almost close enough – and no closer?

JOHN: Whenever we've gotten together, the three or four times that we have . . .

ALMA: As few as that?

JOHN: It's only been three or four times that we've – come face to face. And each of those times – we seemed to be trying to find something in each other without knowing what it was that we wanted to find. It wasn't a body hunger although – I acted as if I thought it might be the night I wasn't a gentleman – at the casino – it wasn't the physical you that I really wanted!

ALMA: I know, you've already . . .

JOHN: You didn't have that to give me.

ALMA: Not at that time.

JOHN: You had something else to give.

ALMA: What did I have?

[JOHN *strikes a match. Unconsciously he holds his curved palm over the flame of the match to warm it. It is a long kitchen match and it makes a good flame. They both stare at it with a sorrowful understanding that is still perplexed. It is about to burn his fingers.* ALMA *leans forward and blows it out, then she puts on her gloves.*]

JOHN: You couldn't name it and I couldn't recognize it. I thought it was just a Puritanical ice that glittered like flame. But now I believe it *was* flame, mistaken for ice. I still don't understand it, but I know it was there, just as I know that your eyes and your voice are the two most beautiful things I've ever known – and also the warmest, although they don't seem to be set in your body at all . . .

ALMA: You talk as if my body had ceased to exist for you, John, in spite of the fact that you've just counted my pulse. Yes, that's it!

You tried to avoid it, but you've told me plainly. The tables have turned, yes, the tables have turned with a vengeance! You've come around to my old way of thinking and I to yours like two people exchanging a call on each other at the same time, and each one finding the other gone out, the door locked against him and no one to answer the bell! [*She laughs.*] I came here to tell you that being a gentleman doesn't seem so important to me any more, but you're telling me I've got to remain a lady. [*She laughs rather violently.*] The tables have turned with a vengeance! – The air in here smells of ether. – It's making me dizzy ...

JOHN: I'll open a window.

ALMA: Please.

JOHN: There now.

ALMA: Thank you, that's better. Do you remember those little white tablets you gave me? I've used them all up and I'd like to have some more.

JOHN: I'll write the prescription for you. [*He bends to write.*]

[NELLIE *is in the waiting-room. They hear her voice.*]

ALMA: Someone is waiting in the waiting-room, John. One of my vocal pupils. The youngest and prettiest one with the least gift for music. The one that you helped wrap up this handkerchief for me. [*She takes it out and touches her eyes with it.*]

[*The door opens, first a crack.* NELLIE *peers in and giggles. Then she throws the door wide open with a peal of merry laughter. She has holly pinned on her jacket. She rushes up to* JOHN *and hugs him with childish squeals.*]

NELLIE: I've been all over town just shouting, shouting!

JOHN: Shouting what?

NELLIE: Glad tidings!

[JOHN *looks at* ALMA *over* NELLIE*'s shoulder.*]

JOHN: I thought we weren't going to tell anyone for a while.

NELLIE: I couldn't stop myself. [*She wheels about.*] Oh, Alma, has he told *you*?

ALMA [*quietly*]: He didn't need to, Nellie. I guessed ... from the Christmas card with your two names written on it!

[NELLIE *rushes over to* ALMA *and hugs her. Over* NELLIE*'s shoulder*

ALMA *looks at* JOHN. *He makes a thwarted gesture as if he wanted to speak. She smiles desperately and shakes her head. She closes her eyes and bites her lips for a moment. Then she releases* NELLIE *with a laugh of exaggerated gaiety.*]

NELLIE: So Alma, you were really the first to know!

ALMA: I'm proud of that, Nellie.

NELLIE: See on my finger! This was the present I couldn't tell you about!

ALMA: Oh, what a lovely, lovely solitaire! But solitaire is such a wrong name for it. Solitaire means single and this means *two*! It's blinding, Nellie! Why, it . . . hurts my eyes!

[JOHN *catches* NELLIE*'s arm and pulls her to him. Almost violently* ALMA *lifts her face; it is bathed in tears. She nods gratefully to* JOHN *for releasing her from* NELLIE*'s attention. She picks up her gloves and purse.*]

JOHN: Excuse her, Miss Alma. Nellie's still such a child.

ALMA [*with a breathless laugh*]: I've got to run along now.

JOHN: Don't leave your prescription.

ALMA: Oh, yes, where's my prescription?

JOHN: On the table.

ALMA: I'll take it to the drug store right away!

[NELLIE *struggles to free herself from* JOHN*'s embrace which keeps her from turning to* ALMA.]

NELLIE: Alma, don't go! Johnny, let go of me, Johnny! You're hugging me so tight I can't breathe!

ALMA: Good-bye.

NELLIE: Alma! Alma, you know you're going to sing at the wedding! The very first Sunday in spring! – which will be Palm Sunday! 'The Voice that Breathed o'er Eden.'

[ALMA *has closed the door.* JOHN *shuts his eyes tight with a look of torment. He rains kisses on* NELLIE*'s forehead and throat and lips.*]

THE SCENE DIMS OUT WITH MUSIC

SCENE XII

In the park near the angel of the fountain. About dusk.

ALMA *enters the lighted area and goes slowly up to the fountain and bends to drink. Then she removes a small white package from her pocket-book and starts to unwrap it. While she is doing this, a* YOUNG MAN *comes along. He is dressed in a checked suit and a derby. He pauses by the bench. They glance at each other.*

A train whistles in the distance. The YOUNG MAN *clears his throat. The train whistle is repeated. The* YOUNG MAN *crosses towards the fountain, his eyes on* ALMA. *She hesitates, with the unwrapped package in her hand. Then she crosses towards the bench and stands hesitantly in front of it. He stuffs his hands in his pockets and whistles. He glances with an effect of unconcern back over his shoulder.*

ALMA *pushes her veil back with an uncertain gesture. His whistle dies out. He sways back and forth on his heels as the train whistles again. He suddenly turns to the fountain and bends to drink.* ALMA *slips the package back into her purse. As the* YOUNG MAN *straightens up, she speaks in a barely audible voice.*

ALMA: The water – is – cool.

THE YOUNG MAN [*eagerly*]: Did you say something?

ALMA: I said, the water is cool.

THE YOUNG MAN: Yes, it sure is, it's nice and cool!

ALMA: It's always cool.

THE YOUNG MAN: Is it?

ALMA: Yes. Yes, even in summer. It comes from deep underground.

THE YOUNG MAN: That's what keeps it cool.

ALMA: Glorious Hill is famous for its artesian springs.

THE YOUNG MAN: I didn't know that.

[THE YOUNG MAN *jerkily removes his hands from his pockets.* ALMA *gathers confidence before the awkwardness of his youth.*]

ALMA: Are you a stranger in town?

THE YOUNG MAN: I'm a travelling salesman.

ALMA: Ah, you're a salesman who travels! [*She laughs gently.*] But you're younger than most of them are, and not so fat!

THE YOUNG MAN: I'm just starting out. I travel for Red Goose shoes.

ALMA: Ah! The Delt's your territory?

THE YOUNG MAN: From the Peabody Lobby to Cat-Fish Row in Vicksburg.

[ALMA *leans back and looks at the* YOUNG MAN *under half-closed lids, perhaps a little suggestively.*]

ALMA: The life of a travelling salesman is interesting ... but lonely.

THE YOUNG MAN: You're right about that. Hotel bedrooms are lonely.

[*There is a pause. Far away the train whistles again.*]

ALMA: All rooms are lonely where there is only one person. [*Her eyes fall shut.*]

THE YOUNG MAN [*gently*]: You're tired, aren't you?

ALMA: I? Tired? [*She starts to deny it; then laughs faintly and confesses the truth.*] Yes ... a little ... But I shall rest now. I've just now taken one of my sleeping tablets.

THE YOUNG MAN: So early?

ALMA: Oh, it won't put me to sleep. It will just quiet my nerves.

THE YOUNG MAN: What are you nervous about?

ALMA: I won an argument this afternoon.

THE YOUNG MAN: That's nothing to be nervous over. You ought to be nervous if you *lost* one.

ALMA: It wasn't the argument that I wanted to win ...

THE YOUNG MAN: Well, I'm nervous too.

ALMA: What over?

THE YOUNG MAN: It's my first job and I'm scared of not making good.

[*That mysterious sudden intimacy that sometimes occurs between strangers more completely than old friends or lovers moves them both.* ALMA *hands the package of tablets to him.*]

ALMA: Then you must take one of my tablets.

THE YOUNG MAN: Shall I?

ALMA: Please take one!

THE YOUNG MAN: Yes, I shall.

ALMA: You'll be surprised how infinitely merciful they are. The prescription number is 96814. I think of it as the telephone number of God!

[*They both laugh. He places one of the tablets on his tongue and crosses to the fountain to wash it down.*]

THE YOUNG MAN [*to the stone figure*]: Thanks, angel. [*He gives her a little salute, and crosses back to* ALMA.]

ALMA: Life is full of little mercies like that, not *big* mercies but comfortable *little* mercies. And so we are able to go on. [*She has leaned back with half-closed eyes.*]

THE YOUNG MAN [*returning*]: You're falling asleep.

ALMA: Oh no I'm not. I'm just closing my eyes. You know what I feel like now? I feel like a water-lily?

THE YOUNG MAN: A water-lily?

ALMA: Yes, I feel like a water-lily on a Chinese lagoon. Won't you sit down?

[*The* YOUNG MAN *does.*]

My name is Alma. Spanish for soul! What's yours?

THE YOUNG MAN: Ha-ha! Mine's Archie Kramer. Mucho gusto, as they say in Spain.

ALMA: Usted habla Español, señor?

THE YOUNG MAN: Un poquito! Usted habla Español, señorita?

ALMA: Me tañbien. Un poquito!

THE YOUNG MAN [*delightedly*]: Ha ... ha ... ha! Sometimes un poquito is plenty!

[ALMA *laughs – in a different way than she has ever laughed before, a little wearily, but quite naturally. The* YOUNG MAN *leans towards her confidently.*]

What's there to do in this town after dark?

ALMA: There's not much to do in this town after dark, but there are resorts on the lake that offer all kinds of after-dark entertainment. There's one called Moon Lake Casino. It's under new management now, but I don't suppose its character has changed.

THE YOUNG MAN: What was its character?

ALMA: Gay, very gay, Mr Kramer ...

THE YOUNG MAN: Then what in hell are we sitting here for? Vamonos!

ALMA: Como, no, señor!

THE YOUNG MAN: Ha-ha-ha! [*He jumps up.*] I'll call a taxi. [*He runs off shouting:* 'Taxi! Taxi!']

[ALMA *rises from the bench. As she crosses to the fountain the grave mood of the play is reinstated with a phase of music. She faces the stone angel and raises her gloved hand in a sort of valedictory salute. Then she turns slowly about towards the audience with her hand still raised in a gesture of wonder and finality as . . .*]

THE CURTAIN FALLS

SMALL CRAFT WARNINGS

To Bill Barnes:
You said to go on, and I went.

TOO PERSONAL?*

The greatest danger, professionally, of becoming the subject of so many 'write-ups' and personal appearances on TV and lecture platforms is that the materials of your life, which are, in the case of all organic writing, the materials of your work, are sort of telegraphed in to those who see you and to those who read about you. So, when you get to the serious organization of this material into your work, people (meaning audiences and critics – all but the few most tolerant whom you naturally regard as the best) have a sort of *déjà vu* or *déjà entendu* reaction to these materials which you have submitted to the cathartic process of your 'sullen craft and art'.

You may justifiably wonder why a man of my years in his profession, recognizing this hazard, has yet been willing to expose himself (with a frequency which seems almost symptomatic of clinical exhibitionism) to all of these interviews and the fewer, but equally personal, exposures on platform and 'the tube'.

I can offer you at least two reasons for this phenomenon. One is probably something with which you will immediately empathize. When one has passed through an extensive period of that excess of privacy which is imposed upon a person drifting almost wilfully out of contact with the world, anticipating that final seclusion of the non-being, there comes upon him, when that period wears itself out and he is still alive, an almost insatiable hunger for recognition of the fact that he is, indeed, still alive, both as man and artist. That's reason number one. The other is rather comical, I'm afraid. You get a devastatingly bad write-up, and you feel that you are washed up for good. Then some magazine editor gets through to you on that phone in the studio of your tropical retreat, the phone that you never pick up till it's rung so persistently that you assume that your secretary and house guests have been immobilized by nerve gas or something of that nature, and

* This was meant to be submitted to the *New York Times* as a pre-opening piece, but they chose to interview me instead – T.W.

this editor speaks to you as sympathetically as the family doctor to a child stricken with a perforated appendix and tells you that he is as shocked as you were by the tasteless exposé-type of interview which appeared about you in a recent issue of some other mag. And then, of course, you forget about work, and you rage yourself into a slather over the iniquities and duplicities of the 'interviewer' referred to. You say, 'Why, that creature was so drunk he didn't know what street I lived on, and the guy that set me up for him laced my martini with sodium pentathol, and all I remember about this occasion is that my head came off my shoulders and hit the ceiling and I heard myself babbling away like an hysteric and I hadn't the slightest notion that he had a concealed tape recorder with him, and later he offered to play bridge with me that night, and he came over again with the tape recorder in some orifice of his body, I presume, and you know I do not see well and you know I like to hold forth to apparently amiable listeners, and I just assume that when they say "I am interested only in your work", that that's what they mean.'

Now the editor has you on the hook.

'That's exactly my reaction to the revolting piece and how abouc letting us do a piece to correct it?'

You grasp at this offer like a drowning rat climbs on to anything that will float it. So you get another write-up. Then after this write-up, which is usually more colourful and better written than the one before, but equally non-serious, if not downright clownish, you feel that it is a life-or-death matter, professionally, with a new play opening somewhere, to correct the hilarious misquotes and exaggerations which embellished the second write-up, and so you go on to others and others. Now at last you have poured out, compulsively and perhaps fatally, all the recent content of your experience which should have been held in reserve for its proper place, which is in the work you're doing every morning (which, in my case, is the writing I do every morning).

Is it or is it not right or wrong for a playwright to put his persona into his work?

My answer is: 'What else can he do?' – I mean the very root-necessity of all creative work is to express those things most involved in his experience. Otherwise, is the work, however well executed, not a manufactured, a synthetic thing? I've said, perhaps repeatedly, that I have two major classifications for writing: that which is organic and that which is not. And this opinion still holds.

Now let me attempt to entertain you once more with an anecdote.

Long ago, in the early forties, I attended a very posh party given by the Theatre Guild. I was comfortably and happily seated at a small table with my dear friend Miss Jo Healy, who was receptionist at the Guild in those days, when a lady with eyes that blazed with some nameless frenzy rushed up to me like a guided missile and seized me by the arm and shrieked to me, 'You've got to meet Miss Ferber, she's dying to meet you.'

Now in those days I was at least pliable, and so I permitted myself to be hauled over to a large table at which were seated a number of Diamond T trucks disguised as ladies.

'Oh, Miss Ferber,' shrieked my unknown pilot, 'this is Tennessee Williams.'

Miss Ferber gazed slowly up and delivered this annihilating one-liner:

'The best that I can manage is a mild "Yippee".'

'Madam,' I said, 'I can't even manage that.'

Now everyone knows, who is cognizant of the world of letters, that Miss Edna Ferber was a creature of mammoth productivity and success. She was good at doing her thing; her novel and picture sales are fairly astronomical, I would guess.

I bring her up because she represents to me the classic, the archetypal, example of a writer whose work is impersonal, at least upon any recognizable level. I cannot see her in the oil fields of Texas with Rock Hudson and the late James Dean. Nor can I see her in any of her other impressive epics. I see her only as a lady who chose to put down a writer who was then young and vulnerable with such a gratuitously malicious one-liner. I mean without provocation, since I had literally been dragged to the steps of her throne.

So far I have spoken only in defence of the personal kind of writing. Now I assure you that I know it can be overdone. It is the responsibility of the writer to put his experience as a being into work that refines it and elevates it and that makes of it an essence that a wide audience can somehow manage to feel in themselves: 'This is true.'

In all human experience, there are parallels which permit common understanding in the telling and hearing, and it is the frightening responsibility of an artist to make what is directly or allusively close to his own being communicable and understandable, however disturbingly, to the hearts and minds of all whom he addresses.

T.W.
26 March 1972

THE CAST

The first English production of this play was at the Hampstead Theatre Club, London, on 29 January 1973. It was directed by Vivian Matalon; the stage setting and costumes were by Saul Radomsky, lighting by Robert Ornbo. On 13 March 1973, the production was transferred to the Comedy Theatre, London. The cast was as follows:

LEONA DAWSON	*Elaine Stritch*
MONK	*Peter Jones*
DOC	*George Pravda*
BILL	*Edward Judd*
VIOLET	*Frances De La Tour*
STEVE	*James Berwick*
QUENTIN	*Tony Beckley*
BOBBY	*Eric Deacon*
TONY, THE COP	*John Bay*

Act One: A bar along the Southern California Coast

Act Two: An hour or two later

ACT ONE

The curtain rises. The sound of ocean wind is heard. The stage is lighted at a very low level.

The scene is a somewhat non-realistic evocation of a bar on the beach-front in one of those coastal towns between Los Angeles and San Diego. It attracts a group of regular patrons who are nearly all so well known to each other that it is like a community club, and most of these regulars spend the whole evening there. Ideally, the walls of the bar, on all three sides, should have the effect of fog rolling in from the ocean. A blue neon outside the door says: 'Monk's Place'. The bar runs diagonally from upstage to down; over it is suspended a large varnished sailfish, whose gaping bill and goggle-eyes give it a constant look of amazement. There are about three tables, with red-checked tablecloths. Stage right there is a juke box, and in the wall at right are doors to the ladies' and gents' lavatories. A flight of stairs ascends to the bar-owner's living quarters. The stairs should be masked above the first few steps.

The bar interior is dimly, evenly lit at rise. At some time in the course of the play, when a character disengages himself from the group to speak as if to himself, the light in the bar should dim, and a special spot should illuminate each actor as he speaks.

MONK *is behind the bar serving* DOC. MONK, *the bar-owner, and* DOC, *who lost his licence for heavy drinking but still practises more or less clandestinely, are middle-aged.*

At a downstage table sits VIOLET, *at her feet a battered suitcase fastened with a rope. Her eyes are too large for her face, and they are usually moist; her appearance suggests a derelict kind of existence; still, she has about her a pale, bizarre sort of beauty. As* LEONA DAWSON *later puts it, she's like a water plant.*

MONK [*to* DOC]: Notice? [*He nods his head.*] Over there?

[DOC *emerges from introspection to glance the way indicated by* MONK. *They both gaze at* VIOLET.]

VIOLET [*singing a bit, self-conscious under their scrutiny*]:

The wheel of fortune
Keeps turning around . . .

[*She can't remember past this.*]

DOC (*voice filtered through booze*]: Oh, yes, she's a noticeable thing. She has a sort of not-quite-with-it appearance. Amorphous, that's the word. Something more like a possibility than a completed creature.

MONK: What I mean is the *suitcase. With* her.

DOC: Oh, yes, the suitcase. Does she think she's in the waiting room of a depot?

MONK: I think she thinks she's moved in here.

DOC: Oh. That's a possible problem for you there.

MONK: You're Goddam right. I'm running a tavern that's licensed to dispense spirits, not a pad for vagrants. You see, they see those stairs. They know I live up there.

DOC: Yep, they see those stairs to the living quarters above, and it hits them dimly that you night need the solace of their companionship up there some nights when they find it convenient to offer it to you, and I don't need to tell you that this solace of companionship is not the least expensive item on the shelves of the fucking supermarket a man of my age has to spend what's left of his life in. Oh, that solace, that comfort of companionship is on the shelves of the market even for me, but I tell you, the price is inflated on it. I had me one last summer. Remember that plump little Chicano woman used to come in here with me some nights last summer? A little wet-leg woman, nice boobs on her and a national monument for an ass? Well, she came to me for medical attention.

[MONK *laughs heartily at this.*

BILL *enters the bar; he comes up to it with an over-relaxed amiability like a loser putting up a bold front: by definition a 'stud' – but what are definitions?*

MONK *mechanically produces* BILL'*s can of Miller's but doesn't open it for him.*]

She had worms, diet of rotten beef tacos, I reckon, or tamales or something. I diagnosed it correctly. I gave her the little bottle and the wooden spoon and I said to her, 'Bring me in a sample of your stool for lab analysis.' She didn't know what I meant. Language barrier. I finally said, 'Señorita, bring a little piece of your shit in the bottle tomorrow.' [*He and* MONK *laugh heartily.*]

[BILL *is worried over the fact his beer can is not opened and served.*]

VIOLET: Hey, Bill . . .

DOC: Some beginning of some romance. Dewormed the lady and laid her in place of payment. Jesus, what a love story. I had her all summer, but in September she met a good-looking young pimp who made her critical of me. She called me a dirty old man, so I let her go.

BILL: Hey, Monk. About that beer.

MONK [*ignoring* BILL]: I don't remember you coming in here with a woman.

DOC: We always sat at a back table arguing over the fair expense of her ass.

BILL: Jesus, Monk, how big a tab has Leona run up here!? For Chrissake! [*He leans across the bar and snatches the can of Miller's from* MONK*'s hand.* MONK *had ignored him only half deliberately and is annoyed by the grab.*]

MONK: Look, I don't run Leona's tab through a computer, since I know she's good for it. If you want the can opened, give it back here. [*He opens the can.*] Now if it was your tab, not hers, I'd worry, but since it's hers, not yours, I don't. O.K.? No offence, no complaint, just . . .

VIOLET: Bill?

BILL: I could tell you some things.

MONK: Why don't you tell 'em to Violet, she's called you three times.

BILL [*glancing at her*]: Hi, Vi.

VIOLET: I had an awful experience today with Mr Menzies at the amusement arcade. [*Sobbing sound.*] Oh, I don't know what to do. Min broke in. Last night. Menzies said I . . . Come over here so I can tell you. Oh, and bring me a beer and a pepperoni, I'm famished. Lonesome and famished.

BILL: You want me to solve both those situations for you?

VIOLET: Yes, please.

BILL [*to* MONK]: Another Miller's and a coupla Slim Jims.

MONK: Yep, I got that message. Have you left Leona?

VIOLET: Bill, where's Leona?

BILL: Crying into a stew in her Goddam trailer.

[MONK *opens another beer, and* BILL *ambles over to* VIOLET *with the pepperonis and beer and the smile he meets the world with. It is a hustler's smile, the smile of a professional stud – now ageing a bit but still with considerable memorabilia of his young charm.*]

VIOLET: Thanks, Bill ...

[MONK *is toying with a radio which is over the bar.*]

RADIO VOICE: Heavy seas from Point Conception south to the Mexican border, fog continuing till tomorrow noon, extreme caution should be observed on all highways along this section of the coastline.

MONK [*ironically, turning off radio*]: Small craft warnings, Doc.

DOC: That's right, Monk, and you're running a place of refuge for vulnerable human vessels, and ...

VIOLET [*closer to* BILL]: Have you left Leona? For good?

BILL: Just till she gets her knickers out of that twist. She had this brother, a faggot that played the fiddle in church, and whenever she's drunk, she starts to cry up a storm about this little fag that she admitted was arrested for loitering in the Greyhound bus station men's room, and if I say, 'Well, he was asking for it,' she throws something at me.

VIOLET [*leaning amorously towards him*]: A man like you.

BILL: A man like me?

VIOLET: A bull of a man like you. You got arms on you big as the sides of a ham. [*She strokes his bare arm.*]

BILL: That ain't all I got big.

VIOLET: You mean what I think?

BILL: If you can't see you can feel.

[*She reaches under the table, and it is obvious that she is feeling him.*]

A man likes appreciation. Now I got a letter this week from a female guv'ment employee in Sacramento who's a Reagan supporter.

VIOLET: Huh?

BILL: Shit. She ain't seen me since '65 but remembers me clearly and wants me back on her aquabed with her, and if you've slept in an aquabed it don't matter who's in it with you.

[*The door bursts open.* LEONA *enters like a small bull making his charge into the ring.* LEONA, *a large, ungainly woman, is wearing white clam-digger slacks and a woolly pink sweater. On her head of dyed corkscrew curls is a sailor's hat which she occasionally whips off her head to slap something with – the bar, a tabletop, somebody's back – to emphasize a point. There are abrupt changes of position at the downstage table at her entrance, but she notices only* BILL *there.*]

LEONA: YOUUUUU . . . MOTHER! I was talkin' to you from the stove and you weren't there!

[BILL *chuckles and winks.*]

Three hours I spent shopping for and preparing a . . . memorial dinner while you watched TV.

BILL: Stew and veg.

LEONA [*lyrically, as a pop-poem*]: Lamb stew with garden fresh vegetables from the Farmer's Market, seasoned with bay leaves, and rosemary and thyme.

BILL: Stew.

LEONA: I'd set up a little banquet table in that trailer tonight, my grandmother's silver and Irish lace tablecloth, my crystal candlesticks with the vine leaves filigreed on 'em in silver which I'd polished, all spit-polished for this memorial dinner, set the candles on either side of my single rose vase containing a single talisman rose just opened, a table like a photo from *House and Garden*. I talk from the stove to no one. I open the fridge to get out the jellied bouillon, madrilene, topped with . . . 'Okayyyy, ready.' I come in and I'm received by the TV set and the trailer door hanging open, and in the confusion I knock over and break my cut-glass decanter of Burgundy, imported.

BILL: I went out for a bottle. You'd kilt a fifth of Imp. She was crying in the stew to save on salt.

LEONA: Without word or a note on the table. You went! Why? For what?

VIOLET: Leona, Bill's not happy tonight, so let him be.

LEONA: Two people's not happy and one of 'em with *reason*! Is that your suitcase with you? Are you thrown out, evicted? A lady of the street? Oh, my God, here's a good one I heard at the shop today about a pair of street-ladies in Dublin. One enters a pub, elegant but pissed, and she says to the barman, 'Two gins for two ladies.' He observes her condition and says, 'Where is the other lady?' 'The other lady,' she says, 'is in the gutter resting.' [*Only she is amused by the story.*] Oh, well, I thought it was funny. [LEONA *sits at table with* VIOLET and BILL.] Violet, dear, will you look at your nails?

VIOLET: I know, the enamel's chipping.

LEONA: Yes! Exposing the dirt.

[*Violet drops her hands under the table.*]

Oh, my God, forget it, forget the whole enchilada. Not worth a thought.

[*No response.*]

Excuse me a moment. I'm going to press one button three times on that multiselector, and Violet, here's an orange stick for your nails ... Don't be depressed. A sure cure for depression is the axe.

VIOLET: I'm not depressed.

LEONA [*laughing*]: Then you must not be conscious. [*She crosses to the juke box.*] I hope nobody objects to the number I play. It's going to be played here repeatedly tonight, appreciated or not. [*She bends over the juke box to find the desired number, which she herself contributed to the 'Classicals' on the box.*] Rock? No! Popular? No! Classicals – yes! Number? Number? Which?

VIOLET: Tell her I'm not depressed.

[VIOLET*'s hand has dropped under the table. It is apparent that she is reaching for* BILL.]

BILL: *She's* depressed ... and depressing. [*Leans back luxuriously in a chair. A look to* LEONA. *He speaks with emphasis, rather than volume.*] ... Not bad, huh? A definite ... personal ... asset?

[MONK *turns up radio. Gets static.*]

LEONA: Do you have to turn that on when I'm ...

[*At this precise moment she is caught by the change in attitudes at the downstage table. Her eyes widen; her hands clench; she takes a couple of paces towards the table and crouches a bit to peer under it. Then quick as a shot:*]

YOUUU CUNT!

[*She charges.*

Violet screams and springs up, overturning her chair.]

MONK: Hold her!

[BILL*'s massive frame obstructs* LEONA, *not only her motion but her view of* VIOLET. BILL *is holding her by both shoulders, grinning into her face.*

The following lines overlap.]

LEONA: OFF HANDS!

MONK: Nope, nope, nope, nope, nope!

LEONA: McCorkle, DON' YOU . . . !

MONK: Keep her at that table!

[*During this* MONK *has crossed from behind the bar.*

VIOLET *has turned about dizzily, then fled into the ladies'.*

LEONA *stamps on* BILL*'s foot. He yells, falls back an instant, releasing her. As she rushes forward, he gives her a hard slap on the butt; she turns to give him battle, and is caught from behind by* MONK. *She kicks at* MONK*'s shin, and gives* BILL *a wallop in the face with her cap.*]

BILL [*rubbing his eyes*]: Goddam, she . . .

MONK: I'm havin' no violence here! Never! None! From no one!

[*A sudden hush falls: a sudden moment of stillness in a* corrida.]

LEONA [*incredulously, profoundly, hurtly, right into* BILL*'s face*]: YOU! Let *her*! In front of me? . . . in PUBLIC! . . . In a BAR!

BILL: What the fuck of it! You hit me right in the eyes with . . .

LEONA [*makes a big-theatre turn and shouts*]: Where *IS* she? Where's she gone? [*Receiving no answer – there is still no sound from* VIOLET*'s place of refuge – she suddenly rushes for the stairs.*]

MONK: Nobody's up my stairs! Come down those . . .

[VIOLET*'s lamentation begins.*]

LEONA: Aw! She's gone to the LADIES'! Change the name on that door.

MONK: I'm operating a place for gents and ladies. [*He is panting a bit.*]

LEONA: Gents and . . . what?

MONK: Ladies.

LEONA: Aw, now, Monk. I thought you run a clean place but don't come on with ... her? Lady? Him? Gent? [*She points towards the ladies' room and then towards* BILL.] There's limits to ...

MONK: Yes. Stay away from ...

[LEONA *had started towards the ladies'.* MONK *blocks her. She throws her head back and utters an apocalyptic outcry. It's like the outcry of all human protest.*]

No more disturbance of ...

LEONA [*drawing herself up heroically as she confronts* MONK *almost nose-to-nose*]: LET ME SET YOU STRAIGHT ABOUT WHAT'S A LADY! A lady's a woman, with respect for herself and for relations of others! HER? IN THERE? WAILING? RESPECT FOR? ... She's got no respect for herself and that is the single respect in which she's correct to! No one could blame her for that! [*She has resumed her pacing and slapping at things with sailor's cap.*] What could she possibly find to respect in herself? She lives like an animal in a room with no bath that's directly over the amusement arcade at the foot of the pier, yeah, right over the billiards, the pinball games, and the bowling alleys at the amusement arcade, it's bang, bang, bang, loud as a TV western all day and all night, and then bang, bang again at eight a.m. It would drive a sane person crazy but she couldn't care less. She don't have a closet, she didn't have a bureau so she hangs her dresses on a piece of rope that hangs across a corner between two nails, and her other possessions she keeps on the floor in boxes.

BILL: What business is it of yours?

LEONA: None, not a Goddam bit! When she was sick? I went there to bring her a chicken. I asked her, where is your silver? She didn't have any silver, not a fork, spoon, or knife, hell, not even a plate, but she ate the chicken, aw, yeah, she ate the chicken like a dog would eat it, she picked it up in her paws and gnawed at it just like a dog. Who came to see if she was living or dead? ME! ONLY! I got her a bureau, I got her a knife, fork, and spoon, I got her china, I got her a change of bed linen for her broken-down cot, and ev'ry day after work I come by that Goddam rathole with a bottle of hot beef bouillon or a chicken or meatloaf to see what she needed and bring it, and then one time I come by there to see what she needed and bring it. The bitch wasn't there. I thought my God she's died or they put her away. I run downstairs, and I heard her screaming with joy in the amusement arcade. She was having herself a ball with a shipload of drunk sailor boys; she hardly had time to speak to me.

BILL: Maybe she'd gotten sick of you. That's a possible reason.

LEONA: It's a possible reason I was sick of her, too, but I'd thought that the bitch was dying of malnutrition, and I thought she was human, and a human life is worth saving or what the shit *is* worth saving. But is she human? She's just a parasite creature, not even made out of flesh but out of wet biscuit dough, she always looks like the bones are dissolving in her.

BILL [*banging his beer bottle on the table*]: DO YOU THINK I BELONG TO YOU? I BELONG TO MYSELF, I JUST BELONG TO MYSELF.

LEONA: Aw, you pitiful piece of ... worthless .. conceit! [*She addresses the bar.*] ... Never done a lick of work in his life ... He has a name for his thing. He calls it Junior. He says he takes care of Junior and Junior takes care of him. How long is that gonna last? How long does he figure Junior is going to continue to provide for him, huh? HUH! ... Forever or *less* than forever? ... Thinks the sun rises and sets between his legs and that's the reason I put him in my trailer, feed him, give him beer-money, pretend I don't notice there's five or ten bucks less in my pocketbook in the morning than my pocketbook had in it when I fell to sleep, night before.

BILL: Go out on the beach and tell that to the sea gulls, they'd be more int'rested in it.

VIOLET [*shrilly, from the ladies' room*]: Help me, help me, somebody, somebody call the po-liiiiice!

LEONA: Is she howling out the ladies' room window?

VIOLET: How long do I have to stay in here before you get the police?

LEONA: If that fink is howling out the ladies' room window, I'm going out back and throw a brick in at her.

MONK: Leona, now cool it, Leona.

LEONA: I'll pay the damage, I'll pay the hospital expenses.

MONK: Leona, why don't you play your violin number on the box and settle down at a table and . . .

LEONA: When I been insulted by someone, I don't settle down at a table, or nowhere, NOWHERE!

[VIOLET *sobs and wails as* STEVE *comes into the bar.* STEVE *is wearing a floral-patterned sports shirt under a tan jacket and the greasy white trousers of a short-order cook.*]

STEVE: Is that Violet in there?

LEONA: Who else do you think would be howling out the ladies' room window but her, and you better keep out of this, this is between her and me.

STEVE: What happened? Did you hit Violet?

LEONA: You're Goddam right I busted that filthy bitch in the kisser, and when she comes out of the ladies', if she ever comes out, I'm gonna bust her in the kisser again, and kiss my ass, I'm just the one that can do it! MONK! DRINK! BOURBON SWEET!

MONK: Leona, you're on a mean drunk, and I don't serve liquor to no one on a mean drunk.

LEONA: Well, you can kiss it, too, you monkey-faced mother. [*She slaps the bar top with her sailor hat.*]

STEVE: Hey, did you hit Violet?

[BILL *laughs at this anticlimactic question.*]

LEONA: Have you gone deaf, have you got wax in your ears, can't you hear her howling in there? Did I hit Violet? The answer is yes, and I'm not through with her yet. [LEONA *approaches the door of the ladies' room.*] COME ON OUT OF THERE, VIOLET, OR I'LL BREAK IN THE DOOR! [*She bangs her fist on the door, then slaps it contemptuously with her cap, and resumes her pacing.*]

[BILL *keeps grinning and chuckling.*]

STEVE: Why did she hit Violet?

LEONA: Why don't you ask *me* why?

STEVE: Why did you hit Violet?

LEONA: I hit Violet because she acted indecent with that son of a bitch I been supporting for six months in my trailer.

STEVE: What do you mean 'indecent'?

LEONA: Jesus, don't you know her habits? Are you unconscious ev'ry night in this bar and in her rathole over the amusement arcade? I mean she acted indecent with her hands on the table. The red enamel had nearly all chipped off the nails and the fingernails, black, I mean *black*, like she'd spend every day for a month without washing her hands after making mud-pies with filthy motherless kids, and I thought to myself, it's awful, the degradation a woman can sink down into without respect for herself, so I said to her, Violet, will you look at your hands, will you look at your fingernails, Violet?

STEVE: Is that why you hit Violet?

LEONA: Goddam it, NO! Will you listen? I told her to look at her nails and she said, oh, the enamel is peeling, I know. I mean the dirtiness of the nails was not a thing she could notice, just the chipped red enamel.

STEVE: Is that why you hit Violet?

LEONA: Shit, will you shut up till I tell you why I hit her? I wouldn't hit her just for being unclean, unsanitary. I wouldn't hit her for nothing that affected just her. And now, if you'll pay attention, I'm going to tell you exactly why I did hit her. I got up from the table to play 'Souvenir'.

STEVE: What is she talking about? What are you talking about?

LEONA: When I come back to the table her hands had disappeared off it. I thought to myself, I'm sorry, I made her ashamed of her hands and she's hiding them now.

STEVE: Is that why you hit Violet?

LEONA: Why do you come in a bar when you're already drunk? No! Listen! It wasn't embarrassment over her filthy nails that had made her take her hands off the table top, it was her old habit, as filthy as her nails. The reason her pitiful hands had disappeared off the table was because under the table she was acting indecent with her hands in the lap of that ape that moved himself into my trailer and tonight will move himself out as fast as he moved himself in. And now do you know why I hit her? If you had balls, which it doesn't look like you do, you would've hit her yourself instead of making me do it.

STEVE: I wasn't there when it happened, but that's the reason you hit her?

LEONA: Yeah, now the reason has got through the fog in your head, which is thick as the fog on the beach.

[VIOLET *wails from the ladies' room.*]

STEVE: I'm not married to Violet, I never was or will be. I just wanted to know who hit her and why you hit her.

LEONA [*slapping at him with her cap*]: Annhh!

STEVE: Don't slap at me with that cap. What do I have to do with what she done or she does?

LEONA: No responsibility? No affection? No pity? You stand there hearing her wailing in the ladies' and deny there's any connection between you? Well, now I feel sorry for her. I regret that I hit her. She can come back out now and I won't hit her again. I see her life, the awfulness of her hands reaching out under a table, automatically creeping under a table into the lap of anything with a thing that she can catch hold of. Let her out of the ladies', I'll never hit her again. I feel too much pity for her, but I'm going out for a minute to breathe some clean air and to get me a drink where a barman's willing to serve me, and then I'll come back to pay up whatever I owe here and say good-bye to the sailfish, hooked and shellacked and strung up like a flag over ... over ... lesser, much lesser ... creatures that never, ever sailed an inch in their ... lives ...

[*The pauses at the end of this speech are due to a shift of her attention towards a young man and a boy who have entered the bar. Her eyes have followed them as they walked past her to a table in the front. She continues speaking, but now as if to herself.*]

... When I leave here tonight, none of you will ever see me again. I'm going to stop by the shop, let myself in with my passkey and collect my own equipment, which is enough to open a shop of my own, write a good-bye note to Flo, she isn't a bad old bitch, I doubled her trade since I been there, she's going to miss me, poor Flo, then leave my passkey and cut back to my trailer and pack like lightning and move on to ...

BILL: Where?

LEONA: Where I go next. You won't know, but you'll know I went fast.

[*Now she forgets her stated intention of going out of the bar and crosses to the table taken by the young man and the boy. The boy,* BOBBY, *wears faded jeans and a sweatshirt on the back of which is lettered 'Iowa to Mexico'. The young man,* QUENTIN, *is dressed effetely in a yachting jacket, maroon linen slacks, and a silk neck-scarf. Despite this costume, he has a quality of sexlessness, not effeminacy. Some years ago, he must have been remarkably handsome. Now his face seems to have been burned thin by a fever that is not of the flesh.*]

LEONA [*suddenly very amiable*]: Hi, boys!

QUENTIN: Oh. Hello. Good evening.

BOBBY [*with shy friendliness*]: Hello.

[BILL *is grinning and chuckling.* VIOLET'*s weeping in the ladies' room no longer seems to interest anyone in the bar.*]

LEONA [*to* BOBBY]: How's the corn growing out there where the tall corn grows?

BOBBY: Oh, it's still growing tall.

LEONA: Good for the corn. What town or city are you from in Iowa?

BOBBY: Goldenfield. It's close to Dubuque.

LEONA: Dubuque, no shoot? I could recite the telephone book of Dubuque, but excuse me a minute, I want to play a selection on the number selector, and I'll come right back to discuss Dubuque with you. Huh? [*She moves as if totally pacified to the juke box and removes some coins from a pocket. They fall to the floor. She starts to bend over to pick them up, then decides not to bother, gives them a slight kick, gets a dollar bill out of a pocket, calling out:*] Monk, gimme change for a buck. [LEONA *crosses to* MONK *at bar, waving a dollar bill.*]

QUENTIN: Barman? ... Barman? ... What's necessary to get the barman's attention here, I wonder.

[LEONA *crosses back to juke box, stage right.* BOBBY *hands* LEONA *the change he's picked up off the floor. She looks for a number on the juke box.*]

MONK: I heard you. You've come in the wrong place. You're looking for the Jungle Bar, half a mile up the beach.

QUENTIN: Does that mean you'd rather not serve us?

MONK: Let me see the kid's draft card.

BOBBY: I just want a Coke.

QUENTIN: He wants a plain Coca-Cola, I'd like a vodka and tonic.

[LEONA *lights up the juke box with a coin and selects a violin number, 'Souvenir'. A look of ineffable sweetness appears on her face, at the first note of music.*]

BILL: Y' can't insult 'em, there's no way to bring 'em down except to beat 'em and roll 'em.

[*The bar starts to dim, and a special spot comes up on* BILL. *The violin music on the juke box plays softly under.*]

I noticed him stop at the door before he come in. He was about to go right back out when he caught sight of me. Then he decided to stay. A piss-elegant one like that is asking for it. After a while, say about fifteen minutes, I'll go in the gents' and he'll follow me in there for a look at Junior. Then I'll have him hooked. He'll ask me to meet him outside by his car or at the White Castle. It'll be a short wait and I don't think I'll have t'do more than scare him a little. I don't like beating 'em up. They can't help the way they are. Who can? Not me. Left home at fifteen, and like Leona says, I've never done a lick of work in my life and I never plan to, not as long as Junior keeps batting on the home team, but my time with Leona's run out. She means to pull out of here and I mean to stay ...

[*The bar is relighted.* LEONA *is still at the juke box. She is leaning against the juke box, listening intently to the music.*]

MONK [*rapping at the ladies'*]: Violet, you can come out, now, she's playing that violin number.

[BILL *and* STEVE *laugh. The bar starts to dim, and a special spot comes up on* STEVE. *The violin number still plays under.*]

STEVE: I guess Violet's a pig, all right, and I ought to be ashamed to go around with her. But a man unmarried, forty-seven years old, employed as a short-order cook at a salary he can barely get by on alone, he can't be choosy. Nope, he has to be satisfied with the Goddam scraps in this world, and Violet's one of those scraps. She's a pitiful scrap, but ... [*He shrugs sadly and lifts the beer bottle to his mouth.*] ... something's better than nothing and I had nothing before I took up with her. She gave me a clap once and tried to tell me I got it off a toilet seat. I asked the doctor, is it possible to get a clap off a public toilet seat, and he said, yes, you can get it that way but you *don't*. [*He grins sadly and drinks again, wobbling slightly.*]

... Oh, my life, my miserable, cheap life! It's like a bone thrown to a dog! I'm the dog, she's the bone. Hell, I know her habits. She's always down there in that amusement arcade when I go to pick her up, she's down there as close as she can get to some Navy kid, playing a pinball game, and one hand is out of sight. Hustling? I reckon that's it. I know I don't provide for her, just buy her a few beers here, and a hot dog on the way home. But, Bill, why's he let her mess around with him? One night he was braggin' about the size of his tool, he said all he had to do to make a living was wear tight pants on the street. Life! ... Throw it to a dog. I'm not a dog, I don't want it. I think I'll sit at the bar and pay no attention to her when she comes out ...

[*The light in the bar comes up to normal level as the spot fades out. After a moment,* VIOLET *comes out of the ladies' room slowly, with a piteous expression. She is dabbing her nostrils with a bit of toilet tissue. Her lips are pursed in sorrow so that she is like a travesty of a female saint under torture. She gasps and draws back a little at the sight of* LEONA*; then, discreetly sobbing, she edges on to a bar stool, and* MONK *gives her a beer.* STEVE *glares at her. She avoids looking at him.* BILL *grins and chuckles at his table.* LEONA *ignores the fact that* VIOLET *has emerged from her retreat. She goes on pacing the bar, but is enthralled by the music.*]

LEONA: My God, what an instrument, it's like a thing in your heart, it's a thing that's sad but better than being happy, in a ... crazy drunk way ...

VIOLET [*piteously*]: I don't know if I can drink, I feel sick at my stomach.

LEONA: Aw, shit, Violet. Who do you think you're kidding? You'll drink whatever is put in the reach of your paws. [*She slaps herself on the thigh with the sailor cap and laughs.*]

VIOLET: I do feel sick at my stomach.

LEONA: You're lucky you're sick at your stomach because your stomach can vomit, but when you're sick at your heart, that's when it's awful, because your heart can't vomit the memories of your lifetime. I wish my heart could vomit, I wish my heart could throw up the heartbreaks of my lifetime, my days in a beauty shop and my nights in a trailer. It wouldn't surprise me at all if I drove up to Sausalito alone this night. With no one . . .

[*She glances at* BILL, *who grins and chuckles.* VIOLET *sobs piteously again.* LEONA *gives* VIOLET *a fairly hard slap on the shoulders with her sailor's cap.* VIOLET *cries out in affected terror.*]

Shuddup, I'm not gonna hit you. Steve, take her off that bar stool and put her at a table, she's on a crying jag and it makes me sick.

STEVE [*to* VIOLET]: Come off it, Violet. Sit over here at a table, before you fall off the bar stool.

LEONA: She hasn't got a mark on her, not a mark, but she acts like I'd nearly kilt her, and turns to a weeping willow. But as for that ape that I put up in my trailer, I took him in because a life in a trailer, going from place to place any way the wind blows you, gets to be lonely, sometimes. But that's a mistake I'll not make again . . . knock wood! [*Knocks table top.*]

STEVE [*wishing to smooth troubled waters*]: Know what that means, to knock wood? It means to touch the wood of the true cross, Leona.

[*He peers gravely and nearsightedly into* LEONA*'s face.*]

LEONA: Yeh, for luck, you need it.

MONK [*to* VIOLET *at bar*]: That's mine! Here's yours. [*She has reached out for* MONK*'s drink.*]

STEVE: Violet, get off that stool and sit at a table.

LEONA You got to move her. She's got to be moved.

[STEVE *accepts this necessity. He supports* VIOLET*'s frail, liquid figure to a table upstage, but her long, thin arm snakes out to remove* MONK*'s drink from the bar top as she goes.*

The phone rings, and MONK *lifts it.*]

MONK: Monk's Place . . . Doc, it's for you.

DOC [*crossing to the end of the bar*]: Thanks, Monk.

MONK: The old Doc's worked up a pretty good practice for a man in retirement.

LEONA: Retirement your ass, he was kicked out of the medical profession for performing operations when he was so loaded he couldn't tell the appendix from the gizzard.

MONK: Leona, go sit at your table.

LEONA: You want responsibility for a human life, do you?

MONK: Bill, I think she's ready to go home now.

LEONA: I'll go home when I'm ready and I'll do it alone.

BILL: I seen a circus with a polar bear in it that rode a three-wheel bicycle. That's what you make me think of tonight.

LEONA: You want to know something, McCorkle? I could beat the shit out of you.

BILL: Set down somewhere and shut up.

LEONA: I got a suggestion for you. Take this cab fare ... [*She throws a handful of silver on the table.*] ... And go get your stuff out of my trailer. Clear it all out, because when I go home tonight and find any stuff of yours there, I'll pitch it out of the trailer and bolt the door on you. I'm just in the right mood to do it.

BILL: Don't break my heart.

LEONA: What heart? We been in my trailer together for six months and you contributed nothing.

BILL: Shit, for six months I satisfied you in your trailer!

LEONA: You never satisfied nothing but my mother complex. Never mind, forget it, it's forgotten. Just do this. Take this quarter and punch number K-6 three times on the juke box.

BILL: Nobody wants to hear that violin number again.

LEONA: I do, I'm somebody. My brother, my young brother, played it as good if not better than Heifetz on that box. Y'know, I look at you and I ask myself a question. How does it feel to've never had anything beautiful in your life and not even know you've missed it? [*She crosses towards the juke box.*] Walking home with you some night, I've said, Bill, look at the sky, will you look at that sky? You never looked up, just grunted. In your life you've had no experiation ... experience! Appreciation! ... of the beauty of God in the sky, so what is your life but a bottle of, can of, glass of ... one, two, three! [*She has punched the violin selection three times.*]

MONK: The Doc's still on the phone.

LEONA: 'Souvenir' is a soft number.

[*The violin number starts to play again on the juke box.*]

DOC [*returning to the bar*]: I've got to deliver a baby. Shot of brandy.

LEONA [*returning to* BILL'*s table*]: It wouldn't be sad if you didn't know what you missed by coming into this world and going out of it some day without ever having a sense of, experience of and memory of, a beautiful thing in your life such as I have in mine when I remember the violin of and the face of my young brother.

BILL: You told me your brother was a fruit.

LEONA: I told you privately something you're repeating in public with words as cheap as yourself. My brother who played this number had pernicious anaemia from the age of thirteen and any fool knows a disease, a condition, like that would make any boy too weak to go with a woman, but he was so full of love he had to give it to someone like his music. And in my work, my profession as a beautician, I never seen skin or hair or eyes that could touch my brother's. His hair was a natural blond as soft as silk and his eyes were two pieces of heaven in a human face, and he played on the violin like he was making love to it. I cry! I cry! ... No, I don't, I *don't* cry! ... I'm proud that I've had something beautiful to remember as long as I live in my lifetime ...

[VIOLET *sniffles softly.*]

When they passed around the plate for the offering at church, they'd have him play in the choir stall and he played and he looked like an angel, standing under the light through the stained glass window. Um-hummm. [*Her expression is rapt.*] ... And people, even the tightwads, would drop paper money in the plates when he played. Yes, always before the service, I'd give him a shampoo-rinse so that his silky hair, the silkiest hair I've ever known on a human head in my lifetime as a beautician, would look like an angel's halo, touched with heavenly light. Why, people cried like I'm crying and the preacher was still choked up when he delivered the sermon. 'Angels of Light', that was it, the number he played that Easter ... [*She sings a phrase of the song.*] Emotions of people can be worse than people but sometimes better than people, yes, superior to them, and Haley had that gift of making people's emotions uplifted, superior to them! But he got weaker and weaker and thinner and thinner till one Sunday he collapsed in the choir stall, and after that he failed fast, just faded out of this world. Anaemia – pernicious . . .

VIOLET [*sobbing*]: Anaemia, that's what I've got!

LEONA: Don't compare yourself to him, how dare you compare yourself to him. He was too beautiful to live and so he died. Otherwise we'd be living together in my trailer. I'd train him to be a beautician, to bring out the homeliness in . . . I mean the, I mean the . . . [*She is confused for a moment. She lurches into a bar stool and knocks it over.*] I mean I'd train my young brother to lay his hands on the heads of the homely and lonely and bring some beauty out in them, at least for one night or one day or at least for an hour. We'd have our own shop, maybe two of 'em, and I wouldn't give you . . . [*She directs herself to* BILL] . . . the time of the day, the time of the night, the time of the morning or afternoon, the sight of you never would have entered my sight to make me feel pity for you, no, noooo! [*She bends over* BILL*'s table, resting her spread palms on it, to talk directly into his face.*] The companionship and the violin of my brother would be all I had any need for in my lifetime till my death-time! Remember this, Bill, if your brain can remember. Everyone needs! One beautiful thing! In the course of a lifetime! To save the heart from colluption!

BILL: What is 'colluption', fat lady?

LEONA: *CORRUPTION!* . . . Without one beautiful thing in the course of a lifetime, it's all a death-time. A woman turns to a slob that lives with a slob, and life is disgusting to her and she's disgusting to life, and I'm just the one to . . .

BILL [*cutting in*]: If you'd rather live with a fruit . . .

LEONA: *Don't say it! Don't say it!* [*She seizes hold of a chair and raises it mightily over her head.* VIOLET *screams.* LEONA *hurls the chair to the floor.*] Shit, he's not worth the price of a broken chair! [*Suddenly she bursts into laughter that is prodigious as her anger or even more, it's like an unleashed element of nature. Several patrons of the bar, involuntarily, laugh with her. Abruptly as it started, the laughter stops short. There is total silence except for the ocean sound outside.*]

VIOLET: Steve, love, get me a hot dog with chili and onion, huh? Or maybe a Whopper.

STEVE: Oh, now you want a Whopper, a king-size burger, now, huh? Always got your hand out for something.

VIOLET: That's a cruel injustice. [*Sobs.*]

STEVE: Stop it!

VIOLET: I'm in paiii-in!

LEONA: Look at her, not a mark on her, but says she's in pain and wants a hot dog with everything on it, and I heard on TV that the Food Administration found insect and rodent parts in some hot dogs sold lately. [*She has been stalking the bar.*] Let her have him for supper! [*Indicates* BILL.]

DOC [*rising from his bar stool*]: Well, I better be going. Somebody's about to be born at Treasure Island.

LEONA: That's my trailer court where I keep my trailer. A baby's about to be born there?

BILL: Naw, not a baby, a full-grown adult's about to be born there, and that's why the Doc had t'brace himself with a coupla shots of brandy.

DOC [*turning about on his bar stool, glass in hand*]: You can't make jokes about birth and you can't make jokes about death. They're miracles, holy miracles, both, yes, that's what both of them are, even though, now, they're usually surrounded by ... expedients that seem to take away the dignity of them. Birth? Rubber gloves, boiled water, forceps, surgical shears. And death? ... The wheeze of an oxygen tank, the jab of a hypodermic needle to put out the panic light in the dying-out eyes, tubes in the arms and the kidneys, absorbent cotton inserted in the rectum to hold back the bowels discharged when the ... the *being stops.* [*During this speech the bar dims, and a special spot comes up on* DOC.] ... It's hard to see back of this cloud of ... irreverent ... paraphernalia. But behind them both are the holy mysteries of ... birth and ... death ... They're dark as the face of a black man, yes, that's right, a Negro, yes. I've always figured that God is a black man with no light on his face, He moves in the dark like a black man, a Negro miner in the pit of a lightless coal mine, obscured completely by the ... irrelevancies and irreverencies of public worship ... standing to sing, kneeling to pray, sitting to hear the banalities of a preacher ... Monk, did I give you my ...?

[*As light comes up in bar, the spot fades out.*]

MONK: Bag? Yeah, here. [MONK *hands a medical kit across the bar.*]

LEONA: I want to know, is nobody going to stop him from going out, in his condition, to deliver a baby? I want to know quick, or I'll stop him myself!

DOC: Thanks. And I'll have a shot of brandy to wash down a Benzedrine tablet to steady my hands.

LEONA: NOBODY, HUH?

DOC: Tonight, as I drove down Canyon Road, I noticed a clear bright star in the sky, and it was right over that trailer court, Treasure Island, where I'm going to deliver a baby. So now I know: I'm going to deliver a new Messiah tonight.

LEONA: The hell you are, you criminal, murdering quack, leggo of that bag!

[LEONA *rushes* DOC *and snatches his bag. She starts towards the door but is blocked by one of the men; starts in another direction and is blocked again. She is then warily approached from three or four sides by* MONK, DOC, BILL, *and* STEVE *as trainers approaching an angry 'big cat'.*

All ad-lib during this, and in the lines that follow, MONK, LEONA, *and* DOC *speak almost simultaneously, while* STEVE *keeps up a continual placating repetition of 'Violet says' and 'Have a beer with us, Leona.'*

The effect should almost suggest a quartet in opera: several voices blended but each pursuing its separate plaint.]

MONK: Don't let her out with ...

DOC: My bag! The instruments in that bag ...

MONK: Steve, Bill, hold her, I can't with my ...

DOC: Are worth and insured for ... over two thousand! If you damage the contents of that bag ... I'll sue you for their value and for slander!

[LEONA *sits on* DOC*'s bag at centre table.*]

LEONA: I'll surrender this bag to you in a courtroom only!

DOC: Very expensive, very, very expensive.

STEVE: Look, she's sitting on Doc's bag. Violet says she's, Leona, Violet wants to, listen, listen, listen Leona, set down and have a beer with us! Violet says she ...

VIOLET: Not at this table, no, no, I'm scared of Leona, she ...

STEVE: Violet, shuddup. Leona? Violet's offered you to a ... drink! Have a drink with us, Leona.

LEONA: I'll stay sitting on it till some action is taken to stop this man from illegal ...

[BILL *squirts a mouthful of beer at her, and she immediately leaps up to strike at him fiercely with the sailor's cap. In that instant* MONK *seizes the bag from the chair and tosses it to* DOC, *who rushes out the door with it.*]

All of you are responsible! ... If he murders a baby tonight and the baby's mother! Is life worth nothing in here? I'm going out. I am going to make a phone call.

[BILL *makes a move to stop her.*]

Don't you *dare* to! Try to!

MONK: Who're you going to call?

STEVE: Who's she going to call?

LEONA [*to* MONK]: That's my business, strictly. I'm not gonna use your phone. [*She charges out the door, and the door is again left open on the sound of surf.*]

MONK: What's she up to?

STEVE: What's she up to, Bill?

BILL [*grinning and shrugging*]: I know what she's up to. She's gonna call the office at Treasure Island and tell 'em the Doc's comin' out there to deliver a baby.

MONK: Well, stop her, go stop her!

STEVE: Yeh, you better stop her.

BILL [*indifferently*]: She's disappeared in the fog.

MONK: She can get the Doc into serious trouble, and his condition's no better than mine is ...

BILL: Shit, they know her too well to pay any attention to her call.

MONK: I hate to eighty-six anyone out of my place; I never have done that in the six years I've run it, but I swear to God, I ... have to avoid ... disturbance.

VIOLET [*plaintively*]: Last week she gave me a perm and a rinse for nothing, and then tonight she turns on me, threatens to kill me.

BILL: Aw, she blows hot and cold, dependin' on whichever way her liquor hits her.

VIOLET: She's got two natures in her. Sometimes she couldn't be nicer. A minute later she ...

MONK [*at the telephone*]: Shut up a minute. Treasure Island? This is Monk speaking from Monk's Place ... Yeah. Now. If you get a phone call out there from Leona Dawson, you know her, she's got a trailer out there, don't listen to her; she's on a crazy mean drunk, out to make trouble for a capable doctor who's been called by someone out there, an emergency call. So I thought I'd warn you, thank you. [MONK *hangs up the telephone.*]

[VIOLET *comes downstage, and the light is focused on her.*]

VIOLET: It's perfectly true that I have a room over the amusement arcade facing the pier. But it wasn't like Leona describes it. It took me a while to get it in shipshape condition because I was not a well girl when I moved in there, but I got it clean and attractive. It wasn't luxurious but it was clean and attractive and had an atmosphere to it. I don't see anything wrong with living upstairs from the amusement arcade, facing the pier. I don't have a bath or a toilet but I keep myself clean with a sponge bath at the washbasin and use the toilet in the amusement arcade. Anyhow it was a temporary arrangement, that's all it was, a temporary arrangement ...

[LEONA *returns to the bar.* BILL *rises quickly and walks over to the bar.*]

LEONA: One two, button my shoe, three, four, shut the door, five, six, pick up sticks ... [*No one speaks.*] ... Silence, absolute silence. Am I being ostracized? [*She goes to the table of* QUENTIN *and* BOBBY.] Well, boys, what went wrong?

QUENTIN: I'm afraid I don't know what you mean.

LEONA: Sure you know what I mean. You're not talking to each other, you don't even look at each other. There's some kind of tension between you. What is it? Is it guilt feelings? Embarrassment with guilt feelings?

BOBBY: I still don't know what you mean, but, uh ...

LEONA: 'But, uh' what?

QUENTIN: Don't you think you're being a little presumptuous?

LEONA: Naw, I know the gay scene. I learned it from my kid brother. He came out early, younger than this boy here. I know the gay scene and I know the language of it and I know how full it is of sickness and sadness; it's so full of sadness and sickness, I could almost be glad that my little brother died before he had time to be infected with all that sadness and sickness in the heart of a gay boy. This kid from Iowa, here, reminds me a little of how my brother was, and you, you remind me of how he might have become if he'd lived.

QUENTIN: Yes, you should be relieved he's dead, then.

[*She flops awkwardly into a chair at the table.*]

QUENTIN [*testily*]: Excuse me, won't you sit down?

LEONA: D'ya think I'm still standing up?

QUENTIN: Perhaps we took your table.

LEONA: I don't have any table. I'm moving about tonight like an animal in a zoo because tonight is the night of the death-day of my brother and . . . Look, the barman won't serve me, he thinks I'm on a mean drunk, so do me a favour, order a double bourbon and pretend it's for you. Do that, I'll love you for it, and of course I'll pay you for it.

QUENTIN [*calling out*]: Barman? I'd like a double bourbon.

MONK: If it's for the lady, I can't serve you.

[BILL *laughs heartily at the next table.*]

QUENTIN: It isn't for the lady, it's for me.

LEONA: How do you like that shit? [*She shrugs.*] Now what went wrong between you before you come in here, you can tell me and maybe I can advise you. I'm practically what they call a faggot's moll.

QUENTIN: Oh. Are you?

LEONA: Yes, I am. I always locate at least one gay bar in whatever city I'm in. I live in a home on wheels, I live in a trailer, so I been quite a few places. And have a few more to go. Now nobody's listening to us, they're involved in their own situations. What went wrong?

QUENTIN: Nothing, exactly. I just made a mistake, and he did, too.

LEONA: Oh. Mistakes. How did you make these mistakes? Nobody's listening, tell me.

QUENTIN: I passed him riding his bicycle up Canyon Road and I stopped my car and reversed it till I was right by his bike and I . . . spoke to him.

LEONA: What did you say to him?

BOBBY: Do you have to talk about it?

QUENTIN: Why not? I said: 'Did you really ride that bike all the way from Iowa to the Pacific Coast?' and he grinned and said, yes, he'd done that. And I said: 'You must be tired?' and he said he was and I said: 'Put your bike in the back seat of my car and come home with me for dinner.'

LEONA: What went wrong? At dinner? You didn't *give* him the dinner?

QUENTIN: No, I gave him drinks, first, because I thought that after he'd had dinner, he might say: 'Thank you, good night.'

BOBBY: Let's shut up about that. I had dinner after.

LEONA: After what?

QUENTIN: After ...

BOBBY: I guess to you people who live here it's just an old thing you're used to, I mean the ocean out there, the Pacific, it's not an *experience* to you any more like it is to me. You say it's the Pacific, but me, I say THE PACIFIC!

QUENTIN: Well, everything is in 'caps' at your age, Bobby.

LEONA [*to* QUENTIN]: Do you work for the movies?

QUENTIN: Naturally, what else?

LEONA: Act in them, you're an actor?

QUENTIN: No. Script writer.

LEONA [*vaguely*]: Aw, you write movies, huh?

QUENTIN: Mostly rewrite. Adapt. Oh, I had a bit of a setback when they found me too literate for my first assignment ... converting an epic into a vehicle for the producer's doxy, a grammar school dropout. But the industry is using me now to make blue movies bluer with ... you know, touches of special ... erotica ... lovely.

[LEONA *laughs.*]

LEONA: Name?

QUENTIN: Quentin ... Miss? [*He rises.*]

LEONA: Leona. Dawson. And he's?

QUENTIN: Bobby.

LEONA: Bobby, come back to the party. I want you back here, love. Resume your seat. [*Resting a hand on the boy's stiff shoulder*] ...

You're a literary gent with the suede shit-kickers and a brass-button blazer and a . . . [*Flicks his scarf.*]

BILL [*leering from bar*]: Ask him if he's got change for a three-dollar bill.

QUENTIN: Yes, if you have the bill.

LEONA: Ignore the peasants. I don't think that monkey-faced mother will serve us that bourbon . . . I never left his bar without leaving a dollar tip on the table, and this is what thanks I get for it, just because it's the death-day of my brother and I showed a little human emotion about it. Now what's the trouble between you and this kid from Iowa where the tall corn blows, I mean grows?

QUENTIN: I only go for straight trade. But this boy . . . look at him! Would you guess he was gay? . . . I didn't, I thought he was straight. But I had an unpleasant surprise when he responded to my hand on his knee by putting his hand on mine.

BOBBY: I don't dig the word 'gay'. To me they mean nothing, those words.

LEONA: Aw, you've got plenty of time to learn the meanings of words and cynical attitudes. Why he's got eyes like my brother's! Have you paid him?

QUENTIN: For disappointment?

LEONA: Don't be a mean-minded mother. Give him a five, a ten. If you picked up what you don't want, it's your mistake and pay for it.

BOBBY: I don't want money from him. I thought he was nice, I liked him.

LEONA: Your mistake, too [*She turns to* QUENTIN.] Gimme your wallet.

[QUENTIN *hands her his wallet.*]

BOBBY: He's disappointed. I don't want anything from him.

LEONA: Don't be a fool. Fools aren't respected, you fool. [*She removes a bill from the wallet and stuffs it in the pocket of* BOBBY*'s shirt.* BOBBY *starts to return it.*] OK, I'll hold it for you till he cuts out of here to make another pickup and remind me to give it back to you when he goes. He wants to pay you, it's part of his sad routine. It's like doing penance . . . penitence.

BILL [*loudly*]: Monk, where's the head?

MONK: None of that here, Bill.

QUENTIN [*with a twist of a smile towards* BILL]: Pity.

LEONA [*turning to* QUENTIN]: Do you like being alone except for vicious pickups? The kind you go for? If I understood you correctly? ... Christ, you have terrible eyes, the expression in them! What are you looking at?

QUENTIN: The fish over the bar ...

LEONA: You're changing the subject.

QUENTIN: No, I'm not, not a bit ... Now suppose some night I woke up and I found that fantastic fish ... what is it?

LEONA: Sailfish. What about it?

QUENTIN: Suppose I woke up some midnight and found that peculiar thing swimming around in my bedroom? Up the Canyon?

LEONA: In a fish bowl? Aquarium?

QUENTIN: No, not in a bowl or aquarium: free, unconfined.

LEONA: Impossible.

QUENTIN: Granted. It's impossible. But suppose it occurred just the same, as so many impossible things *do* occur just the same. Suppose I woke up and discovered it there, swimming round and round in the darkness over my bed, with a faint phosphorescent glow in its big goggle-eyes and its gorgeously iridescent fins and tail making a swishing sound as it circles around and around and about right over my head in my bed.

LEONA: Hah!

QUENTIN: Now suppose this admittedly preposterous thing did occur. What do you think I would say?

LEONA: To the fish?

QUENTIN: To myself and the fish.

LEONA: ... I'll be raped by an ape if I can imagine what a person would say in a situation like that.

QUENTIN: I'll tell you what I would say, I would say: 'Oh, well ...'

LEONA: ... Just 'Oh, well'?

QUENTIN: 'Oh, well' is all I would say before I went back to sleep.

LEONA: What I would say is: 'Get the hell out of here, you goggle-eyed monstrosity of a mother,' that's what I'd say to it.

MONK: Leona, let's lighten it up.

QUENTIN: You don't see the point of my story?

LEONA: Nope.

QUENTIN [*to* BOBBY]: Do *you* see the point of my story?

[BOBBY *shakes his head.*]

Well, maybe I don't either.

LEONA: Then why'd you tell it?

QUENTIN: What is the thing that you mustn't lose in this world before you're ready to leave it? The one thing you mustn't lose ever?

LEONA: . . . Love?

[QUENTIN *laughs.*]

BOBBY: Interest?

QUENTIN: That's closer, much closer. Yes, that's almost it. The word that I had in mind is surprise, though. The capacity for being surprised. I've lost the capacity for being surprised, so completely lost it, that if I woke up in my bedroom late some night and saw that fantastic fish swimming right over my head, I wouldn't be really surprised.

LEONA: You mean you'd think you were dreaming?

QUENTIN: Oh, no. Wide awake. But not really surprised. [*The special spot concentrates on him. The bar dims, but an eerie glow should remain on the sailfish over the bar.*] There's a coarseness, a deadening coarseness, in the experience of most homosexuals. The experiences are quick, and hard, and brutal, and the pattern of them is practically unchanging. Their act of love is like the jabbing of a hypodermic needle to which they're addicted but which is more and more empty of real interest and surprise. This lack of variation and surprise in their . . . 'love life' . . . [*He smiles harshly*] . . . spreads into other areas of . . . 'sensibility?' [*He smiles again.*] . . . Yes, once, quite a long while ago, I was often startled by the sense of being alive, of being *myself, living*! Present on earth, in the flesh, yes, for some completely mysterious reason, a single, separate, intensely conscious being, *myself*: *living*! . . . Whenever I would feel this . . . *feeling*, this . . . shock of . . . what? . . . self-realization? . . . I would be stunned, I would be thunderstruck by it. And by the existence of everything that exists, I'd be lightning-struck with astonishment

... it would do more than astound me, it would give me a feeling of panic, the sudden sense of ... I suppose it was like an epileptic seizure, except that I didn't fall to the ground in convulsions; no, I'd be more apt to try to lose myself in a crowd on a street until the seizure was finished ... They were dangerous seizures. One time I drove into the mountains and smashed the car into a tree, and I'm not sure if I *meant* to do that, or ... In a forest you'll sometimes see a giant tree, several hundred years old, that's scarred, that's blazed by lightning, and the wound is almost obscured by the obstinately still living and growing bark. I wonder if such a tree has learned the same lesson that I have, not to feel astonishment any more but just go on, continue for two or three hundred years more? ... This boy I picked up tonight, the kid from the tall corn country, still has the capacity for being surprised by what he sees, hears and feels in this kingdom of earth. All the way up the canyon to my place, he kept saying, *I can't believe it, I'm here, I've come to the Pacific, the world's greatest ocean!* ... as if nobody, Magellan or Balboa or even the Indians had ever seen it before him; yes, like he'd discovered this ocean, the largest on earth, and so now, because he'd found it himself, it existed, now, for the first time, never before ... And this excitement of his reminded me of my having lost the ability to say: 'My God!' instead of just: 'Oh, well.' I've asked all the questions, shouted them at deaf heaven, till I was hoarse in the voice box and blue in the face, and gotten no answer, not the whisper of one, nothing at all, you see, but the sun coming up each morning and going down that night, and the galaxies of the night sky trooping onstage like chorines, robot chorines: one, two, three, kick, one two, three, kick ... Repeat any question too often and what do you get, what's given? ... A big carved rock by the desert, a ... monumental symbol of worn-out passion and bewilderment in you, a stupid stone paralysed sphinx that knows no answers that you don't but comes on like the oracle of all time, waiting on her belly to give out some outcries of universal wisdom, and if she woke up some midnight at the edge of the desert and saw that fantastic fish swimming over her head ... y'know what she'd say, too? She'd say: 'Oh, well' ... and go back to sleep for another five thousand years. [*He turns back; and the bar is relighted. He returns to the table and adjusts his neck-scarf as he speaks to* BOBBY.] ... Your bicycle's still in my car. Shall I put it on the sidewalk?

BOBBY: I'll go get it.

QUENTIN: No. You will find it here, by the door. [*Desires no further exposure to* BOBBY.]

LEONA [*to* BOBBY]: Stay here awhile ... Set down. He wants to escape.

BOBBY: From me? [*Meaning 'Why?'*]

LEONA [*visibly enchanted by* BOBBY, *whom she associates with her lost brother*]: Maybe more from himself. Stay here awhile.

BOBBY: ... It's ... late for the road. [*But he may resume his seat here.*]

LEONA: On a bike, yeh, too late, with the dreaded fog people out. Y'know, I got a suggestion. It's sudden but it's terrific. [*She leans across the table, urgently.*] Put your bike in my trailer. It's got two bunks.

BOBBY:Thank you but ...

LEONA: It wouldn't cost you nothing and we'd be company for each other. My trailer's not ordinary, it's a Fonda deluxe, stereo with two speakers, colour TV with an eight-inch screen, touchamatic, and baby, you don't look well fed. I'm a hell of a cook, could qualify as a pro in that line, too.

BILL [*to* STEVE]: What a desperate pitch. I was the wrong sex. She wants a fruit in her stinkin' trailer.

LEONA: Nothing stunk in my trailer but what's out now ... He can't understand a person wanting to give protection to another, it's past his little reception. [*To* BOBBY] Why're you staring out into space with visibility zero?

BOBBY [*slowly, with a growing ardour*]: I've got a lot of important things to think over alone, new things. I feel new vibes, vibrations, I've got to sort out alone.

LEONA: Mexico's a dangerous country for you, and there's lonely stretches of road ... [*She's thinking of herself, too.*]

BOBBY: [*firmly but warmly to her*]: Yes ... I need that, now.

LEONA: Baby, are you scared I'd put the make on you?

[BILL *grunts contemptuously but with the knowledge that he is now truly evicted.*]

I don't, like they say, come on heavy ... never, not with ... [*She lightly touches* BOBBY'*s hand on the table.*] *This* is my touch! Is it *heavy*?

[BOBBY *rises.* QUENTIN *is seen dimly, setting the bicycle at the door.*]

BOBBY: That man didn't come on heavy. [*Looking out at* QUENTIN.] His hand on my knee was just a human touch and it seemed natural to me to return it.

LEONA: Baby, his hand had ... ambitions ... And, oh, my God, you've got the skin and hair of my brother and even almost the eyes!

BILL: Can he play the fiddle?

BOBBY: In Goldenfield, Iowa, there was a man like that, ran a flower shop with a back room, decorated Chinese, with incense and naked pictures, which he invited boys into. I heard about it. Well, things like that aren't tolerated for long in towns like Goldenfield. There's suspicion and talk and then public outrage and action, and he had to leave so quick he didn't clear out the shop. [*The bar lights have faded out, and the special spot illuminates* BOBBY.] A bunch of us entered one night. The drying-up flowers rattled in the wind and the wind-chimes tinkled and the ... naked pictures were just ... pathetic, y'know. Except for a sketch of Michelangelo's David. I don't think anyone noticed me snatch it off the wall and stuff it into my pocket. Dreams ... images ... nights ... On the plains of Nebraska I passed a night with a group of runaway kids my age and it got cold after sunset. A lovely wild young girl invited me under a blanket with just a smile, and then a boy, me between, and both of them kept saying 'love', one of 'em in one ear and one in the other, till I didn't know which was which 'love' in which ear or which ... touch ... The plain was high and the night air ... exhilarating and the touches not heavy ... The man with the hangup has set my bike by the door. [*Extends his hand to* LEONA. *The bar is relighted.*] It's been a pleasure to meet a lady like you. Oh, I've got a lot of new adventures, experiences, to think over alone on my speed iron. I think I'll drive all night, I don't feel tired. [BOBBY *smiles as he opens the door and nods good-bye to Monk's Place.*]

LEONA: Hey, Iowa to Mexico, the money ... here's the money!

[*She rushes to the door, but* BOBBY *is gone with his bicycle.*]

BILL: He don't want a lousy five bucks, he wants everything in the wallet. He'll roll the faggot and hop back on his bike looking sweet and innocent as her brother fiddling in church.

[LEONA *rushes out, calling.*]

STEVE: The Coast is overrun with 'em, they come running out here like animals out of a brushfire.

MONK [*as he goes to each table, collecting the empty cans and bottles, emptying ash trays on a large serving tray*]: I've got no moral objections to them as a part of humanity, but I don't encourage them here. One comes in, others follow. First thing you know you're operating what they call a gay bar and it sounds like a bird cage, they're standing three deep at the bar and lining up at the men's room. Business is terrific for a few months. Then in comes the law. The place is raided, the boys hauled off in the wagon, and your place is padlocked. And then a cop or gangster pays you a social visit, big smile, all buddy-buddy. You had a good thing going, a real swinging place, he tells you, but you needed protection. He offers you protection and you buy it. The place is reopened and business is terrific a few months more. And then? It's raided again, and the next time it's reopened, you pay out of your nose, your ears, and your ass. Who wants it? I don't want it. I want a small steady place that I can handle alone, that brings in a small, steady profit. No buddy-buddy association with gangsters and the police. I want to know the people that come in my place so well I can serve them their brand of liquor or beer before they name it, soon as they come in the door. And all their personal problems, I want to know that, too.

[VIOLET *begins to hum softly, swaying to and fro like a water plant. When* MONK *finishes cleaning off the tables, he returns behind the bar. The bar lights dim, and his special spot comes up.*]

I'm fond of, I've got an affection for, a sincere interest in my regular customers here. They send me post cards from wherever they go and tell me what's new in their lives and I am interested in it. Just last month one of them I hadn't seen in about five years, he died in Mexico City and I was notified of the death and that he'd willed me all he owned in the world, his personal effects and a two-hundred-fifty-dollar savings account in a bank. A thing like that is beautiful as music. These things, these people, take the place of a family in my life. I love to come down those steps from my room to open the place for the evening, and when I've closed for the night, I love climbing back up those steps with my can of Ballantine's ale, and the stories, the jokes, the confidences and confessions I've heard that night, it makes me feel not alone . . . I've had heart attacks, and I'd be a liar to say they didn't scare me and don't still scare me. I'll die some night up those steps, I'll die in the night alone, and I hope it don't wake me up, that I just slip away, quietly.

[LEONA *has returned. The light in the bar comes up but remains at a low level.*]

LEONA: . . . Is there a steam engine in here? Did somebody drive in here on a steam engine while I was out?

MONK [*returning from his meditation*]: . . . Did what?

LEONA: I hear something going huff-huff like an old locomotive pulling into a station. [*She is referring to a sound like a panting dog. It comes from* BILL *at the unlighted table where* VIOLET *is seated between him and* STEVE.] . . . Oh, well, my home is on wheels . . . Bourbon sweet, Monk.

MONK: Leona, you don't need another.

LEONA: Monk, it's after midnight, my brother's death-day is over, I'll be all right, don't worry. [*She goes to the bar.*] . . . It was selfish of me to wish he was still alive.

[*A pin-spot of light picks up* VIOLET*'s tear-stained and tranced face at the otherwise dark table.*]

. . . She's got some form of religion in her hands . . .

CURTAIN

ACT TWO

An hour later. 'Group singing' is in progress at the table stage right. LEONA *is not participating. She is sitting moodily at the bar facing front.*

VIOLET: 'I don't want to set the world on fii-yuh.'

STEVE: 'I don't want to set the world on fii-yuh.'

VIOLET: I like old numbers best. Here's an oldie that I learned from my mother. [*She rises and assumes a sentimental look.*]
'Lay me where sweet flowers blos-som,
Where the dainty lily blows
Where the pinks and violets min-gle,
Lay me underneath the rose.'

LEONA: Shit. Y'don't need a rose to lay her, you could lay her under a cactus and she wouldn't notice the diff-rence.

[BILL *crosses to the bar for a beer.*]

I guess you don't think I'm serious about it, hitting the highway tonight.

[BILL *shrugs and crosses to a downstage table.*]

Well, I am, I'm serious about it. [*She sits at his table.*] An experienced expert beautician can always get work anywhere.

BILL: Your own appearance is a bad advertisement for your line of work.

LEONA: I don't care how I look as long as I'm clean and decent . . . and *self-supporting.* When I haul into a new town, I just look through the yellow pages of the telephone directory and pick out a beauty shop that's close to my trailer camp. I go to the shop and offer to work a couple of days for nothing, and after that couple of days I'm in like Flynn, and on my own terms, which is fifty per cent of charges for all I do, and my tips, of course, too. They like my work and they like my personality, my approach to customers. I keep them laughing.

BILL: You keep me laughing, too.

LEONA: ... Of course, there's things about you I'll remember with pleasure, such as waking up sometimes in the night and looking over the edge of the upper bunk to see you asleep in the lower. [BILL *leaves the table. She raises her voice to address the bar-at-large.*] Yeah, he slept in the lower 'cause when he'd passed out or nearly, it would of taken a derrick to haul him into the upper bunk. So I gave him the lower bunk and took the upper myself.

BILL: As if you never pass out. Is that the idea you're selling?

LEONA: When I pass out I wake up in a chair or on the floor, oh, no, the floor was good enough for me in your opinion, and sometimes you stepped on me even, yeah, like I was a rug or a bug, because your nature is selfish. You think because you've lived off one woman after another woman after eight or ten women you're something superior, special. Well, you're special but not superior, baby. I'm going to worry about you after I've gone and I'm sure as hell leaving tonight, fog or no fog on the highway, but I'll worry about you because you refuse to grow up and that's a mistake that you make, because you can only refuse to grow up for a limited period in your lifetime and get by with it ... I *loved* you! ... I'm not going to cry. It's only being so tired that makes me cry.

[VIOLET *starts weeping for her.*]

VIOLET: Bill, get up and tell Leona good-bye. She's a lonely girl without a soul in the world.

LEONA: I've got the world in the world, and McCorkle don't have to make the effort to get himself or any part of him up, it's easier to stay down. And as for being lonely, listen, ducks, that applies to every mother's son and daughter of us alive, we were given warning of that before we were born almost, and yet ... When I come to a new place, it takes me two or three weeks, that's all it takes me, to find somebody to live with in my home on wheels and to find a night spot to hang out in. Those first two or three weeks are rough, sometimes I wish I'd stayed where I was before, but I know from experience that I'll find somebody and locate a night spot to booze in, and get acquainted with ... friends ... [*The light has focused on her. She moves downstage with her hands in her pockets, her face and voice very grave as if she were less confident that things will be as she says.*] And then, all at once, something wonderful happens. All the past disappointments in people I left behind me, just disappear, evaporate from my mind, and I just remember the good things, such as their sleeping faces, and ... Life! Life! I never just said, 'Oh, well,' I've always said 'Life!' to life, like a song to God, too, because I've lived in my lifetime and not been afraid of ... changes ... [*She goes back to the bar.*] ... However, y'see, I've got this pride in my nature. When I live with a person I love and care for in my life, I expect his respect, and when I see I've lost it, I GO, GO! ... So a home on wheels is the only right home for me.

[VIOLET *starts towards* LEONA.]

What is she doing here?

[VIOLET *has weaved to the bar.*]

Hey! What are *you* doing here?

VIOLET: You're the best friend I ever had, the best friend I ... [*She sways and sobs like a* religieuse *in the grip of a vision.*]

LEONA: What's that, what're you saying?

[VIOLET *sobs.*]

She can't talk. What was she saying?

VIOLET: ... BEST ... !

LEONA: WHAT?

VIOLET: ... *Friend!*

LEONA: I'd go further than that, I'd be willing to bet I'm the *only* friend that you've had, and the next time you come down sick nobody will bring you nothing, no chicken, no hot beef bouillon, no chinaware, no silver, and no interest and concern about your condition, and you'll die in your rattrap with no human voice, just bang, bang, bang from the bowling alley and billiards. And when you die you should feel a relief from the conditions you lived in. Now I'm leaving you two suffering, bleeding hearts together, I'm going to sit at the bar. I had a Italian boy friend that taught me saying, '*Meglior solo que mal accompanota*', which means that you're better alone than in the company of a bad companion.

[*She starts to the bar, as* DOC enters.]

Back already, huh? It didn't take you much time to deliver the baby. Or did you bury the baby? Or did you bury the mother? Or did you bury them both, the mother and baby?

DOC [*to* MONK]: Can you shut up this woman?

LEONA: Nobody can shut up this woman. Quack, quack, quack, Doctor Duck, quack, quack, quack, quack, quack!

DOC: I'M A LICENSED PHYSICIAN!

LEONA: SHOW *me your licence. I'll shut up when I see it!*

DOC: A doctor's licence to practise isn't the size of a drunken driver's licence, you put it in a wallet, you hang it on the wall of your office.

LEONA: Here is your office! Which wall is your licence hung on? Beside the sailfish or where? Where is your licence to practise hung up, in the gents', with other filthy scribbles?!

MONK: Leona, you said your brother's death-day was over and I thought you meant you were . . .

LEONA: THOUGHT I MEANT I WAS *WHAT?*

MONK: You were ready to cool it. BILL! . . . Take Leona home, now.

LEONA: Christ, do you think I'd let him come near me?! Or near my trailer?! Tonight?! [*She slaps the bar several times with her sailor cap, turning to the right and left as if to ward off assailants, her great bosom heaving, a jungle-look in her eyes.*]

VIOLET: Steve, if we don't go now the King-burger stand will shut on us, and I've had nothing but liquids on my stomach all day. So I need a Whopper tonight.

[BILL *laughs.*]

STEVE: You'll get a hot dog with chili and everything on the way home. Get me . . . get me . . . get me. Grab and grope. You disgrace me! . . . your habits.

VIOLET: You're underdeveloped and you blame me.

LEONA [*looking out*]: Yes . . . [*She slaps something with her cap.*] *Yes!*

VIOLET: What did she mean by that? Another sarcastic crack?

LEONA: When I say 'yes' it is not sarcastic . . . It means a decision to act.

MONK: The place is closing so will everybody get themselves together now, please.

VIOLET: I do have to have something solid. Too much liquids and not enough solids in the system upsets the whole system. Ask the Doc if it don't. Doc, don't it upset the system, liquids without solids? All day long?

[DOC *has been sunk in profoundly dark and private reflections. He emerges momentarily to reply to* VIOLET*'s direct question.*]

DOC: If that's a professional question to a doctor whose office is here ... [*A certain ferocity is boiling in him and directed mostly at himself.*] My fee is ... another brandy. [*He turns away with a short, disgusted laugh.*]

MONK: Something wrong, Doc?

[VIOLET *has crossed to* BILL, *as a child seeking protection.*]

DOC: Why, no, what could be wrong? But a need to put more liquid in my system ...

LEONA [*convulsively turning about*]: Yes ... *yes!* [*This no longer relates to anything but her private decision.*]

BILL [*to himself*]: I'm not about to spend the night on the beach ...

VIOLET: [*leaning towards* BILL]: I am not neither, so why don't we check in somewhere? Us, two, together?

STEVE: I heard that.

LEONA: Yes ... *yes!*

MONK: I said the place is closing.

VIOLET: Let's go together, us three, and talk things over at the King-burger stand.

STEVE: Being a cook I know the quality of those giant hamburgers called Whoppers, and they're fit only for dog food.

VIOLET: I think we better leave, now. [*Extends her delicate hands to both men.*] Steve? Bill? [*They all rise unsteadily and prepare to leave.*] Bill, you know I feel so protected now. [VIOLET, STEVE, *and* BILL *start out.*]

LEONA [*stomping the floor with a powerful foot*]: Y' WANT YOUR ASS IN A SLING BEFORE YOU'RE LAID UNDER THAT ROSE?

VIOLET [*shepherded past* LEONA *by* STEVE *and* BILL]: If we don't see you again, good luck wherever you're going.

[*They go out to the door.*]

LEONA [*rushing after them*]: That's what she wants, she wants her ass in a sling!

[*She rushes out the door. A moment or two later, as* MONK *looks out, and above the boom of the surf,* VIOLET*'s histrionically shrill outcries are heard. This is followed by an off-stage quarrel between* LEONA *and a night watchman on the beach. Their overlapping, ad-lib dialogue* *continues in varying intensity as background to the business on stage: 'If you don't settle down and come along peaceful-like, I'm going to call the wagon! . . .' 'Do that, I just dare you to do it – go on, I just dare you to call the wagon! I want to ride in a wagon – it's got wheels, hasn't it – I'll ride any Goddam thing on wheels! . . .' 'Oh, no – listen, lady, what's your name anyhow? . . .' 'I'm just* the *one to do it! . . . I tell you my name? I'm going to tell you my name? What's your name?* I *want your name! Oh boy, do I want your name! . . .' 'Listen, please, come on, now, let's take this thing easy . . .' 'I've been drinking in this bar, and it's not the first time you . . .' 'Let's go! You raise hell every night! . . .' 'Every night! This isn't the first time – I've been meaning to report you! Yes, I'm going to report you! Yes, how's that for a switch? . . .' 'I'm just trying to do my duty! . . .' 'I live in a home on wheels, and every night you try to molest me when I come home! . . .' 'No! You're wrong – you're always in there drinking and raising hell and . . .' 'Yeah, but you let criminals go free, right? . . .' 'No, I don't! . . .' 'People can't walk in the street, murdering, robbing, thieving, and all I do is have a few Goddam drinks, just because it's my brother's death-day, so I was showing a little human emotion – take your hands off me! . . .' 'Come on now! . . .' 'Don't you put your hands on a lady like me! . . .' 'No, I'm not! . . .' 'I'm a Goddam lady! That's what I am, and you just lay off! . . .' 'I've had enough of this! . . .' 'Every night I come out here, you're looking for free drinks, that's what's the matter with you! . . .' 'I've never had a drink in my life, lady! . . .' 'You never had a drink in your life! . . .' 'No, I haven't, I've . . .' 'Show me your identification, that's what I want to see! . . .' 'I'm just trying to do my duty . . .' 'Look here, old man . . .' 'I don't know why I have to put up with an old dame like you this way . . .' 'Oh! – Oh! – Why you Goddam son of a! . . .' 'Now! . . .' 'Don't you talk to me like that . . .' 'I'm not talking to you, I'm telling you to come over here and let me get you to the telephone here! . . .' 'You've been harassing that man Monk! . . .' 'I'm not harassing anybody! . . .' 'You're not harassing anybody? . . .' 'You come over to this Monk's Place every night and raise hell, the whole damn bunch of you, and a poor man like me trying to earn a few dollars and make a living for his old woman and . . .' 'Let me see your identification! What precinct are you from? . . .' 'Oh, yeah . . .' 'Go on, I want that identification, and I want that uniform off you, and that badge . . .' 'You won't do anything of the sort! . . .' 'Oh, yeah . . .' 'Yes, I'm doing my job, what I'm doing is legal! . . .' 'I happen to have more influence up at that station than you . . . Goddam pig! . . .' 'I haven't done nothing to you, I'm just trying to do my job . . .' 'Do your job? . . .' 'Yes, and you're giving me a lot of hard time! . . .' 'There's raping and thieving and criminals and robbers walking the streets, breaking store fronts, breaking into every bar . . .' 'Well, that's not my – listen, lady! I'm just the night watchman around this beach here. I'm just on the beach nights, I don't have anything to do with what's going on somewhere else in the city, just on this beach! . . .' 'You don't know what's going on on the beach . . .' 'I know what's going on on the beach, and it's you and that crowd drinking every night, raising hell! . . .' 'We're not raising hell every night! . . .' 'If I was your husband, golly, I – I – by God I would take care of you, I wouldn't put up with your likes, you and that crowd drinking every night! . . .' 'I like that uniform you've got on you, and I'm gonna have it! . . .' 'Why do you have to pick on a little man like me for? . . .' 'I've seen you sneaking around, Peeping Tom, that's what you are! . . .' 'No, that's not so! . . .' 'I've seen you sneaking around looking in ladies' windows . . .' 'That's not true! I'm just trying to do my duty! I keep telling you . . .' 'Yeah, peeping in windows . . .' 'No! . . .' 'Watching people undress . . .' 'No! You . . .' 'I've seen you, you lascivious old man! . . .' 'I've seen you taking these young men over to your trailer court and making studs out of them! . . .' 'Yeah! – Yeah! – Yeah! – Men, that's what I take to my trailer! I wouldn't take a palsied old man like you! . . .' 'You know damn well I wasn't trying to get you to . . . ! I was trying to get you to this telephone box, where I was going to! . . .' 'You will not be able to, old man! . . .' 'Listen, Miss, I asked you to give me your identification! You give me your identification so I can tell who you are! . . .' 'I want your identification! I've seen you, I've seen you sneaking around the trailer court, I've seen you looking in windows . . .' 'Oh, that's a lie! I never did a thing like that in all my life, I go to church. I'm a good Christian man! . . .' 'Oh yeah! Yeah! Yeah! . . .' 'I could take you in if I were younger, I wouldn't* have *to call the highway patrol, but I'm going to do that right now! . . .' 'Listen, Holy Willie! I've seen your likes in church before! I wouldn't trust you with a ...' 'A little church wouldn't do you any harm neither! ...' 'Old man ... Yeah! Yeah! ...' 'I've seen you with those young studs! ...' 'Doesn't that make you excited? ...' 'No, by God, it doesn't! ...' 'Is that your problem? ...' 'No, I don't have none! You're the one with the hang-ups and problems –* you *are a problem! You hang out here all night in that damn Monk's Place! ...' 'I've got my own man, I don't have to worry about any other man, I got my own man in my trailer! ...' 'Anyone want to spend the night with you, he must be a pig then, he must be some kind of pig living with you! ...' 'Fat old bag of wind, don't you talk to me! ...' 'Look, I'm tired of talking to you, by God, I've put up with you all I'm going to! I told you I was going to call the highway patrol! ...' 'I've seen the way you look at me when you ...' 'That's a lie! – I never ...' 'Yeah! Yeah! ...' 'I – I ...' 'I've seen you skulking around in the dark, looking in windows! ...' 'I don't need your kind! I've got a good woman at home, and she takes care of me, she takes good care of me! If I can get this job done and you'll just settle down and be quiet, we wouldn't have all this noise! ...' 'Does your wife know about the girls you go out with? ...' 'You're trying to incriminate me! ...' 'Does she know about that? ...' 'I know what you're trying to do ...' 'I've seen you ...' 'Trying to get me in trouble! Trying to get me to lose my job here! ...' 'I know what you holy boys are like! ...' 'Why don't you go back in there and raise some more hell with those young studs? ...' 'I ain't doing that neither ...' 'If you'd be quiet! ...' 'Stop harassing! ...' 'I ain't harassing nothing! ...' 'Every time you want a drink, yes? ...' 'I don't, I don't ...'*]

MONK [*to* DOC]: Goddam, she's left her suitcase.

DOC [*musing darkly*]: ... Done what?

MONK: She's left that bag in here, which means she's coming back.

DOC: Aw, yeah, a guarantee of it, she's going to provide you with the solace of her companionship up those stairs to the living quarters. [*He faces out from the bar.*] Y'know, that narrow flight of stairs is like the uterine passage to life, and I'd say that strange, that amorphous-looking creature is expecting to enter the world up the uterine passage to your living quarters above. [*He rises, chuckling darkly.*] Is the toilet repaired in the gents' room?

MONK [*listening to noises outside*]: Yeh, plumber fixed it today.

[DOC *sighs and lumbers heavily the way pointed by the chalk-white hand signed 'GENTS' off stage right.*

MONK *crosses to the door to assess the disturbance outside.* BILL *rushes into the bar.*]

BILL: For Chrissake, get an ambulance with a strait jacket for her.

MONK: You mean you can't hold her, you stupid prick?

BILL: No man can hold that woman when she goes ape. Gimme a dime, I'm gonna call the Star of the Sea psycho ward.

MONK: Don't put a hand on that phone.

[VIOLET *now rushes in the door. She continues her histrionic outcries.*]

VIOLET: They're callin' the wagon for her, she's like a wild thing out there, lock the door, don't let her at me. Hide me, help me! Please! [*She rushes towards the stairs.*]

MONK: Stay down those stairs, pick up your luggage, I'll ... I'll ... call a taxi for you.

VIOLET: Steve done nothin' to ... nothin' ... Just run!

[*Altercation rises outside.* VIOLET *rushes into the ladies'.* MONK *closes the door and bolts it.* DOC *returns from the gents', putting on his jacket. His pant cuffs are wet.*]

DOC: The toilet still overflows.

[STEVE *calls at the locked door.*]

STEVE: Vi'let? Monk?

[MONK *admits him.* STEVE *enters with a confused look about, two dripping hot dogs in his hand.*]

STEVE: Vi'let, is Vi'let, did Vi'let get back in here?

MONK: Yeh, she's back in the ladies'. [MONK *closes door.*]

STEVE [*shuffling rapidly to the ladies'*]: Vi'let? Vi'let? Hear me?

MONK: No. She don't.

STEVE: Vi'let, the King-burger's closed. So I couldn't get a Whopper ... I got you two dogs, with chili and sauerkraut. You can come out now, Leona's getting arrested. Violet screamed for help to a cop that hates and hassles me ev'ry time I go home.

MONK: Those dogs you're holding are dripping on the floor.

DOC: Committing a nuisance ...

STEVE: Vi'let, the dogs'll turn cold, the chili's dripping off 'em. You can't stay all night in a toilet, Vi'let.

VIOLET [*from the ladies'*]: I can, I will, go away.

STEVE: She says she's gonna stay all night in a toilet. Wow ... I mean ... wow. [*Starts eating one of the hot dogs with a slurping sound.*]

MONK: If she's called the law here I want her to shut up in there.

STEVE: Vi'let, shut up in there. Come out for your dog.

VIOLET: Take your dog away and leave me alone. You give me no protection and no support a'tall.

[DOC *utters a laugh that is dark with an ultimate recognition of human absurdity and his own self-loathing.*]

MONK [*touching his chest*]: ... Doc? ... Have a nightcap with me.

DOC: Thanks, Monk, I could use one.

MONK [*leaning back in chair and tapping his upper abdomen*]: Angina or gastritis, prob'ly both.

DOC: In that location, it's gas.

MONK: What happened at Treasure Island?

DOC [*sipping his 'shot'*]: Tell you when I ... get this ... down.

BILL: Time ... runs out with one and you go to another. Got a call from a woman guv'ment employee in Sacramento. She's got a co-op in a high-rise condominium, lives so high on the hog with payoffs an' all she can't see ground beneath her.

MONK: Why're you shouting, at who?

BILL: Nobody's ever thrown McCorkle out.

MONK: Unusual and not expected things can happen.

[LEONA *is heard from off stage: 'Okay, you make your phone call, and I'll make mine.'*]

So, Doc, how'd it go at the trailer camp?

[*He and* DOC *are seated in profile at the downstage table.* STEVE *and* BILL *are silhouetted at the edge of the lighted area.*]

DOC: The birth of the baby was at least three months premature, so it was born dead, of course, and just beginning to look like a human baby ... The man living with the woman in the trailer said, 'Don't let her see it, get it out of the trailer.' I agreed with the man that she shouldn't see it, so I put this foetus in a shoe box ... [*He speaks with difficulty, as if compelled to.*] The trailer was right by the beach, the tide was coming in with heavy surf, so I put the shoe box ... and contents ... where the tide would take it.

MONK: ... Are you sure that was legal?

DOC: Christ, no, it wasn't legal ... I'd barely set the box down when the man came out shouting for me. The woman had started to haemorrhage. When I went back in the trailer, she was bleeding to death. The man hollered at me, 'Do something, can't you do something for her!'.

MONK: ... Could you?

DOC: ... I could have told the man to call an ambulance for her, but I thought of the probable consequences to me, and while I thought about that, the woman died. She was a small woman, but not small enough to fit in a shoe box, so I ... I gave the man a fifty-dollar bill that I'd received today for performing an abortion. I gave it to him in return for his promise not to remember my name ... [*He reaches for the bottle. His hand shakes so that he can't refill his shot-glass.* MONK *fills it for him.*] ... You see, I can't make out certificates of death, since I have no legal right any more to practise medicine, Monk.

MONK: ... In the light of what happened, there's something I'd better tell you, Doc. Soon as you left here to deliver that baby, Leona ran out of the bar to make a phone call to the office at Treasure Island, warning them that you were on your way out there to deliver a baby. So, Doc, you may be in trouble ... If you stay here ...

DOC: I'll take a Benzedrine tablet and pack and ...

MONK: Hit the road before morning.

DOC: I'll hit the road tonight.

MONK: Don't let it hit you. [*Stands to shake.*] G'bye, Doc. Keep in touch.

DOC: G'bye, Monk. Thanks for all and the warning.

MONK: Take care, Doc.

STEVE: Yeh, Doc, you got to take care. Bye, Doc.

BILL: No sweat, Doc, g'bye.

[DOC *exits.*]

MONK: That old son of a bitch's paid his dues ...

[*Altercation rises outside once more: 'I'm gonna slap the cuffs on you! ...' 'That does it, let go of me, you fink, you pig!' Approach of a squad car siren is heard at a distance.*]

Yep, coming the law!

BILL: I don't want in on this.

STEVE: Not me neither.

[They rush out. Squad car screeches to a stop. LEONA *appears at the door, shouting and pounding.]*

LEONA: MONK! THE PADDY WAGON IS SINGING MY SONG!

[MONK *lets her in and locks the door.]*

MONK: Go upstairs. Can you make it?

[She clambers up the steps, slips, nearly falls. POLICEMAN *knocks at the door.* MONK *admits him.]*

Hi, Tony.

TONY: Hi, Monk. What's this about a fight going on here, Monk?

MONK: Fight? Not here. It's been very peaceful tonight. The bar is closed. I'm sitting here having a nightcap with . . .

TONY: Who's that bawling back there?

MONK [*pouring a drink for* TONY]: Some dame disappointed in love, the usual thing. Try this and if it suits you, take the bottle.

TONY [*He drinks.*]: . . . O.K. Good.

MONK: Take the bottle. Drop in more often. I miss you.

TONY: Thanks, g'night. [*He goes out.*]

MONK: Coast is clear, Leona. [*As* MONK *puts another bottle on the table,* LEONA *comes awkwardly back down the stairs.*]

LEONA: Monk? Thanks, Monk. [*She and* MONK *sit at the table.* VIOLET *comes out of the ladies' room.*]

VIOLET: Steve? . . . Bill? [*She sees* LEONA *at the table and starts to retreat.*]

LEONA: Aw, hell, Violet. Come over and sit down with us, we're having a nightcap, all of us, my brother's death-day is over.

VIOLET: Why does everyone hate me? [*She sits at the table: drinks are poured from the bottle.* VIOLET *hitches her chair close to* MONK'*s. In a few moments she will deliberately drop a matchbook under the table, bend to retrieve it, and the hand on* MONK'*s side will not return to the table surface.*]

LEONA: Nobody hates you, Violet. It would be a compliment to you if they did.

VIOLET: I'd hate to think that I'd come between you and Bill.

LEONA: Don't torture yourself with an awful thought like that. Two people living together is something you don't understand, and since you don't understand it you don't respect it, but, Violet, this being our last conversation, I want to advise something to you. I think you need medical help in the mental department and I think this because you remind me of a ... of a ... of a plant of some kind ...

VIOLET: Because my name is Violet?

LEONA: No, I wasn't thinking of violets, I was thinking of water plants, yeah, plants that don't grow in the ground but float on water. With you everything is such a ... such a ... well, you know what I mean, don't you?

VIOLET: Temporary arrangement?

LEONA: Yes, you could put it that way. Do you know how you got into that place upstairs from the amusement arcade?

VIOLET: ... How?

LEONA: Yes, *how* or *why* or *when*?

VIOLET: ... Why, I ... [*She obviously is uncertain on all three points.*]

LEONA: Take your time. And *think*. How, why, when?

VIOLET: Why, I was ... in L.A., and ...

LEONA: Are you sure you were in L.A.? Are you sure about even that? Or is everything foggy to you, is your mind in a cloud?

VIOLET: Yes, I was ...

LEONA: I said take your time, don't push it. Can you come out of the fog?

MONK: Leona, take it easy, we all know Violet's got problems.

LEONA: Her problems are mental problems and I want her to face them, now, in our last conversation. Violet? Can you come out of the fog and tell us how, when, and why you're living out of a suitcase upstairs from the amusement arcade, can you just ...

MONK [*cutting in*]: She's left the amusement arcade, she left it tonight, she came here with her suitcase.

LEONA: Yeah, she's a water plant, with roots in water, drifting the way it takes her.

[VIOLET *weeps.*]

And she cries too easy, the water works are back on. I'll give her some music to cry to before I go back to my home on wheels and get it cracking up the Old Spanish Trail. [*She rises from the table.*]

MONK: Not tonight, Leona. You have to sleep off your liquor before you get on the highway in this fog.

LEONA: That's what you think, not what I think, Monk. My time's run out in this place. [*She has walked to the juke box and started the violin piece.*] ... How, when, and why, and her only answer is tears. Couldn't say how, couldn't say when, couldn't say why. And I don't think she's sure where she was before she come here, any more sure than she is where she'll go when she leaves here. She don't dare remember and she don't dare look forward, neither. Her mind floats on a cloud and her body floats on water. And her dirty fingernail hands reach out to hold on to something she hopes can hold her together. [*She starts back towards the table, stops; the bar dims and light is focused on her.*] ... Oh, my God, she's at it again, she got a hand under the table. [LEONA *laughs sadly.*] Well, I guess she can't help it. It's sad, though. It's a pitiful thing to have to reach under a table to find some reason to live. You know, she's worshipping her idea of God Almighty in her personal church. Why the hell should I care she done it to a nowhere person that I put up in my trailer for a few months? I wish that kid from I-oh-a with eyes like my lost brother had been willing to travel with me, but I guess I scared him. What I think I'll do is turn back to a faggot's moll when I haul up to Sausalito or San Francisco. You always find one in the gay bars that needs a big sister with him, to camp with and laugh and cry with, and I hope I'll find one soon ... it scares me to be alone in my home on wheels built for two ... [*She turns as the bar is lighted and goes back to the table.*] Monk, HEY, MONK! What's my tab here t'night?

MONK: Forget it, don't think about it, go home and sleep, Leona. [*He and* VIOLET *appear to be in a state of trance together.*]

LEONA: I'm not going to sleep and I never leave debts behind me. This twenty ought to do it. [*She places a bill on the table.*]

MONK: Uh-huh, sure, keep in touch ...

LEONA: Tell Bill he'll find his effects in the trailer-court office, and when he's hustled himself a new meal ticket, he'd better try and respect her, at least in public ... Well ... [*She extends her hand slightly.* MONK *and* VIOLET *are sitting with closed eyes.*] ... I guess I've already gone.

VIOLET: G'bye, Leona.

MONK: G'bye ...

LEONA: 'Meglior solo', huh, ducks? [LEONA *lets herself out of the bar.*]

MONK: ... G'bye, Leona.

VIOLET: ... Monk?

MONK [*correctly suspecting her intent*]: You want your suitcase, it's ...

VIOLET: I don't mean my suitcase, nothing valuable's in it but my ... undies and ...

MONK: Then what've you got in mind?

VIOLET: ... In *what*?

MONK: Sorry. No offence meant. But there's taverns licensed for rooms, and taverns licensed for liquor and food and liquor, and I am a tavern only licensed for ...

VIOLET [*overlapping with a tone and gesture of such ultimate supplication that it would break the heart of a stone*]: I just meant ... let's go upstairs. Huh? Monk? [MONK *stares at her reflectively for a while, considering all the potential complications of her taking up semi- or permanent residence up there.*] Why're you looking at me that way? I just want a temporary, a night, a ...

MONK: ... Yeah, go on up and make yourself at home. Take a shower up there while I lock up the bar.

VIOLET: God love you, Monk, like me. [*She crosses, with a touch of 'labyrinthitis', to the stairs and mounts two steps.*] Monk! ... I'm scared of these stairs, they're almost steep as a ladder. I better take off my slippers. Take my slippers off for me. [*There is a tone in her voice that implies she has already 'moved in' ... She holds out one leg from the steps, then the other.* MONK *removes her slippers and she goes on up, calling down to him:*] Bring up some beer, sweetheart.

MONK: Yeh, I'll bring some beer up. Don't forget your shower. [*Alone in the bar,* MONK *crosses downstage.*] I'm going to stay down here till I hear that shower running, I am not going up there till she's took a shower. [*He sniffs the ratty slipper.*] Dirty, worn-out slipper still being worn, sour-smelling with sweat from being worn too long, but still set by the bed to be worn again the next day, walked on here and there on – pointless – errands till the sole's worn through, and even then not thrown away, just padded with cardboard till the cardboard's worn through and still not thrown away, still put on to walk on till it's . . . past all repair . . . [*He has been, during this, turning out lamps in the bar.*] Hey, Violet, will you for Chrissake take a . . . [*This shouted appeal breaks off with a disgusted laugh. He drops the slipper, then grins sadly.*] She probably thinks she'd dissolve in water. I shouldn't of let her stay here. Well, I won't touch her, I'll have no contact with her, maybe I won't even go up there tonight. [*He crosses to open the door. We hear the boom of the ocean outside.*] I always leave the door open for a few minutes to clear the smoke and liquor smell out of the place, the human odours, and to hear the ocean. Y'know, it sounds different this late than it does with the crowd on the beach-front. It has a private sound to it, a sound that's just for itself and for me. [MONK *switches off the blue neon sign. It goes dark outside. He closes door.*]

[*Sound of water running above. He slowly looks towards the sound.*]
That ain't rain.

[*Tired from the hectic night, maybe feeling a stitch of pain in his heart (but he's used to that),* MONK *starts to the stairs. In the spill of light beneath them, he glances up with a slow smile, wry, but not bitter. A smile that's old too early, but it grows a bit warmer as he starts up the stairs.*]

CURTAIN